Small Differences

McGILL-QUEEN'S STUDIES IN THE
HISTORY OF RELIGION

G.A. Rawlyk, Editor

Volumes in this series have been supported by the
Jackman Foundation of Toronto.

1 Small Differences
Irish Catholics and Irish Protestants, 1815-1922
An International Perspective

Donald Harman Akenson

2 Two Worlds
Protestant Culture of Nineteenth-Century
Ontario

William Westfall

3 An Evangelical Mind
Nathanael Burwash and the Methodist
Tradition in Canada, 1839-1918

Marguerite Van Die

4 The Dévotes
Women and Church in Seventeenth-Century
France

Elizabeth Rapley

5 The Evangelical Century
College and Creed in English Canada from
the Great Revival to the Great Depression

Michael Gauvreau

6 The German Peasants' War and Anabaptist
Community of Goods

James M. Stayer

Small Differences

Irish Catholics and Irish Protestants, 1815–1922 An International Perspective

DONALD HARMAN AKENSON

McGill-Queen's University Press
Montreal & Kingston • London • Buffalo

Gill and Macmillan
Dublin

© McGill-Queen's University Press 1988
ISBN 0-7735-0636-5 (cloth)
ISBN 0-7735-0858-9 (paper)

Legal deposit first quarter 1988
Bibliothèque nationale du Québec

First paperback edition 1991

Printed in Canada on acid-free paper

Published in Ireland by
Gill and Macmillan Ltd
Goldenbridge, Dublin 8
With associated companies in Auckland, Delhi,
Gaborone, Hamburg, Harare, Hong Kong,
Johannesburg, Kuala Lumpur, Lagos, London,
Manzini, Melbourne, Mexico City, Nairobi,
New York, Singapore, Tokyo

British Library Cataloguing in Publication Data

Akenson, Donald Harman
    Small differences : Irish Catholics and Irish
    Protestants, 1815-1922: an international perspective.
    1. Ireland. Catholics. Relations with protestants,
    history. 1. Title.
    305.6
    ISBN 0-7171-1876-2

Canadian Cataloguing in Publication Data

Akenson, Donald Harman, 1941-
    Small differences : Irish Catholics and Irish
    Protestants, 1815-1922: an international perspective
    (McGill-Queen's studies in the history of religion)
    Includes bibliographical references and index.
    ISBN 0-7735-0858-9 (McGill-Queen's University Press)
    ISBN 0-7171-1876-2 (Gill and MacMillan)
    1. National characteristics, Irish. 2. Catholics –
    Ireland. 3. Protestants – Ireland. 4. Ireland –
    Social life and customs - 19th century. 5. Ireland –
    Social life and customs – 20th century. 1. Title.
    11. Series.
    DA959.A44 1991   305.891'62   C91-090012-4

To Curtis B. Akenson

"*Oh dear, not the **Irish** Christians again!*"

By kind permission of the editors of *Punch*

Contents

Figures and Tables   ix

List of Appendixes   x

Preface   xi

Acknowledgments   xiii

1 Perspective   3
2 Some Empirical Tests   15
3 Clean Laboratories   42
4 Seeming Contrarieties   86
5 Keeping Separate: Boundary Maintenance
   Systems   108
6 Systems of Belief   127

Appendixes   151

Notes   195

Index   233

Figures and Tables

FIGURES

1 Irish Religious Distributions, 1834–1911 6
2 Irish Illiteracy Rates, 1861–1911 7
3 Religion and Occupation, Adult Males, 1861 21
4 Excess of Female Life Expectancy over Male Life Expectancy, 1900–27 39
5 Proportion of Irish-born Persons Living Outside Ireland, 1841–1921 43
6 Emigration from Ireland (excluding Great Britain), 1815–1920 46
7 Occupations of Male Adults, by Place of Birth, Australia, 1921 70
8 Religious Persuasion and Child-bearing, Australia, 1911 76
9 Place of Birth and Child-bearing, Australia, 1911 78
10 Canadian Proportion of Irish Migration to North America, 1825–71 89
11 Irish Linguistic Preferences, 1851–1911 137

TABLES

1 Occupations Grouped by Percentage of Protestants and Catholics Employed 20
2 Irish Emigration to Great Britain, 1876–1920 51
3 Proportion of Catholics in Total Australian Population, 1851–1921 63
4 Persons of Irish Ethnicity living in Rural Areas: Canada, 1871–1931 92

Appendixes

A Irish Religious Distributions, 1834 153
B Irish Census of Religion, 1861 155
C Irish Religious Denominations,
    1861–1911 157
D Irish Illiteracy Rates, 1861–1911 158
E Religion and Occupation of Adult Irish
    Males, 1861 159
F The 1861 Irish Census of Occupations 160
G Excess of Female Life Expectancy at Birth
    Over Male Life Expectancy 181
H Permanent Residence of Irish-born Persons,
    1841–1921 182
I Emigration from Ireland, 1815–1920 183
J Male Adult Occupational Types and Place of
    Birth, Australia, 1921 184
K Occupation and Place of Birth, Males, New
    South Wales, 1901 185
L Occupation and Religion, Males, New South
    Wales, 1901 187
M Religious Persuasion and Average Number
    of Children, Australia, 1911 189
N Place of Birth and Average Number of
    Children, Australia, 1911 190
O Migrants from Irish Ports to British North
    America, 1825–52 191
P Total Irish Migrants to British North
    America, 1853–71 192
Q Linguistic Preference of the Irish Population,
    1851–1911 193

Preface

I began writing this book more than twenty years ago, but only within the last three years have I had the wit to realize that this was what I have been doing. My intellectual debt to individual scholars and friends who have talked and corresponded with me over the years is great, but is much too wide to particularize. In any case, not everyone who has helped me would want to be associated with this study, for it inevitably is a very high-risk enterprise.

Irish historians, like members of the middle class everywhere, usually avoid talking about divisive issues, and thus really important matters are sidestepped. The cultural differences between Protestants and Catholics are so central to modern Irish history that to evade them leaves a great black hole in the nation's story. Controversial and emotionally divisive as this matter is in Irish life, I think that as historians we can engage it and other such volatile issues successfully. Of course we must argue a bit, but we can do so according to the academic equivalent of the Marquis of Queensbury rules. The alternative is either to continue to avoid central topics in Irish history or to turn every disagreement on a controversial subject into an eye-gouging alley-fight; the first is not responsible scholarship and the second is not civilized.

This is a reflective essay in that it tries to draw together several earlier monographs, but it also contains a large amount of new data and several hypotheses that I hope other scholars will find worth their investigation. Although much of the material in this book is derived from the social sciences and from their way of thinking – particularly from the logic of experimental design – quantitative data are presented very simply. There is nothing here that cannot be comprehended by someone who has sat through elementary algebra: no regressions, no beta weights, no multiple classification analyses, just simple arithmetic, and one or two correlations. This simplicity is important. The general run of historians for the most part tends to ignore the conclusions of quantitative historians, because of the opaque way their material usually is presented. (Less frequently, but no less unfortunately, sometimes general historians meekly accept what quantitative historians say, because they fear the embarrassment of asking the wrong question.) In this study, if simple arithmetic and logical sequences based upon that arithmetic do not make a point clearly, the fault is mine, not the reader's.

Further to suit the tastes of those who do not enjoy quantitative thought, complex tables are included in the text as little as possible, and, visual presentation of data is done instead. The data on which the various illustrative figures are based is found in detail in the appendixes, along with a specification of the source of those data.

Some readers may not like the fact that I write quite a bit about the nature of the evidence that comes to hand. Grappling about in the dirt, trying to sort out shards of evidence from the detritus of history's midden, is not high prestige work, and it sometimes seems to be reserved for those who are beneath the salt in the intellectual feast. But it is unavoidable: if one is to write honestly about history – and especially, about a topic that is at once eminently controversial and simultaneously delicate from an evidentiary viewpoint – one has to discuss in detail how one gets answers.

By detailing the primary source material that is available, I am pointing not only to sources that are apt to be useful to future researchers, but I am also giving those who disagree with me a chance to use the data to frame alternative hypotheses. An open debate on such an important matter can only advance our collective understanding of Irish history, particularly if it is conducted with a strong sense of evidence and with the civilized good humour that characterizes the best of Irish letters.

Acknowledgments

For direct support in preparing this volume, I am very happy to acknowledge the John Simon Guggenheim Memorial Foundation, the Ministry of State for Multiculturalism, the Social Sciences and Humanities Research Council of Canada, the Australian National University, and the School of Graduate Studies and Research, Queens University, Kingston, Ontario. The views expressed, however, do not necessarily reflect the position or policy of any of those agencies.

Small Differences

CHAPTER ONE

Perspective

The French moralist and social observer, Jean de la Bruyère, was right when he wrote in 1688 that "the exact opposite to what is generally believed is often the truth."[1]

One of the things that everyone knows is that Irish Catholics and Irish Protestants were, and are, fundamentally different from each other. These differences have long been noted not only in the Irish homeland, but in the places abroad where the Irish settled. There are literally hundreds of books and thousands of periodical articles, scholarly and popular, that either take the fact of Irish Catholic-Protestant differences for granted or seek to amplify the theme by illustration and anecdote. This book is an effort at examining what everybody knows.

The frame-dates for this study are 1815 and 1922. The first, 1815, marks the end of the Napoleonic era in Europe and the subsequent maritime peace that permitted the modern phase of Irish migration to the several new worlds. This flow made the nineteenth-century Irish the most internationally dispersed of the European national cultures. Although there were annual variations in the rate of emigration, from 1815 onwards migration out of Ireland attracted both Protestants and Catholics proportionately, in approximately equal numbers.[2] Thus, each group had globe-circling connections.

The second date, 1922, marks not only the independence of the twenty-six counties of southern Ireland, but the close of a very tense period in the relations of Irish Protestants and Irish Catholics and two sets of violent events. One of these was the "Belfast pogroms" of 1920–2. These are misnamed, for they were not pogroms in the full European sense of the word, but they were nasty and long lasting periods of riot and intimidation. Each side bloodied the other, but the Catholics, being the weaker of the parties in Belfast, suffered most of the consequences. In 1920–2, roughly 200 Catholics were killed by

Protestants and about 100 Protestants by Catholics. No count was kept of the number of persons maimed or of the houses burned, but it was estimated that 9,000 Catholics were driven from their jobs between mid-1920 and early 1922, many of them in the skill-intensive and well-paid Belfast shipyards.[3]

There was a parallel campaign in the south of Ireland and that against Protestants. Unlike the northern episode, this was mostly a rural affair and it consisted of hectoring, intimidating, burning, and murdering isolated Protestants, most, but not all, of whom were owners of small town businesses or of relatively large farms. These actions were not part of the considered policy of the Irish national movement of the time and republican leaders, Michael Collins especially, tried without success to stop them. These atrocities were for the most part spontaneous and local and they derived not from political ideology but from the deep and free-flowing stream of sectarian hatred that runs through Irish history of that era. A precise tally of Protestant victims of these outrages for the entire period 1920–2 is not available, but between early December 1921 and late March 1923, 192 houses and residences belonging to the Protestant minority in southern Ireland were destroyed.[4] The real effect of anti-Protestant intimidation and of the pinching-in upon Protestants in cultural and employment matters by the new Free State government (particularly in educational policy and in hiring in the new civil service) became clear in 1926 when the first census of southern Ireland was taken. It revealed that thousands of Protestants had decided they had no future in Catholic Ireland and had left: in 1911 there had been 327,000 Protestants in what eventually became the Irish Free State, but by 1926 there were only 221,000.[5] This, and not the events in Belfast in 1920–2, or, indeed in 1969–72, represents the biggest movement of population in twentieth-century Irish history.

Such unpleasant events are a logical result of Ireland's sectarian division, but not the only possible outcome. The subject of Catholic-Protestant differences is less stark, more textured, and is characterized by large gray sectors and by confusingly lentiginous areas. The differences between Irish Catholics and Irish Protestants, though strongly held, were for the most part not violent. In many local and in myriad social situations, the two groups got on peaceably together, the surface amity being like the thin ice on a newly frozen pond. There always have been Irishmen who publically claimed that it made no difference to them if a person is Protestant or Catholic and one can accept such statements as being sincere – even as one notes that a person making such a claim knew, and Ireland being what it is, could not help but know, the religious background of the person to whom he was making this declaration. In Ireland, everyone, even the least sectarian individual, always has taken note of religious persuasion.

Implicit in this study is a paean of respect to the work of the late Provost F.S.L. Lyons and to that of Professor Emeritus J.C. Beckett. Each scholar produced an elegant volume on aspects of the Irish Protestant traditions: Beckett's *The Anglo-Irish Tradition* (London: Faber and Faber) was published in 1976 and Lyons's *Culture and Anarchy in Ireland, 1890–1939* (Oxford: Clarendon Press) in 1979. Although primarily about the Anglo-Irish (meaning, crudely, people who were for the most part of English origin and of Anglican religious affiliation), both volumes include a considerable amount of comparative material, explicit and implicit, about the differences between Protestants and Catholics in Ireland.

I am paying these two graceful works of scholarship the compliment of not attempting to go over once again the ground that they covered so well. Instead of concentrating on high culture, as did those two studies, I am focusing upon a demotic pattern of behaviour and upon the everyday culture of the bulk of the Irish people. If a study of putative religious differences is to be more than a wandering anamnesis of material in the darker recesses of the folk mind, much of the work must be demographic in nature. That is, one must collect evidence of behaviour that covers large numbers of cases.

Of course, within the Protestant faith there are several groups, of which the most important in Ireland are the Anglicans, the Presbyterians, and, to a lesser degree, the Methodists. The differences between and among these groups (and their own subsects) is not inconsequential, but at the level of generalization being sought here, one can treat them in most circumstances as a single group. This is true to contemporary usage, for whatever their differences, the Protestant denominations shared a conception of themselves as distinctly non-Roman Catholic in religion and antinationalist in politics. That the aggregation of the Protestants is historically legitimate is shown by the actions of the Irish Free State which, immediately after independence, began collecting its demographic data in two master categories: Catholic and non-Catholic. At times, I shall refer to the various Protestant denominations separately, but only where they have a significant deviation in behaviour one from another.

Considering how religiously sensitized the Irish always have been, the basic demographic data for much of the nineteenth century are disappointingly thin. The first Irish religious census was conducted in 1834, and, strictly speaking, it was not a direct census but a re-enu-

Figure 1
Irish Religious Distributions, 1834–1911

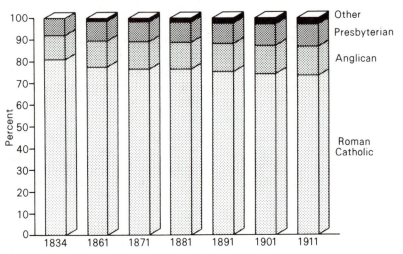

Source: See Appendixes A, B, and C.

meration. There had been a personal census in 1831, but it had included no query on religion. In 1834 a royal commission was established to investigate the state of "religious and other instruction" in Ireland. This was tied into contemporary efforts to curb the temporalities of the Established Church and, naturally, there was a good deal of curiousity about how many adherents there were to the various Irish denominations. The royal commissioners adopted the sensible expedient of having the 1831 census returns sent back to the original enumerators and from them an indication of the religious affiliation of each person who had been living in Ireland in 1831 was provided. This method was not perfectly accurate for any given parish, but on the aggregate level it can be taken as giving a fair representation of the situation.[6] (The results are summarized in Appendix A.)

From a modern viewpoint, the chief drawback of the 1834 data is that the geographic categories employed were those of the diocesan boundaries of the Established Church and these are not immediately familiar to most present-day readers. The next Irish religious census, that of 1861, obviated this problem by using civil boundaries. (See Appendix B.) It is somewhat surprising – and regrettable – that there was no Irish religious census in 1851. This was the only time that any kind of religious enumeration was tried for England, Wales, and Scotland and a great opportunity for accurate religious comparisons was

Figure 2
Irish Illiteracy Rates, 1861–1911

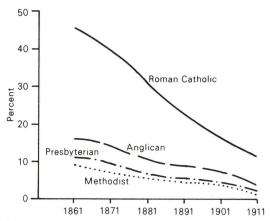

Source: See Appendix D.

lost by Ireland's nonparticipation. It occurred because of the belief of the under-secretary for Ireland, Thomas Larcom, that each enumerator would inflate the number of persons of his own denomination. Thus, rather than yield to sectarian competition, the Irish Census Act specifically forbade the inclusion of a religious question on the census form.[7] Larcom's worries were not generally shared and in the 1861 census and in subsequent decennial enumerations, a religious query was included. The census takers' standards of conduct were carefully monitored and there is no indication of any significant bias in the religious sections of the 1861 census or of its successors. The religious distribution for the years 1834 through 1911 (the last census of united Ireland) are given in Figure 1. (See also Appendix C.)

Those data are merely descriptive and one wishes to know how the various religious affiliations compared on economic and cultural matters. Here the going becomes difficult. One can, for example, note the cross-tabulations of religious denomination and of illiteracy in Ireland, as is done in Figure 2.

Assuming that one accepts the census officials' definition of illiteracy (and that is a separate and complex problem) what can one legitimately conclude from the cross-tabulations? Very little, except that Roman Catholics tended to be more frequently illiterate than were Protestants and that their illiteracy rate dropped more rapidly than did that of any group during the second half of the nineteenth century and the first decade of the twentieth. But whether or not illiteracy and Catholicism are in any way causally related is impossible to say. The positive relationship of the two variables could be (and, indeed, probably is) a function of other, unseen, factors.

This example brings us to the heart of any empirical investigation of the historical differences between Irish Catholics and Irish Protestants.

In the first instance, one is trying to uncover differences between Protestants and Catholics that are of a *significant magnitude*. This emphasis upon magnitude is important, because historians, like academicians in most disciplines, are given to teasing out small comparisons until they seem to become major contrasts. Here we must focus only upon significantly large differences, not mere distinctions. Obviously one is not here using "significant" in the statistical sense, and what is a significant difference between the two groups is a matter of judgment. Were one to find out that the average Catholic in, say, 1900 took in 3,400 calories a day and the average Protestant 3,300, it probably would not be a difference of significant magnitude to allow any conclusion about nutritional levels, religion, and economic status.

Second, one is looking for differences that are *causally important*. Conceivably, there are differences between Protestants and Catholics that have no referents in the real world. For instance, it is theoretically possible that a multimillion dollar study of the fingerprint patterns of the two groups in present-day Ireland would show that a certain pattern of swirls and crests was markedly more frequent in one group than in the other. That would be fascinating, but unless the differences could be shown to be causally related to some differences in the behaviour of the two groups, they would be for the purposes of this study meaningless epiphenomena.

This raises a third, related, point: that one must continually work at distinguishing *association* (or correlation) from *causation*. In the case of Irish Catholics and Protestants this is especially important, because there are numerous adventitious adhesions to their religious identities. To return to the case of the seeming propensity for illiteracy among the Catholics: it is highly probable that one could establish satisfactorily (and demonstrate statistically) that the apparent differences between Protestants and Catholics were entirely a function of social class and had no causal connection to religion. That is, if one held social class constant, one would find that Catholics were no more likely than were Protestants to have been illiterate. On many such issues, if one holds constant the economic substructure by employing a good experimental design, the differences in the cultural superstructure are seen to be nonexistent.

Holding-everything-constant, of course, is a great problem for historians. Unlike present-day social scientists, we do not have the luxury of designing experiments that clearly isolate causal variables: we have to work with whatever data have been left to us. There exist statistical techniques that are helpful, but in most instances we are thrown back on the logical tools that have governed intellectual discourse since classical times. In practical terms, as historians we have two problems. One of these is analogous to the problem of *multicollinearity* in statistical work. This occurs when the variations in potential explanatory factors are so similar that it is difficult to distinguish their separate effects. Most collective historical phenomena are multicollinear to some degree and so inevitably one has to make decisions as to when the collinearity is so severe as to make one abandon the investigation. There is, however, no clear cut point at which one makes this decision and each historian must be his own judge.

In dealing with these difficult matters of historical method, there are three fallacious ways of thinking that are devoutly to be avoided. (Indeed, there are a myriad of ways of falling into error, but these three are the most invidious in Irish social history and are nearly endemic.) The first is the fallacy of viewing a subset as if it were a whole. One should not discuss a subset of any body of data until one places it in the context of the entire body from which it is drawn. Sometimes a subset will be almost perfectly representative of the larger body from which it is taken. This is the case in a well-designed random sample. If one has such a sample – say of the heads of household of the 1901 census of Ireland – one can use it to delineate significant differences between Catholics and Protestants in that sample and do so with the confidence that, within the statistical limits of one's procedure, the sample represents accurately the characteristics of the whole Irish population. One cannot do this, however, in the case of nonrandom subsets; skewed samples give skewed results. The fallacy of misusing subsets has been most frequent in studies of Irish-Catholic urban communities, particularly those of the diaspora-Irish in North America. Local studies can be immensely rewarding, but only if generalizations are drawn from them with great care.

Second, one needs to be wary of the fallacy of false relativism. To return to the earlier example of the cross-tabulations of religion and illiteracy in Ireland in 1901 it might (conceivably) be shown:

1 that in 1901 among Catholics of middle class origin, there was a three percent illiteracy rate and among Protestants of the same class a 2.5 percent rate;
2 therefore, it could accurately be concluded that in this social class the Catholics had a relatively higher propensity for illiteracy.

It would be absurd, however, to discuss Catholicism and illiteracy in such a way as to equate the two – "illiterate Catholics" – because in fact the overwhelming majority were literate. Put in this extreme form, one wonders how responsible historians ever could fall into such a way of thinking, but actually it is quite common in Irish studies. For example, until recently, in studies of the Irish in British North America it was common to describe the Irish Catholics as engaged in urban occupations and the Irish Protestants as engaged in rural employment. This stemmed from the fact that the Catholics had a slightly greater propensity to live in cities than did the Protestants, but actually the great majority of both groups settled and worked in the countryside. In such a manner, accurate statements of relative differences are misinterpreted so that they become inaccurate statements of absolute matters.

Third, when dealing with issues as volatile and complex as is religion in Ireland, one should be chary of direct contemporary evidence on the subject, particularly by contemporary "expert" witnesses. Contrasts between Protestants and Catholics were easily drawn in the nineteenth and early twentieth centuries and this was especially prevalent because it was an age that was given to thinking about cultural differences in racial terms. Just as it was easy for nineteenth-century Englishmen to draw stereotypic differences between the Anglo-Saxon and the Celt,[8] it was easy for Irishmen of both faiths to believe in and testify to the existence of stereotypic differences between Irish people, Protestant and Catholic. That is why one searches for broadly based demographic data that were collected in as neutral a fashion as possible (such as is the case with censuses). If one finds that widely-based demographic data clash with the opinion of contemporaries, then one should not feel uneasy about rejecting the contemporary viewpoint: after all, expert contemporary testimony once held that the sun revolved around the earth. The way a people believe that their world is structured, and the way it actually is, often are different. Emile Durkheim in his classic *The Elementary Forms of the Religious Life* noted that "there are societies in Australia and North America where space is conceived in the form of an immense circle, because the camp has a circular form, and this spatial circle is divided up exactly like the tribal circle, and is in its image."[9] The same sort of thing occurred in Ireland.

In an engagingly honest preface to a study of electoral politics in twentieth-century Ireland, a Canadian political scientist admitted that "my attention was drawn to Ireland by footnotes. Over and over again the literature of comparative politics noted simply 'except Ireland.' " Whatever the topic – ideological splits, electoral systems – "the observation was the same: except Ireland. The question that puzzled me was, Why should this be so?"[10]

When one turns to twentieth-century Irish historical writings, one is struck with a similar observation: except Ireland. Unlike the historiography of western Europe and of Great Britain, Irish historical writing is dominated by an unspoken, but pervasive, cultural determinism. Most European and British historical writing today assumes implicitly that economic substructures and the social configurations based on those structures (such as class and ideology) are the fundamental strata of historical reality. Yet, most Irish historians, whether discussing Irish politics, nationalism, the colonial relationship of England and Ireland, the achievement of Catholic equality under the law, the establishment of an Irish peasant proprietorship, adopt a stance in which culture and national self-assertion are the ultimate explanations of events. With rare exceptions, this vaguely spiritual sense underlies the work of even the most outwardly empirical of writers and is all the more pervasive for its being largely unconscious.

Occasionally, scholars have made explicit the cultural determinism that usually is only implicit, and in such instances the results have been stimulating if not entirely convincing. The most extreme example of this approach is that of the Dutch historical geographer M.W. Heslinga, whose *The Irish Border as a Cultural Divide* (Assen: Van Gorcum, 1971) argues that the cultural differences between Ulster and the rest of Ireland have been simply the extension across the Irish sea of cultural differences that exist in Great Britain. The border between "the north" and "the south" is taken to be primarily a cultural, rather than a geographic, divide and the north is seen as an area of Scottish cultural hegemony, the south as an area of English cultural domination. Not surprisingly, this interpretation does not appeal to most Irish historians because it explains the cultural history of modern Ireland without much reference to Irish culture.

The most compelling example of recent work produced from an overtly cultural-deterministic viewpoint is *Ireland's English Question*, by Patrick J. O'Farrell, the brilliant Australian historian of Ireland. This wonderfully idiosyncratic and spikey study not only posits that culture, not economics, is the driving engine of Irish history – "the economic interpretation of Irish history, whether propounded by conservative Unionists, or radicals, or Christian Socialists, has always been superficial"[11] – but that Irish Catholicism is the very heart of Irish culture. Within this rubric, the colonial relationship of England and Ireland is perceived largely as a footnote to that great volta voce in western history, the Protestant reformation.

Since the mid-1970s, a number of highly competent younger scholars have introduced into Irish historical studies many of the methods, if not the prevailing econo-socio deterministic assumptions, employed in other western historiographies. Samuel Clark, in his tour de force on the *Social Origins of the Irish Land War* (Princeton: Princeton University Press, 1979), has established the absolute necessity of employing social class as an explanatory factor if one is to deal adequately with the political culture of nineteenth-century Ireland.[12] The methods of North American microhistory have been adopted by the American scholar Kevin O'Neill in *Family and Farm in Pre-Famine Ireland: The Parish of Killashandra*.[13] In this study of the only Irish parish for which pre-Famine manuscript census data survive, O'Neill employs economic modelling to explain the changing family patterns of an Irish-Catholic community. And, in a ground-breaking series of articles, A.C. Hepburn of the University of Ulster has analyzed the intersecting matrices of occupation, class, and religion in Belfast in the late nineteenth and early twentieth centuries.[14]

One could name several other studies of impressive rigour and innovative technique. The interesting point, however, is what is missing: there has yet to be a successful classical Marxist analysis of Irish life or of any of its major components. This is strange within the context of British and of European historical writing, for the Marxist analysis is common and is frequently highly insightful. Admittedly, the early years of the present Ulster trouble, from 1969 onwards, brought forth a spate of Marxist-derived works – but these ranged from the merely unsuccessful to the truly awful.[15] Even when employed by serious scholars rather than polemicists, Marxist analysis has not worked very well in explaining Irish historical phenomena. This is particularly ironic because both Marx and Engels had a sympathetic interest in Irish history.[16]

For at least a century and a quarter it has been commonplace for observers of Irish life to note that the differences between Protestants and Catholics in Ireland have nothing to do with religion per se and everything to do with divergent cultural traditions or with economic discrimination. This may well be true. The difficulty is that attempts to obtain a broader perspective on Irish religious differences frequently have exchanged the shackles of an overly narrow definition of religion for the gyves of an unconscious racism. Take, for example, the observations of Friedrich Engels (no religious-determinist, certainly) about the Irish-Catholic peasant, a creature he greatly admired:

The Irishman is a light-hearted, cheerful, potato-eating child of nature. Straight from the moorland, where he grew up under a leaky roof, fed on weak tea and short commons, he is suddenly flung into our [English] civilisation . . .

His half-wild upbringing and the wholly civilised surroundings in which he finds himself later, engender an internal conflict, a continuous irritation, a rage which constantly smoulders within him, making him capable of anything.[17]

Such men could fuel a revolution, Engels at first thought, but by the late 1860s he began to have misgivings about the Catholic peasant. These reservations, like his praise, he expressed racially stereotypically. "The worst about the Irish," he wrote to Karl Marx, "is that they become corruptible as soon as they stop being peasants and turn bourgeois. True, this is the case with most peasant nations. But in Ireland it is particularly bad."[18]

Less animated social analysts than Engels showed the same caste of mind when dealing with Irish-Catholic culture. Sidney and Beatrice Webb took a "working honeymoon" in Dublin in 1892 and systematically read about and observed Irish life. They wrote a joint letter to their close friend Graham Wallas: "We will tell you about Ireland when we come back. The people are charming but we detest them, as we should the Hottentots – for their very virtue. Home Rule is an absolute necessity in order to depopulate the country of this detestable race."[19]

If cultural stereotyping, bordering on racism, has characterized many of the communist and socialist observers of the Irish from the late nineteenth century onwards,[20] it has also been evinced by their opposite number, the historical empiricists. William Forbes Adams published in 1932 a remarkable study, *Ireland and the Irish Emigration to the New World from 1815 to the Famine*. He had a fine thirst for primary data. Unlike his precedessors in the field of emigration history (and, alas, unlike most of his successors), he actually examined the primary emigration data and, before developing conclusions about the nature of the Irish diaspora, he equilibrated for shortcomings in the primary records. Yet, when dealing with the cultural background of the Irish migrants to the New World, he fell into the same sort of semiracial thinking that characterized the early communists and socialists.

Differences of religion in 1815 were on the whole less important than differences of race in determining the character of the emigrants and both were most marked among the lower classes. The Scots-Irish peasants of Ulster, and to a lesser extent the English and Welsh settlers in Leinster, had retained habits and traits which set them apart from the native Irish, and checked the growth of common sympathies or the realization of common interests. They were energetic, moderately clean, and less volatile and susceptible to mass emotion than their mercurial neighbours. A stern and narrow morality cut them off from a whole range of popular entertainment, from friendly fighting and the enjoyment of harpers. But the most vital distinction lay in that indefinite quality called morale. The Ulster peasant inherited something of the dour pride and stoicism of his ancestors. The native Irish had developed no such armor, and the self pity, the unending note of sorrow which has sounded in their literature from its earliest days, deepened and strengthed after 1815.[21]

In various forms, this sort of stereotyping, done without adequate evidence, persists to this day.[22] Undeniably, religious and cultural differences have existed among segments of the Irish population. The problem is to find real differences, to demonstrate them if possible with broadly based empirical data, and to mark clearly the gaps in the data. What is required as a first step is a set of clear tests of Catholic-Protestant differences.

CHAPTER TWO

Some Empirical Tests

For many Irish historians this may be the balking point, for it involves trying to replace anecdotes about religious matters with broadly based empirical evidence. Since we are examining the possible influence of religion on the behaviour of the entire body of the Irish people, we must collect data on as wide a basis as possible: sometimes, getting to the heart of what counts involves counting.

The reason that one must cast a wide evidentiary net was well expressed by that most rebarbative of social scrutineers, Kingsley Amis's Fat Englishman: "Most patterns are illusions based on insufficient evidence. An observer seeing red and black at roulette coming up alternately six times each might conclude that he'd found a pattern, this was how it always went. Then red comes up twice running. End of pattern."[1]

In practical terms, there are three broadly based tests of Protestant-Catholic differences that one might apply to nineteenth- and early twentieth-century Ireland. These are occupational stratigraphy, family structure, and the treatment of women.[2] Because the word "empirical" has come to have a bad connotation in some quarters – it is a term of derogation referring to work that is merely empirical in the sense of being uninformed by theory – I should make it clear what is intended here. By empirical tests of differences between Protestants and Catholics, I mean to indicate the examination of large, systematic, and comprehensive bodies of data that permit one to test theoretical hypotheses, to evaluate the robustness of rival theories, and to improve those existing systems of theory that have proven value.

One of the few things on which there is general agreement among social anthropologists is that significant differences in culture produce significant differences in economic behaviour. For instance, Israeli and Lebanese farmers share a common agricultural topography and soil structure, yet their exploitation of these resources is radically different and that difference is rooted in the contrasting patterns of Israeli and Lebanese culture.[3]

There is a long, if not at present very popular, tradition in European historical writing which argues that fundamental economic structures are in considerable degree shaped by cultural patterns (and, in turn, these economic structures determine secondary cultural patterns). The benchmark of this tradition is Max Weber's *The Protestant Ethic and the Spirit of Capitalism* (1904) which is one of those volumes that is too often guyed and too rarely actually read. Far from being simplistic, this work is nothing less than an attempt to discover the psychological underpinnings that facilitate the development of capitalist economic life. Like most scholarly landmarks of the past, it has fallen into disfavour not so much through its being disproved as its having become disapproved of: that is, it became unfashionable.[4] A derivative and well known exposition of a parallel argument to Weber's was presented in 1922 in the Holland Lectures by R.H. Tawney and this eventually became the widely read *Religion and the Rise of Capitalism* (1926).[5]

These two works, and the tradition that they represent, fit in well with the dominant assumptions of Irish historical writing, for although they are not culturally deterministic, they can easily be misread that way. In their emphasis upon religion as the central pivot of culture (at least insofar as economic behaviour is concerned), they obviously have direct relevance to nineteenth- and twentieth-century Ireland which was one of the most religiously sensitized nations in the western world. Nevertheless, these works, although not entirely ignored, did not find their way into the core of Irish historiography because they easily led to two hypotheses that are (in my opinion) implausible, but which were embarrassing for Irish scholars even to state: (1) that Ireland in the nineteenth and early twentieth centuries was economically backward not chiefly because of British rule, or lack of industrial resources, but because of the economic inertia of the dominant Catholic culture; and (2) that the reason Protestants in Ireland were better off than were Catholics was not because of structural discrimination, but because of the greater economic initiative engendered by Protestant religious tenets.

The rough edges of the Weber-Tawney approach were smoothed away by David McClelland in *The Achieving Society*, one of the most ambitious, if confusing, scholarly works of the past thirty years. McClelland, a Harvard psychologist, tried to explain why certain societies have done better in material terms than have others. What would account for what he called "overachievement in the economic sphere"?[6] Overachieving cultures to McClelland were those such as the Jews in America, and the offshore Chinese in southeast Asia. Significantly, McClelland proceeded from operational premises directly opposed both to those of traditional historians and to those of most economists. He pointed out that almost all explanations of economic growth – whether by economic theorists or by historians – are not empirically or systematically testable. "The fact is that traditions for gathering evidence for or against a general proposition in economics and history are different from what they are in the behavioural sciences. . . . In a word, the behavioural scientist follows . . . the tradition of the logic of experimental design as established by R.A. Fisher (1951) and others, whereas *the economist and historian ordinarily follow an older scholarly tradition which relies heavily on the logic of the extreme case, on the citing of key examples, and on the opinion of outstanding authorities*."[7] Instead he proposed that the cultural-economic history of western society be constructed through the creation of objective measures of the variables that were thought to be important.

McClelland posited that economic behaviour was strongly related to an hypothetical construct he called "n Achievement." Crudely, this can be equated with the "achievement motive" that is common to a group or culture. Through quite elaborate tests, McClelland measured n Achievement among several disparate groups, ranging from school children in Orissa Province, India, to Japan, to Germany. (Separate scores were derived for German Protestants and German Catholics.) Then, armed with two sets of independent data (one having to do with the economic performance of various groups, the other with the culturally determined need for achievement), he ran off masses of regressions and found that in general, societies with a high cultural need for achievement had a higher level of economic attainment. This conclusion was not tautological, for his experimental design guaranteed that his two variables were independent of each other. But neither was the conclusion in itself very illuminating. What was more interesting was that McClelland suggested that cultures which taught that the gods scorned those who tried hard, which taught fatalism in the face of life's exigencies, which glorified the random but played down prudent risk, were not the economic overachievers.

As related to Protestants and Catholics, McClelland seemed to be working out a means of showing not only that Weber fundamentally was right, but the mechanisms whereby he was. That is, if one takes Weber's hypothesis, that certain forms of Protestantism led to the growth of modern capitalism, it was, using McClelland's terms, through raising n Achievement level among Protestant children. And how was that done? Through child-rearing patterns that emphasized (at least relative to Catholic practices) self-reliance, high expectations of success, and encouraged a moderate anti-authoritarianism. McClelland claimed to have found widespread differences between Catholic and Protestant child rearing, but he cautioned that these differences frequently were cancelled out by local effects, particularly social class.

McClelland's big barmbrack of a book is now rarely read in its entirety, but parts of it still strike a resonant chord with economic historians, with historians of the traditional school. David Landes, who wrote the latest, one of the best, and, perhaps, the last "good old-fashioned economic history" of the industrial revolution, adopted the central viewpoint, if not the syntax of his Harvard colleague. In *The Unbound Prometheus*, Landes argued that at the heart of the industrial revolution was technological innovation and that this sprang from "the Faustian sense of mastery over man and nature"[8] that ran through certain European cultures. Mostly, these were Protestant cultures.

This tradition – represented but not limited to the line of Weber-Tawney-McClelland-Landes – has not been assimilated into the historiography of the Irish homeland. Indeed, save for one brief moment in the early twentieth century, the issue of Catholic-Protestant economic differences has not been clearly engaged. That moment followed the publication of a volume of essays by Sir Horace Plunkett, entitled *Ireland in the New Century* (London: John Murray, 1904). In this book, Plunkett pointed to various Irish cultural practices that stood in the way of economic growth. He was anything but carping or censorious (his record as founder of the Irish cooperative movement put his motives and actions as a promoter of economic development beyond reproach), but he was an Irish Protestant discussing the behaviour of Irish Catholics, and his words hit a raw nerve. In particular, his comments about extravagance in church building among the Catholics and upon the Catholic reliance upon authority in religious and secular matters, demanded riposte, and in *Catholicity and Progress in Ireland* (London: Kegan Paul, Trench, Trubner and Co., 1905), M. O'Riordan damned Plunkett as a short-sighted Protestant on the one hand, and, on the other, argued that there was nothing in the Catholic faith that impeded economic development. There, unfortunately, the debate ended. As is frequently the case in Ireland, the debate now was religiously polarized and rational discussion impossible. Subsequent Irish scholars learned from this affray that they had best avoid the discussion of religious allegiance and economic behaviour.

Significantly, although the tradition of Weber-Tawney-McClelland-Landes has not been assimilated into the historiography of the Irish homeland, it has been taken up by historians of the Irish migrants to the United States of America. A general, if not universal, consensus concerning the Irish Catholics in America has emerged whereby it is held that (1) for the period beginning with the Great Famine and ending with the start of the twentieth century, the Irish-Catholic immigrants did not do very well in U.S. society and (2) that one of the main reasons was that they were culturally handicapped, in that the culture they brought with them did not place enough emphasis upon individualism, upon rational control of circumstances and money, and upon commercial success. Some historians ascribed this alleged cultural backwardness to the character of Irish Catholicism, others to the Gaelic culture, others to the general economic underdevelopment of Ireland, and others to English imperialism.[9] There is a strong implied contrast in all these theories for, if the Catholics were relatively disadvantaged, then the Protestants were advantaged.

Whether or not this America-derived framework will find its way into the historical work of the Irish at home is uncertain. It is perhaps indicative of the Irish resistance to such an idea, that one of the better general studies of the phenomenon of nineteenth- and twentieth-century economic and social change, J.J. Lee's *The Modernization of Irish Society, 1848–1918* states epigrammatically that "it is as difficult to find convincing evidence of a Catholic ethic in Dublin as of a Protestant in Belfast."[10] Lee argues that in fact "Irish Catholicism, far from being fatalistic and other-worldly, displayed an obsession with the materialistic which might have made less institutionally religious societies squirm with envy."[11]

Nevertheless, there is a large body of demographic data that on surface examination seems to confirm the view that Catholicism was an economic handicap. The first year for which one can provide reliable population-wide data on Catholic-Protestant differences is 1861. Table 1 is a resetting of a contemporary Irish presentation of some of the data from the 1861 census. It makes with efficiency the point that higher status professions tended to be dominated by Protestants, as were some of the skilled trades. (For reference, recall that in 1861 Catholics were somewhat less than 78 percent of the population and, if they had been randomly distributed among occupations, would have formed 78 percent of any given job category.)

It is more revealing, however, to deal with the entire occupational profile of the main religious denominations, as is done in Figure 3. (The categorization is done for males only, because the classification of rural females was done too imprecisely in 1861 to allow meaningful analysis).

Even given the coarseness of contemporary categories, the table

Table 1
Occupations Grouped by Percentage of Protestants and Catholics
Employed, 1861

% Protestant		% Catholic
100		0
	needle makers, linen thread makers, damask designers, artisans in pearl	
90		10
	nobles, barons, knights, baronets, cotton weavers, army surgeons, flax yarn makers	
80		20
	land agents, teachers of Irish, bankers, insurance agents, photographers, army officers, druggists, factory overseers, surgeons, authors, barristers	
70		30
	house agents, judges, physicians, linen and damask weavers, attorneys and solicitors, engravers, saddlers, merchants	
60		40
	watch makers, landed proprietors, portrait painters, artists, gunsmiths, weavers, poor-law clerks, coast guards, mill workers, prison officers, apothecaries	
50		50
	embroiderers, excise officers, rent collectors, postmasters, engineers, hotel keepers, clerks, drapers, flax dressers, grocers, parish clerks, factory workers	
40		60
	milliners, shirt makers, pawnbrokers, leather dealers, sculptors, pensioners, painters, glassers and decorators, constabulary and metropolitan police, saddlers and harness makers, process servers	
30		70
	gate keepers, letter carriers, stewards, dressmakers, shopkeepers, skilled weavers, coat makers, carpenters, farmers, loaders, housekeepers	
23		77
	brick layers, rope and twine makers, carters, seamstresses	
20		80
	flax spinners, tanners, bootbinders, musicians, publicans, bakers, blacksmiths, tailors, knitters, stablemen, domestic servants, prostitutes, waiters, butchers, thatchers, basketmakers, slaters, charwomen, farm laborers, fishermen	
10		90
	tobacconists, peddlers, cattle dealers, wool weavers, masons, chimney sweeps, old clothes dealers, carriage brokers, brogue makers	
0		100

Source: Adapted from A. Hume, *Results of the Irish Census of 1861* (London: Rivingtons, 1864), 51.

Figure 3
Religion and Occupation, Adult Males, 1861

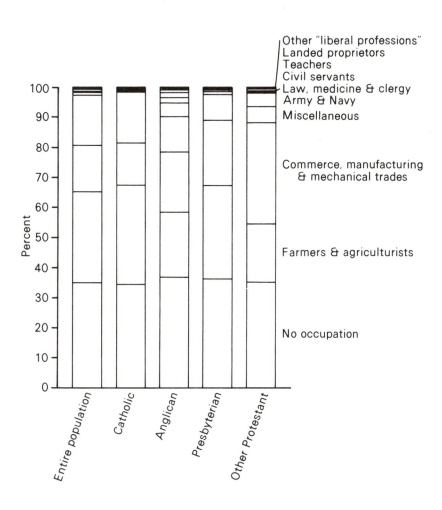

shows markedly diverging denominational profiles. Catholics were underrepresented sharply among landed proprietors, but were slightly overrepresented among farmers (a category that included small tenant farmers). There were proportionately fewer Catholics than Protestants in the liberal professions and in the military. Most significantly, within the context of nineteenth-century Ireland as a "modernizing" society, Catholics were underrepresented in commerce, manufacturing, and the mechanical trades. (The contrast here to the "other Protestant" category, Quakers and Congregationalists for the most part, is particularly striking.) The size of the "miscellaneous" and the "no occupation" categories (which account for more than half of the total returns) means that one can draw only the most tentative conclusions, but, nevertheless, the data are better than none at all. Thus, in Appendix F, I have given the Catholic/non-Catholic breakdown of virtually all occupations defined by the 1861 census takers. Without belabouring the details of this sometimes fascinating enumeration (were there really only seven brothel keepers in all of Ireland and all of these Catholics?), it is undeniable that within each sector of production and each service activity, the higher ranks and more "modern" jobs tended to have an overrepresentation of Protestants: not a monopoly, or anything close to it, but an overrepresentation.

To explain this phenomenon does not require anything so complex as McClelland's n Achievement factor or demand recourse to Weber's hypothesis, but only reference to a well-known Irish tragedy: the penal laws of the eighteenth century. In some ways, the Irish penal code is one of the most puzzling problems in Irish history and, considering its importance, one which is remarkably little studied. The "code" was not really a legal code, but an overlapping snarl of statutes enacted in the late seventeenth and early eighteenth centuries. It was the sort of legislation that was common in contemporary Europe where religious wars between nations led to domestic persecution of suspect religious groups. The Irish penal code differed from the European template, however, in that the Irish penalties were imposed on a religious majority by a religious minority. The adherents of the Established Church imposed penalties upon the Catholics (and to a minor degree upon Presbyterians and other Protestant dissenters). For two further reasons, the Irish penal code is extremely puzzling. The first is because it is not clear what was the motivation behind its imposition: was it intended to turn Ireland into a Protestant nation or, rather, to beggar the Catholic population? And, second, how strongly the code was enforced still has yet to be adequately investigated. Nevertheless, the overall effects are clear: by inhibiting Catholic land ownership, by prohibiting Catholic entry into most of the higher professions, by taking away the Catholic's right to vote, and by prohibiting Catholic membership in parliament, the code radically reduced the economic and social status of the Roman Catholic population of Ireland. Although most of the code had been removed from the statute books by 1793, when the Catholics again got the franchise and thus reacquired the fundamental weapon for protecting their common interests, elements remained in effect until the mid-nineteenth century.[12]

That the legacy of this discrimination against the Catholics, rather than anything in the values and attitudes of their religion, accounts for their relatively lower socioeconomic profile as compared to Protestants in 1861 is a sensible suggestion. This hypothesis has the advantage of being simple, and of being based upon well documented structural discrimination. To anyone familiar with the history of the blacks in the United States, it has the additional weight of analogy: over a century and a quarter after the abolition of slavery, the socioeconomic effects of that severe form of structural discrimination are still being felt. As W. Arthur Lewis has observed, "most subordinate racial or ethnic groups are deficient in entrepreneurship, as, for example, the Afro-Americans and many Third World peoples."[13]

Thus, one need not turn to the cultural characteristics of Irish Catholicism – its alleged fatalism, its supposed excessive authoritarianism, its putative smothering communalism – to explain the occupational stratigraphy of Ireland in 1861. One must realize, however, that there were things that were associated with Irish Catholics – specifically, a comparatively lower socioeconomic status and underrepresentation in "modern" jobs – that could easily be mistaken by contemporaries as being caused by the Catholic culture. That is a confusion of association and causation.

To escape the procrustean structural problem, imposed by the legacy of structural discrimination against the Catholics, one would like to take the life history of large numbers of Catholics and Protestants who were at the same point in life's race (as indicated, for example, by their having the same occupation and being of roughly the same age) and seeing how much mobility upwards or downwards there was on the economic scale over a period of ten or twenty years. Assuming that one kept everything equal (that is, controlled for such things as rural-urban bias and so on), the differing rates of social mobility would then potentially reflect significant cultural differences in attitudes to work, to risk, and to modernization, in the two groups being studied: at least a prima facie case for a cultural interpretation would have been made. Unfortunately, although this kind of study is possible in some countries, it cannot be done in Ireland, for the manuscript census forms (upon which such research would have to be based) were destroyed for 1861, 1871, 1881, and 1891. Thus only 1901 and 1911 offer potential occasion for study. (The Irish censuses after 1911 are permanently sealed, so 1911 is the last possible year of study.)[14]

The most impressive – but, unfortunately disappointing – study of early twentieth-century Irish census data is that conducted by A.C. Hepburn of the University of Ulster. He drew off a large random sample of Belfast households (5,461) and linked the information on the individual census forms to residential and other data. He found that, in 1901, there was a high degree of residential segregation of Catholics in Belfast and that this was almost as high as was found among black Americans in the mid-twentieth century. Not only were the Catholics excluded from the worker-elite, but their situation seemed to be growing not better, but worse.[15] This is an excellent scholarly study, and is a great aid to historians who wish to understand the period in which Ulster unionism was crystallizing into the adamantine rock it has become, but it is disappointing for our present purposes because it shows that the degree of anti-Catholic discrimination in the northeast of Ireland in the early twentieth century was so great that one cannot conduct controlled observations of Protestant and Catholic socioeconomic behaviour under equal conditions.[16] And, one cannot simply drop out the northeast from any controlled study, for it was the one part of Ireland that was part of the British commercial and industrial revolution of the nineteenth century and, therefore, the only place where one might have an opportunity to observe contrasting attitudes to modern economic change among the major religious groups.[17]

Thus, we have arrived at an impasse. As a social laboratory, Ireland developed too little nineteenth-century data and, thanks to the pyrotechnics of governmental bureaucrats and of Irish revolutions, much of what there was has been destroyed. And the Belfast material for the early twentieth century reveals a social laboratory that is too charged, too discriminatory to allow reliable information about the effect of Protestant and Catholic cultures upon economic activities.

If, in the nineteenth and early twentieth centuries, Catholic and Protestant cultures were fundamentally different, then their family structures should have been demonstrably different. Mid-twentieth-century studies of the demographic patterns of Northern Ireland and of the Irish Republic have revealed that across all social levels Protestant and Catholic families differed. For instance, in 1971 Roman Catholic marital fertility in Northern Ireland was two-thirds higher than was Protestant, a differential that is significant by any standard. Crucially, this marked tendency for Catholics to have larger families ran right through the social spectrum. At all levels of socioeconomic background, Catholics in Northern Ireland registered higher fertility levels than did Protestants.[18] On a related matter, the age of marriage, material for 1961 for both Northern Ireland and for the Irish Republic showed that at all age levels Catholic men and Catholic women were more apt to be unmarried than were Protestant men and Protestant women.[19] Admittedly, there was no control for social class on these 1961 data, but, seemingly, a picture emerged of Irish Catholics marrying later in life than did Protestants, but, when they did marry, having larger families. Looking at the 1971 data, Cormac O'Grada posed an apposite judgment. "We are left with the 'cultural' explanation that Catholics have inherited or developed a different set of values as regards fertility and family size."[20]

It would be convenient if we could project this judgment back into the nineteenth century (or even into the early twentieth century), for then we would have taken a major step toward discovering wherein Protestant and Catholic actually differed in the past.[21] However, the one thorough study of this phenomenon in a rural area, O'Grada's reworking of the manuscript census data for counties Londonderry and Tyrone for the year 1911, prevents our doing any such thing. O'Grada's study, a very rigorous piece of work, involved the linking of information of 1,500 farming families and 700 farm labourer families, to the 1911 manuscript census sheets. He collected information on age, religion, occupation, literacy, and property holding. He then cross-tabulated the data and ran regressions, with the following results. First, it was found that farm labourers had somewhat larger families than did farm operators, which is to say that the poorer one was, the more apt one was to have a large family. Second, because Catholics were overrepresented among the poorer classes, this poverty factor influenced their marital fertility level. But, third – and most important – "the large fertility gap so widely noted today [between Protestants and Catholics] was absent in the rural areas surveyed in this study. In these areas at least, *all* confessional groupings registered much higher marital fertility."[22] Specifically, completed Catholic households were on the average larger than Protestant ones by about one-third of a child, a difference easily accounted for by class factors. And, fourth, what little difference there was between Protestant and Catholic family size disappeared when one looked at couples who had been married longest. "The confessional gap hardly existed at all for those couples who had married before the mid-1880s."[23]

That held for a rural area. A complementary study of the Belfast area for 1901 came to the same conclusion, that differences in family structure between Protestants and Catholics is a relatively recent phenomenon: "We know that the greater propensity of Catholics to have large families is a trend which has emerged only during the twentieth century," is A.C. Hepburn's summary of that research.[24] Thus, both rural and urban data indicate that the present-day large differences in family structure began from very small differences that emerged late in the nineteenth century and in the early twentieth. As O'Grada suggests, "finding out just when and why the small gap grew is an interesting historical problem, awaiting inter-disciplinary research."[25] For our present purposes, the germane point is that the available data suggest that nineteenth- and early twentieth-century Protestants and Catholics did not have divergent family patterns, but, rather, that they held a single common pattern.[26]

That is the most reasonable supposition for the post-Famine era, but what about the pre-Famine period? Irish demographic history in the nineteenth century is a complex field and, because of the sketchiness of pre-Famine Irish data, one of considerable speculation. At the risk of burlesquing a complex debate, the dominant view of the pre-Famine situation is as follows: that (1) in common with the dominant pattern in western Europe, the family was nuclear, not extended. Although on occasion two generations shared the same house (and masters and servants did so also), the building blocks of the Irish family were the father, mother, and unmarried children; (2) marriage occurred most frequently in the mid-twenties. That is, the common European pattern of relatively late marriage prevailed; (3) because most small farmers were willing to subdivide their land among their children, the economic constraints against marriage, while significant, were not crippling; (4) there was, in comparison to other European countries, relatively little in the way of "illicit love" by which is meant sexual activity resulting in either illegitimacy or prenuptial pregnancy; and (5) within marriage there was a high fertility rate.[27]

By the time of the Great Famine, a demographic shift was in train. Exactly what the Famine had to do with this is indeterminate. An earlier generation of historians used the Famine to explain virtually everything in nineteenth-century Irish social history: it was *the* watershed. Then, in the 1960s a group of revisionists, led by S.H. Cousens and by R.D. Crotty, pushed the opposite viewpoint. Cousens showed that much of the allegedly lost pre-Famine social structure continued to exist in large fragments in the west of Ireland late into the nineteenth century. Crotty argued that the Famine did not in any way affect Irish agricultural development. For a time, it was fashionable to refer dismissively to the Famine. The pendulum has swung part of the way back, however, and it now is the prevailing view among specialists in the field that major social and demographic shifts indeed had begun in several locales well before the Famine, but that the Famine was important: it served to confirm and to accelerate changes that otherwise probably would have taken decades to complete.[28]

The resultant post-Famine family structure may be summarized as follows: (1) the Irish family remained nuclear and, indeed, became more so, for "stem family" ideology became overwhelmingly dominant. Under the stem family system, only one child per generation inherited the family's main economic interest, be it farm or small town shop. Consolidation, not division of farms, became the rule;[29] (2) the age of marriagè rose, so that in the Irish Free State by the year 1926 (the first date for which data are available) it was thirty-five years of age for men, far above the European average;[30] (3) the Irish became the most celibate people in the western world. "Celibacy" in this case refers not to the renunciation of sexuality in the theological sense, but is a demographer's term for spinsterhood and bachelorhood;[31] (4) by European standards there was very little illicit love, and, if anything, less than in pre-Famine times;[32] (5) as a result of the restrictions on marriage and on nonmarital love, Ireland became the most sexually repressed society in the modern world and some scholars tie this to Ireland's extremely high rate of mental illness, particularly schizophrenia;[33] (6) within marriage the fertility rate was amazingly high;[34] (7) the combination of the stem family system (which precluded subdivision of small farms), the absence of an industrial sector outside of Ulster, and the high rate of marital fertility, meant that a very high rate of emigration was induced; (8) uniquely in Europe, Ireland underwent an absolute decline in population from the mid-nineteenth century until the mid-twentieth.[35]

Thus, Ireland's family history in the nineteenth century is so striking that it is easy to think of it as totally unique. Yet one should not be so taken by the character of Ireland's post-Famine population decline and by the extreme form of frequent celibacy and late marriage to forget that the Irish simply were exhibiting a national version of an international pattern, the "European marriage pattern." In common with the rest of western Europe – and in contrast to most of the rest of the world – Ireland was adopting a social template that consisted in a late average age of marriage and of the acceptance of a fairly large number of persons in each generation as unmarried.[36] The shift from the pre-Famine to the post-Famine family pattern can be seen as part of a general western phenomenon that is usually denominated as "the demographic transition." This is a set of changes in family life, the result of which was the replacement of a society characterized by high birth rates and high death rates, by one with low birth rates and low death rates. The Irish reached the same demographic result as did most western nations – although, admittedly, they took an unusual route in getting there.

While it is necessary to generalize about Ireland's demographic family pattern, it is well to remind oneself continually that the overall pattern subsumes many striking sectorial variations – that is, variations of class, geography, and local culture.[37] It is obvious, but easy to forget, that when rural people move to cities, a shift frequently occurs in their family patterns: usually, they marry earlier and have smaller families. This contributes to major regional differences between parts of Ireland, especially when, as in the case of the Belfast region, city life was associated with the quickly modernizing world of the British industrial revolution. Even in rural areas, and even if one considers only persons of a single religion, there are major differences in dominant sexual and familial practices. Sean Connolly investigated the illegitimacy and prenuptial pregnancy rates of several Catholic parishes and came to the conclusion that there were considerable variations between different parts of the country even within the Catholic faith.[38]

When spelled out clearly, the existence of these demographic fractures seems obvious enough, but they return us to a discussion of one of the great unspoken subjects in Irish history: the differences, if any, between Protestants and Catholics in matters of sexual behaviour and family formation. We are here dealing with the nineteenth and early twentieth centuries, but the question of sexual practice and religion is so embarrassing to the Irish sensibility that historians of Ireland have not dealt with this issue. To the extent that it is approached at all, Protestant-Catholic differences are taken to have been in the nineteenth and early twentieth centuries what the conventional wisdom holds about present-day differences: that (1) Protestants are less apt than Catholics to have large families; (2) that Protestants are less apt to remain celibate, in the demographer's sense, all of their life, and (3) that in general Protestants are easier with sexual matters than are Roman Catholics, which is to say that they are more prone to engage in nonmarital sex and, simultaneously, to be less neurotic about sexual activity. There may well be some truth in these impressions as they reflect present-day Ireland, but there is no such evidence for the last century and there is a good deal of inferential material that suggests a near identity of sexual practices.

The general failure to address such an important social and cultural matter is best exemplified by the work of the late Kenneth Connell, the very scholar who could have dealt with it most directly. A pioneering neo-Marxist, Connell was interested in the way that economic and class structure affected family formation. Religion entered the picture as an enforcer of economically determined patterns. Connell's major body of work is a study of sexual and family practices among Irish Catholics in the largest class in Irish society, small farmers and labourers. Protestants are not mentioned and one has only three alternatives: to assume that there were too few Protestant small farmers and labourers to matter (a viewpoint which the 1861 occupational data make untenable), to assume that the Protestant pattern was identical with the Catholic (which may be true, but that demands evidentiary demonstration), or to assume that, in contrast to the rigorous morality of the Catholics, the Protestants were looser morally and have always been. This last suggestion is rather embarrassing when put so boldly, but my own suspicion is that this is the belief that prevails among professional scholars of Ireland (Connell included). This belief has a long tradition and one finds it in even the most open minded of individuals. One sees it in its formative stages reflected in the *Reminiscences* of the Rev. Walter McDonald, the long-time (1888–1920) head of the graduate faculty of Maynooth Seminary and himself the victim of suppression by his superiors of many of his writings for their liberal character:

The school [that McDonald attended] at Carrick was very "mixed," comprising boys and girls, Protestants and Catholics. There were at the school – attending during the day – some other Protestant lads, from Carrick, who shall be nameless as they were very bold and rough and, when the master's eye was off them, did things which no Catholic boy would do, in the presence of girls. I was too young to take harm at the time, and it may be, of course, that it was by accident that the boys who did those things were Protestants; but it is a fact that so they were. Though ninety-five percent of the boys were town-bred and Catholic, not one of them was ever guilty of such conduct.[39]

This belief in Protestant moral laxity can be traced in a virtually straight line right up to the recent works of Sean Connolly who has written an outstanding study of Irish-Catholic folk religion before the Famine. A first-rate scholar, and certainly not given to conscious stereotypes, even Connolly falls into the dominant mode. At one point he posits "that attitudes to sexual misbehaviour were more lax in parts of Ulster than elsewhere in the country" and the areas he points to were Protestant areas.[40] Connolly does this on the basis of an ordnance surveyor's comments on East Antrim, drawn up by a man who held strong prejudices against the "Scotch" of the area, and he does so in the face of published data from local parish registers which disprove the surveyor as a fully reliable direct witness. The point here is that if a scholar who is one of the best minds of his generation makes these kind of stereotypic assumptions, based on very weak evidence, then all of us must be very wary of falling into the same trap – the more so because stereotyping such as Connolly practised is not the product of intentional historical malfeasance, but of unintentional and unconscious misfeasance.

The laminae of resistance to dealing seriously with possible differences in familial-sexual patterns between Catholics and Protestants is made all the more durable because rigorous work on the topic is hard to do. Governmental registration of births began in 1864, and anything before that date has to rest on circumstantial evidence or non-random sampling. Before 1864 one relies on the work of Kenneth Connell, as modified by later scholars. Connell's "Illegitimacy before the Famine" has held the field for a full two decades. Its argument is as follows. First, he suggests that in 1864, when civil registration of birth started, Ireland already had a very low illegitimacy rate. Second, using evidence from the great Poor Law Commission of 1833–6 that had been directed by the sometime Drummond Professor of Political Economy at Oxford, Archbishop Richard Whately,[41] Connell argued that sanctions against illicit sex were so great as to make illegitimacy and even fornication unattractive. Third, Connell massaged some of the data from the Poor Law Commission to permit him to make guesses about illegitimacy rates in several locales. In more than half the cases he came up with figures of less than 2 percent illegitimacy, which compares to an English rate of between 4 and 6 percent in the late eighteenth and early nineteenth centuries.[42]

Connell's work is a brilliant piece of historical rhetoric, but it leads less to conviction than to reflection. On most of his doubtful points he may well be right, but many of his modes of argument are unsettling. In the first place, as David Miller has noted, Connell ignored data from the first few years of civil registration which implied that illegitimacy was not uniformly low (and thus that controls on nonmarital sex were not as strong as Connell believed). Miller suggests that illegitimacy in the early 1860s was declining from a considerably higher level that had pertained in pre-Famine years.[43] At minimum, Connell's belief that the ideology of sex was the same throughout the nineteenth century becomes very shaky once Miller's point is assimilated.

Second, Connell's attempt to obtain illegitimacy rates from the evidence given before the 1883–6 Poor Law Commission was heroic, but questionable. He was able to calculate illegitimacy rates, or a near-surrogate, for fifty-one parishes. In only two of these cases does information come from the Anglican rector, so presumably (but not absolutely necessarily) the figures of illegitimate births are in most instances for Roman Catholics. These figures are then compared to a total number of births that in most cases is inferred (not directly observed), from the total (both Catholic and Protestant) population of each individual parish, as shown in the 1841 census. This procedure understates the illegitimacy rate because (a) it compares in most instances Catholic illegitimacy with the total number of Catholic and Protestant births and (b) because the population of most parishes in Ireland was higher in 1841 than in the early 1830s (the base for collecting evidence on illegitimate births).[44]

In a curious exercise, Connell destroys much of his own work. In the parishes in which he had drawn up his derived data (as specified by the procedure above), he found that in more than half of his cases, the illegitimacy rate was below 2 percent. However, he had a number of parishes in which he had direct data on both the total number of baptisms in the parish (thus he did not need to infer a number of births) and on the number of illegitimate children who were baptized. For these parishes he found a low of 3.0 percent illegitimacy and a high of 6.7 percent, and these, if anything, understated the actual illegitimacy rate somewhat.[45] Thus, the most telling argument against the reliability of Connell's derived figures that show an extremely low illegitimacy rate are his own direct evidence figures that show Ireland's pre-Famine rate to have been as high as that of England at the time of the Napoleonic wars.[46]

Connell's third technique was to argue, based on the Poor Law Commission evidence, that because the penalties for illicit sex were reported to be so stern, there was very little of it. This is not logically compelling – there were Draconian laws against sheep stealing in eighteenth-century England, but sheep kept disappearing – but at least it is based on direct testimony. Yet, while granting that almost all of the Poor Law Commission witnesses were in agreement that bastard children and unmarried mothers had a very hard life in Irish society, one should note two cautionary points. The first of these is that most of the information on nonmarital sexual activity was generated in a set of queries and in collections of oral testimony that focused on the subject of bastard and deserted children. Thus "failures in chastity" were inevitably mentioned within the context of bastardy, so it is hardly surprising that in the witnesses' testimony illicit love and its punishment frequently were equated. The structure of the questioning guaranteed that, and therefore one is viewing in this testimony the presuppositions of the persons who structured the collection of evidence. Second, even given this strong loading towards emphasizing the virtues of the Irish peasant (by forcing an emphasis upon the sanctions against illicit love and its bitter fruit, the illegitimate child) a counter theme ran through much of the testimony, and this Connell and his successors have ignored. Witnesses frequently suggested that Irish society tolerated an alternative to the chaste-until-marriage ideal. This was a train of events where premarital sexual activity led to pregnancy and thence to marriage. Many of the witnesses before the Poor Law Commission said that in the usual case of premarital pregnancy, the father married the girl. Thus, pregnancy was a way station to marriage and to social acceptability, not to social disaster. That pregnancy was so viewed is confirmed by the widely distributed reports that accusing the father of an unborn child (or, if already born, of an illegitimate child) of rape was a common way for a girl to force a man to marry her.[47] In most cases, however, the prosecution of the court was not necessary, for the parish priest and the girl's family usually brought sufficient pressure to induce the father to come to the altar.[48]

The moral economy that prevailed among the Irish small-farming and labouring classes was much more complex than Connell recognized. One of the shrewdest (if overstated) summaries of this moral economy is found in the strangely ignored writings of John Revans, whose *Evils of the State of Ireland* was published in 1835. Revans was a man of strong, but very well informed opinions: he had been the secretary of the Poor Law Inquiry for England and Wales and subsequently was one of the secretaries of the Poor Law Commission in Ireland, with whom he had a falling out over their final report: he believed that an English-style poor law should be introduced into Ireland, while the commissioners did not. Revans recognized that the sexual and filial structure of Ireland could be understood only if one takes as one's fundamental datum, the marginal position of women in nineteenth-century Irish society: "the inability of a woman of any age to earn her own subsistence makes her most desirous to be married. Women require a husband to maintain them whilst young and children to maintain them while old. It is evident therefore that besides the usual motives of marriage, there are in Ireland many powerful additional ones."[49] Given that the alternative to marriage was a penurious life at best and near-starvation at worst, it was natural that young women made strenuous attempts at attracting a husband. According to Revans: "The peasant women constantly seek illicit intercourse with a view to inducing marriage."[50] And this works through the following mechanisms:

The clergy of all persuasions seem invariably to recommend (which is equivalent to enforcing) marriage in all cases of previous intercourse provided the woman has previously borne a good character. Should the injunctions of the clergy fail to induce the man to marry, the friends of the woman frequently threaten violence, which threat is often successful. In case the persuasions of the clergy and the threats of the male relations fail, the woman has still another resource – she swears or threatens to swear rape against him. This practice is extremely common in Ireland and is mostly successful.[51]

Considering that as a secretary of the Poor Law Commission Revans had read or heard as much testimony on this subject as had anyone in Ireland, one cannot simply throw out his summation. Actually, Kenneth Connell stated that in the case of premarital pregnancy "marriage to the father was perhaps her likeliest fate,"[52] and then he dropped the subject.

This is understandable because Connell's recognition that most premarital pregnancy was not reflected in the illegitimacy data meant that his argument for premarital chastity, based as it was in considerable part on the allegedly low incidence of illegitimacy, is considerably vitiated. And, when one realizes that, given the position of Irish women, marriage was not an unfortunate "fate" (Connell's word) but the goal of most women, then the whole Connellite picture of the effectiveness of sanctions against nonmarital sex virtually disappears. Of course, one can accept his observation that a bastard child and its mother were treated harshly in Irish society, but one must always remember that, though there was a price for sexual risk, there was a strong valiance in the opposite direction. Premarital pregnancy could result in a young girl being ruined for life. Much more often, though, it resulted in her standing before the altar with a husband and thus, through him and through the children of their union, she acquired the only insurance against life's disasters that a woman could acquire in Irish peasant society.

As David Miller has noted, without some careful microanalysis of individual parishes it is impossible to tell what the rates of illegitimacy propounded before 1864 really mean.[53] Such analysis is available for nine Catholic parishes and for one Presbyterian one. Crucially, in each case there is information not only upon illegitimacy, but upon the related phenomenon of premarital pregnancy. Let us examine first the

Catholic data. In the late 1970s Sean Connolly analyzed the parish registers of eight Roman Catholic parishes and incorporated with that study the results of previous research done in 1942 by Lee and Mac-Carthaigh.[54] The registers of these nine parishes permitted a calculation of illegitimacy and prenuptial pregnancy rates from 1821 onwards and in some cases the data stretched as far back as the mid-eighteenth century. As one would expect, there was considerable variation among the nine parishes, but, that noted, two general conclusions may be drawn from these data. The first is that the illegitimacy rate among practising Catholics was low. Overall, between 1821 and 1860, it ran between 2.1 percent and 2.5 percent. Admittedly, these figures probably somewhat underestimate the full extent of illegitimacy in the various communities (in 1864, the first full year of civil registration, the national rate was 3.8 percent), because women frequently moved parish as a means of avoiding the stigma of their condition and the overall trend of these moves was away from rural parishes to urban areas. Also, the data were for baptized children, and wholly unrepentant sinners would not have had their bastard children recorded in the church's records. Nevertheless, even if one assumes that the illegitimacy rates derived from the Roman Catholic parish records need to be inflated by as much as 50 percent, the level of bastardy that they reflect still is low. Connell points out that in the last decade of the century, the rate in England was 4.1 percent and, interestingly, the highest known number was for Portugal, a Catholic country, 12.1 percent.[55] Thus, these nine microstudies seem to confirm Connell's view.

The second inference one draws from Connolly's collection of parish records runs in the opposite direction. This is the report that just over 10 percent of the Catholic women whose marriages were recorded and whose children subsequently were baptized, came to the altar pregnant. Probably one should adjust these figures upwards, for the same reasons that one would adjust upwards the illegitimacy rates: not all illegitimate babies were baptized and, further, girls who were to give birth to bastard children drifted towards the larger urban areas. However, *even* if one accepts a roughly 10 percent premarital pregnancy rate as being the "real" rate, it does not confirm the view that Connell (and to a lesser extent, Connolly) have propounded concerning the unusually low incidence of sexual activity among Irish Catholics.

By way of context, it is worth noting that in spite of Connell's emphasis upon the seeming uniqueness of Irish-Catholic sexual asceticism, the rate is not unusual. A study of a society that more than most is comparable to pre-Famine Ireland – namely the Catholic province of Quebec in the eighteenth and nineteenth centuries – shows that in the district of Sorel, for which an excellent microstudy is available, the

Catholic premarital conception rate varied from 4.5 percent to 8.4 percent, according to the period being studied, but in any case was markedly lower than the Irish-Catholic rate.[56] Thus, we are not here dealing with an unprecedented phenomenon.

Nor, despite the prevailing, historical viewpoint, are we viewing a case of great sexual asceticism. How could this be? In the first instance because not all conceptions come to term. In the modern society, as late as the 1980s, approximately one-third of all conceptions are spontaneously terminated; as Angus McLaren argues, the rate was certainly much higher in early times.[57] Also, as is well known, underdeveloped countries today have a much higher spontaneous abortion rate than do developing ones. Thus, a reasonable guess would be that in mid-nineteenth century Ireland, only one-half of all pregnancies resulted in live births. Hence, *even* if one does not correct the baptismal record for underreporting, it is fair to suggest that one out of five Irish-Catholic women had been pregnant at some time before their marriage.

There is more to the argument than that. A women does not usually become pregnant the first time she has sexual intercourse. Or, the second, or, likely, the twentieth. A study of twentieth-century America showed that on average twenty-five to fifty acts of coitus are required for one conception.[58] And, undoubtedly, the ratio of coition-to-pregnancy was greater in mid-nineteenth century Ireland, because standards of diet and health practices were lower than in twentieth-century America. Where this information leads is obvious. Accepting the guess that roughly 20 percent of Catholic women were pregnant at some time before their marriage, and that roughly three to four dozen acts of sexual intercourse were necessary in the average pregnancy, then (1) those girls who became pregnant probably had been quite sexually active and (2) a probably large additional number of girls were sexually active, but not to the point where the odds caught up with them. (And this assumes no practice of birth control, though that is unlikely: coitus interruptus was well known in western rural societies). The unavoidable conclusion is that although Catholic Ireland in the middle of the nineteenth century may have been sexually controlled, it was far from being sexually ascetic.

Thus, the train of logic that dominates Irish historiography as it concerns Catholic family practices before the Famine does not work. Instead of a pattern of low illegitimacy and, therefore, low sexual activity, one has a pattern of a significant degree of premarital sexual activity, combined with fairly low illegitimacy (although not as low as usually is suggested). The heavy sanctions against having children out of wedlock may have reduced sexual activity somewhat, but, more

often it converted illicit sexual activity into an avenue of family formation. As long as the parish priest was willing to marry the young
fornicators – and the evidence is overwhelming that most of the
priests would do so – then the low illegitimacy rate was in no way an
indication of sexual asceticism. This pattern was predicated upon first,
tacit priestly cooperation, and, second, the availability of land through
subdivision of holdings by either set of parents of the young people.
Later in the nineteenth century, as subdivision became less and less
the common practice, stronger inhibitions on marriage arose, and,
further, the Catholic clergy became much more vigilant, indeed obses-
sively so, about lapses from morality. But that was in the future: to
push back into the first two-thirds of the nineteenth century a pattern
that existed most clearly around the turn of the twentieth century, is
inappropriate.

What about the Protestants? Kenneth Connell, in an observation
that revealed the strong stereotypic mindset with which he operated,
stated that an Irish priest "demonstrated (*not simply to his own satisfac-
tion*) early in the present century, 'Orangeism and illegitimacy go
together ... bastards in Ireland are in proportion to the Orange
Lodges.' "[59] This is so silly as not even to be offensive. The one Protestant microstudy available comes from a Presbyterian area, Islandmagee, Country Antrim. Along with its neighbouring parish of Raloo,
and the town of Carrickfergus, this is denominated as being a part of
the country where Protestant standards of sexual behaviour were
more lax than was generally the case.[60] The results from this supposed
nursery of vice are unsettling. The long-serving minister of the First
Presbyterian Church, Islandmagee, had a fascination with premarital
pregnancy and kept very good records of the actual date of birth of
each child. In the period 1845 to 1867, 13.5 percent of women married
in the church were pregnant.[61] (Since Islandmagee was not socially or
economically traumatized by the Famine, this figure would be representative of the entire nineteenth century.) This figure is effectively
the same as is that found by Connolly for the nine Catholic parishes:
Connolly's proxy for premarital pregnancy, in my judgment, was
slightly less inclusive because he counted only cases where children
were baptized less than nine and a half months after their parents'
marriage, so that the children of malingerers who came to be baptized
late were tallied as being "normal" births no matter what the actual
birth date was; the Islandmagee figures are direct data and count
births that actually took place within eight months, one week, of
marriage.[62] There is no profit in arguing the precise equilibration
needed to turn one set of figures into the other; the real point is that
within the limits of the very sketchy data available to us, illicit love

probably played a considerable, and almost identical, part in both the Protestant and Catholic systems of family formation. The Presbyterians of Islandmagee who showed a fair degree of premarital sexual activity also had a very low illegitimacy rate; indeed, probably lower than for most Catholic parishes.[63]

Stereotypic ways of thinking about familial practices of the two main Irish religious groups not only distorts our vision by obfuscating the probability that the pre-Famine Catholic was much less sexually ascetic than usually is assumed, it also makes us miss the fact that the Protestants, and particularly their clergy, could at times be just as antisexual as any of their Catholic counterparts. The image of the late nineteenth-century Catholic priest out beating the hedge rows for courting couples has become such a dominant motif that one forgets that the Protestant clergy had methods of enforcing sexual morality that would have made the Catholic priests envious. For instance, take the case of the Presbyterian congregation in the village of Ballycarry in the parish of Templecorran (or, as more commonly known locally, "Broadisland"), County Antrim. This is just adjacent to Islandmagee and is in the part of Ulster said to be a hotbed of sexual promiscuity in the first half of the nineteenth century. There, the kirk session records show, it was the practice of the clergy to have notorious local sinners sit in a special pew of shame facing the congregation. This punishment was imposed in the case of a couple who engaged in fornication and those who came to the altar with the girl pregnant. The number of Sundays the sinners were required to sit in the pew of shame were calibrated according to the degree of their sins. This kind of social control was common in Presbyterian parishes. What is singular is the record of this congregation dealing with a young female from Ballycarry who became pregnant by a married man. She refused to reveal his identity, although, as she became visibly more pregnant, the minister and kirk elders increasingly pressed her, so that he could be brought to book. Still, she refused. When her time of delivery came, she made the short journey to Islandmagee to have the baby there, away from prying religious authorities. The kirk elders, however, found her and waited upon her while she was in childbirth. It was a hard labour and she needed the intervention of a midwife, but the elders prevented the poor woman from receiving any aid until, torn with pain, she surrendered and gave them the name of the father of the as-yet-unborn child.[64]

Until there is a great deal more evidence of significant differences between the attitudes of Protestants and Catholics, the cautious conclusion of Joseph Lee seems justified. "In the comparative context, the similarities between the sexual and marital mores of Irish Catholics and Protestants were far more striking than the local differences on which polemicists loved to linger."[65] Further, when large scale studies of nineteenth-century family and sexual patterns eventually are compiled, I suspect that the seeming difference between Catholics and Protestants will not be attributable to substantive cultural factors, but to the intersection of time lag and of social class.

Why?

If one finds convincing (as do most demographers of Ireland) the argument that what can loosely be called the "post-Famine demographic shift" (to extremely high rates of celibacy, very late marriage age, very little illicit love, very high marital fertility, and very high emigration rates) is chiefly ascribable to an economic transition, namely the long-term replacement of the practice of subdividing farms with the practice of consolidation of farm holdings and of parents passing them intact to a single representative of the younger generation – and *if* one finds satisfactory (as do most economic historians of nineteenth-century Ireland) the suggestion that throughout the nineteenth century the class of large farmers held a disproportionately high number of Protestants and, also, that Protestants were underrepresented in the landless labouring class – *then* it may reasonably be suggested that the "post-Famine" family pattern of the Irish nation was simply the writing large of a pattern that previously had characterized the Protestant farmers of Ireland: keeping their land intact, passing it on to a single heir, severely limiting the formation of new families in cases where the new family would not have sufficient economic resources to live reasonably well, and extruding (by emigration abroad or to find work in the city, the military, or the colonial service) those children who did not inherit the family's landed holding. As post-Famine Catholic farms came, as economic units, to resemble Protestant farms, the family patterns determined by those economic units became closer and closer.[66]

The way that a society, or a culture within a society, treats women is not independent either of economic structure or of patterns of family formation, but it is a separate diagnostic tool for defining substantive differences between cultural groups. This is both a promising and a volatile topic in Irish history, because of the provocative work of Robert E. Kennedy Jr in *The Irish: Emigration, Marriage, and Fertility* (Berkeley: University of California Press, 1973). Kennedy presents the thesis that in the nineteenth and twentieth centuries, the Irish treated their women badly, if one may be permitted a gender-offensive, but accurate, depiction of his viewpoint. The lines of his argument are

Figure 4

Excess of Female Life Expectancy over Male Life Expectancy, 1900–27

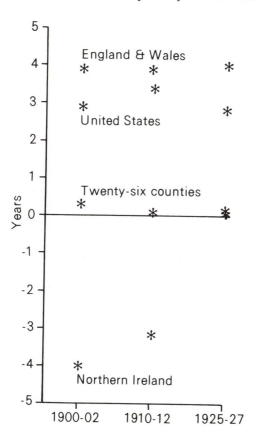

Source: See Appendix G.

admirably clear. As a starting point, he notes that in western society women live longer than do men. This, he believes, is primarily the result of biological factors, but the exact cause is irrelevant to his argument. The important point is that the dominant western pattern gives women a longer life span, so that can be taken as a cross-cultural norm. As compared to this norm, Kennedy notes that Irish women in the nineteenth and early twentieth centuries did not live much longer than did men, and, in some parts of Ireland, lived less long. The Irish pattern resembles more closely that of Bulgaria or of India than it does Great Britain or the United States.

From the relative shortness of the life span of Irish women, Kennedy concluded that they were badly treated in comparison to those of most western nations. The specific mechanisms of this ill treatment, Kennedy suggests, were founded on a strong pattern of male dominance among the Irish, one so strong that it resulted in relatively high female mortality. He cites, as evidence, specific practices: the men eating first in rural households and thereby getting the better and more nutritious food; men keeping the income from the sale of animals and for cash crops for their own use; men being required to look after the needs of the wife and family only after taking care of the needs of the farm, the livestock, and their own personal indulgences; sons being given preferential treatment and daughters being shoved aside, and this holding in both rural and urban areas; women in rural areas being required to do heavy agricultural labour, as well as housework.[67]

One might want to take issue with Kennedy's evidence for the generality of some of these practices, but the structure of his argument is compelling. As with any logic-train, however, one must compare it to possible alternatives. For instance, how important is the fact that in the years studied by Kennedy, the Irish were near or at the top of the marital fertility table? Given that until very recently, childbirth was the single most common cause of female death, the relatively low Irish female life span may largely have been a result of frequent exposure to the risks of child bearing. That point, however, can be subsumed into Kennedy's logic-train and thereby leave it intact: all that the defender of the Kennedy thesis need do is suggest that high marital fertility was another evidence of excessive male dominance and that it worked in concert with other male-imposed practices that Kennedy describes.

More important is the well known phenomenon that, relative to other western European countries, Ireland had a very large population outflow and in the nineteenth and early twentieth centuries, Ireland – alone among western countries – sent abroad approximately equal numbers of men and women.[68] This out-migration acted as a filter in a twofold sense: the least healthy, most disadvantaged, did not gather enough momentum even to try to leave and, further, from roughly mid-nineteenth century onwards, most recipient nations had health screening procedures to keep out sickly migrants. Thus, the relatively high outflow of Irish women (as compared to other European countries) was perforce an outflow of the healthier women within Irish society. Therefore, the statistical phenomenon of the seemingly shorter life span of the Irish woman as compared to the European norm, was a chimera. It was a reflection not of excessive ill treatment by Irish men, but of the strongest, healthiest, toughest women leaving for more promising shores. This was a particularly salient process because Irish female migration was overwhelmingly a rural phenomenon and it is to rural family patterns that Kennedy points most directly in inferring the Irish abuse of women.

Although Kennedy's method is invalid as a form of international comparison, it still might work if limited to making comparisons within Irish society. One notable characteristic of Irish social statistics is that they show that women in the north of Ireland lived shorter lives (using male life span as the norm) in the years 1890–1912 than did women in the twenty-six counties that eventually became the Irish Free State. This might indicate a higher level of male dominance and of female abuse among Protestants at an empirically demonstrable level.

The trouble is, this quick jump to cultural difference leaves out the relationship of social class and life expectancy, and particularly, the north's religious structure. The women most vulnerable to the kinds of life reducing male dominance that Kennedy posits (particularly poor nutrition and excessively heavy labour) were centred in the poorest classes, right at the poverty line. (Middle class men may have been patronizing, but they certainly fed their wives well and they hired servants for the heavy work.) And the poor in the north tended to be strongly loaded towards being Catholics. So, the figures for the north could mean that there was an extremely high degree of female abuse by Irish Catholics.

As a basic rule of social history, when one indicator produces two diametrically opposite results, as in this case, it is the indicator that is at fault. For the period here under study, the life expectancy calculations as an indicator of female abuse do not work.[69]

Does this mean that the patterns of male dominance cited by Kennedy did not exist? They existed, in kind if not in degree as argued by Kennedy, and they are well documented elsewhere by other scholars.[70] But, for the most part, a reasonable supposition is that most Irish males, Protestant and Catholic alike, were very hard on the women of their society – as were males all over the western world.

Thus, the major empirical social indicator of cultural differences that are employed in many countries give unclear results when employed in nineteenth- and twentieth-century Ireland. Either they indicate no significant differences (and thus, should be taken as *positive* indications of fundamental *similarities* between the two religious groups), or they yield no decipherable results at all.

CHAPTER THREE

Clean Laboratories

Given the volatile character of so much of Irish sectarian relations, it would be best to assume for the moment *not* that Protestants and Catholics were essentially similar peoples, but that there is something wrong with the laboratory in which we have been working. Not only are the sources of Irish empirical data severely limited, but it may be that our situation is similar to that of a laboratory scientist who is trying to conduct an experiment concerning the character of the earth's gravitational field in a building that is located, say, on the line of the San Andreas Fault. The ambient conditions are too excited to permit meaningful readings on the instruments. If we accept that assumption, it means that the simple questions we have been asking about the Irish Protestants and Catholics – were they really different on any major empirical social index? – cannot be answered in the homeland.

The trick, then, is to get out, to move the lab. That is not a jocular suggestion. If one defines "the Irish" as comprising all persons born in Ireland, then in the nineteenth and early twentieth centuries, much of the history of the Irish happened outside of Ireland. As Figure 5 indicates, in the last decade of the nineteenth century, 38.8 percent of the Irish-born were living in certain specified countries outside of Ireland and, when one adds to that the numbers living in other countries for which enumerations are not available, it is clear that four out of every ten Irish-born persons was living abroad.[1]

Any realistic social and cultural history of Ireland has to take these people into account and not merely as an exit number. An Irish historiography that focuses only on the Irish in Ireland would be neither Irish nor history. To a considerable extent, Irish life in the second half of the nineteenth and the early twentieth centuries had its horizons set by the prospect of emigration and although not everyone left,

Figure 5
Proportion of Irish-born Persons Living Outside Ireland, 1841–1921

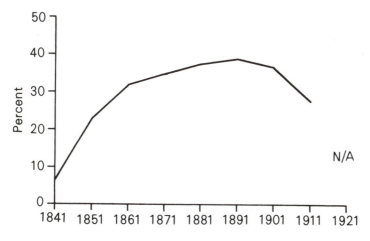

Source: See Appendix H

everyone's viewpoint was strongly influenced by its possibility. As David Fitzpatrick of Trinity College, Dublin, has observed, "growing up in Ireland meant preparing oneself to leave it."[2]

Therefore, the emigration experience is two things at once: an important thing in itself as part of the collective-life-history of everyone born in Ireland and, simultaneously, a laboratory whose data cast light, reflexively, indirectly, but clearly, on some of the darker recesses of Irish cultural patterns at home. Professor Joseph Lee has argued that "the development of emigrant communities in new environments is the closest one can come to constructing a national laboratory, to isolate the relative importance of heredity and environment in moulding a peoples' character."[3] As I have argued elsewhere, this is particularly true in frontier communities, such as mid-nineteenth century Australia, New Zealand, and Canada, where the migrants were erecting a new economic and social order, in which process they brought to the fore, in a clear and observable fashion, the inherent and central aspects of the economic and social systems of their time, and of their own place in those systems.[4]

A suitable response to the suggestion that emigrant communities give one a series of natural laboratories that will reveal truths about the homeland that otherwise would be unobservable is to ask, how representative was the emigrant of the society that he left? Professor Patrick O'Farrell has responded as follows: "Contemporaries always contended that it was the flower of the country, the bone and sinew, that left, but evidence on this is uncertain and contradictory. But such documentation as exists – and the sheer volume of emigration – indicates that emigrants ranged from utter paupers to the reasonably affluent, from misfits to the enterprising; there seems no reason to regard emigrants as anything other than tolerably representative of the range of Irish society."[5]

O'Farrell probably is correct in making this assertion, but for the purposes of this study he need not be: it will suffice if the emigrants were comparable groups of Protestants and of Catholics, wherever they were sliced from the home society. One recalls that in the homeland the greatest problem in comparing Catholics and Protestants was to hold constant such things as social class and regional economic differentials. One of the helpful things about studying emigrants is that the emigration process was itself a great standardizer. That is, the process of emigration was a filter and through the hard empiricism of human experience it gives us something that is unobtainable by statistical manipulation: it provides historians with comparable sets of Protestants and Catholics, sets that can be legitimately compared and, where appropriate, contrasted.

The great standardizer? Consider:[6] Emigration, even to Great Britain, was beyond the personal resources of the poorest and they had no chance at all of making it to North America, much less to Australia. On the other hand, the very rich, with the exception of the odd rapscallion son who was sent abroad, had no need to leave Ireland. There emerged, thus, what can be conceived of as the "emigrating class," consisting of individuals in the broad middle band of Irish society who made prudent calculations of where their future interests best lay and who then followed these calculations, sometimes to the ends of the earth. This is not to gainsay the fact that at certain times, especially during the Great Famine, circumstances pressed very hard upon the emigrants. Yet, even during the Famine, it was not the very poorest, the people who had no options and little strength left who migrated, but individuals with at least meagre economic resources in hand.[7] These people used their last shillings to pay passage away from Ireland. Even the so-called "pauper migrants," whose numbers were only a tiny portion of the emigrant stream, were selected not from the sick and utterly destitute, but from among the poor who, through strength of character, still were unbroken.

Nineteenth- or early twentieth-century emigrants shared several general (if not, of course, universal) characteristics. For one thing, they knew how money worked. These people were not the lumpenprols of the subsistence agricultural economy, but rather small farmers or the offspring of farmers who were being forced away from home by the increasingly common practice of land consolidation, or were agricultural labourers who through prudent application had saved enough money for passage. Also, as a group, they had a solid acquaintance with the way that the system of representative government worked in the English-speaking world, and also with the nature of British-derived court systems. And, most important, they spoke English.[8] This, more than anything else, gave them an advantage over emigrants from non-English speaking European countries. Although it has long been the fashion to denigrate the abilities or resources of the Irish emigrants of the nineteenth and early twentieth centuries, it seems to me that they were remarkable for their shrewdness and adaptability.

As a group, Protestants were important numerically every place that Catholics were. Protestants migrated from Ireland in close to the same proportions as did Roman Catholics,[9] and comprised as large a proportion of the emigrant streams as they did of the homeland's population.[10] Thus, there should be ample opportunity for comparing the two groups.

The general outline of Irish emigration in the nineteenth and early twentieth centuries can be sketched easily enough, albeit not with quite the sharpness one would wish. After 1798, there was some politically motivated emigration, including the forced exile of United Irishmen, but general migration did not begin in earnest until after the end of the Napoleonic wars. Numbers multiplied in the 1830s and became a flood in the Famine years. Thereafter, the general, but irregular, pattern was towards a diminution in emigration in absolute numbers, although these numbers still represented a serious leeching of the Irish home population.

Figure 6 provides a representation of Irish emigration from 1815 to 1920 and it is a useful guide – provided that one recognizes its necessary imperfections.[11]

There were no official estimates for the years 1815-24 and those from 1825-51, inclusive, are shaky. It was only in the spring of 1851 that comprehensive and systematic enumeration of emigrants began. As Deirdre Mageean has noted, "the period from the beginning of the nineteenth century to the Famine ... lacks reliable estimates of even total emigration."[12] Even from 1852 onwards the total outflow was underestimated, because it was not until 1876 that figures on permanent migration to England and Scotland were obtained. And even after 1876, when standards of accuracy were at their best, one still

Figure 6
Emigration from Ireland (excluding Great Britain), 1815–1920

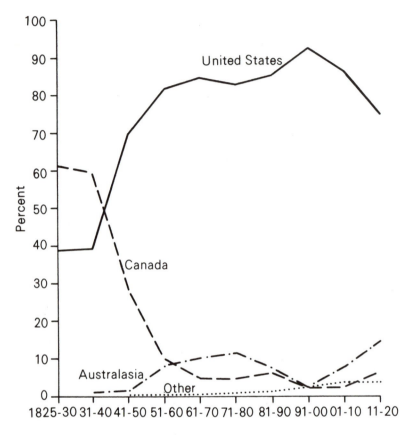

Source: See Appendix I

finds that figures on the number of migrants to any given country vary considerably, depending on whether one uses the totals collected when the migrants left Ireland or the figures compiled by officials of the recipient countries.[13]

Although statistics indicating the county of origin in Ireland of the emigrants were compiled from May 1851 onwards, the leading authority on their use finds them wanting: "For another quarter-century they were to remain highly misleading."[14] Thus, only from 1876 onwards can one discuss with any confidence the geographic origin of the migrants, although there are promising attempts at indirect calculation of these matters from the Famine onwards.[15]

Nor, as mentioned earlier, can one gain direct indication from any official sources of the religious persuasion of the migrants. Only indirect estimates are possible.

This mention of the deficiencies in the Irish emigration data should not be misinterpreted. It is a warning against depending too much on material from the home country, but it is not an indication of insuperable difficulties. It points us to the indigenous data bases that exist in several of the countries to which the Irish migrated. The overseas nations not only are the laboratories that permit us to make the observations we wish to draw, but also contain the data libraries that we need to document those observations.

No reasonable scientist would begin playing with the machines, twirling the dials, and watching the flashing lights in a laboratory in a totally random manner, for at the end of the day he would have collected a great deal of data, but to no end. One needs to focus on a problem, and, where possible, have a specific set of hypotheses that requires testing. Although there are scores of interesting ones about the overseas Irish, the hypotheses that I shall here test concern only the potential differences between Protestants and Catholics.

Fortunately, there is a rich literature, a virtual conventional wisdom, about the nature of Irish culture that has been developed largely, if not entirely, by historians employed in American universities. This is part of a massive body of work on the Irish in the United States.[16] The American literature far exceeds in volume that which deals with all the rest of the Irish diaspora. The useful characteristic of the great body of research on the Irish in the United States is that is has implicitly developed a consensus (not a universal one, but very nearly) about the background of people in the Old World. That is, as an ancillary aspect of chronicling the Irish in the United States, American historians have developed an historiography of nineteenth- and early twentieth-century Irish society.

The American scholars have suggested a syndrome of characteristics said to have been exhibited by the Catholics of Ireland, and that these attributes influenced the migrants' behaviour in the New World. The literature that adumbrates these characteristics rarely refers directly to Protestants, but the contrast is implicit and is pervasive and universally understood: the Irish Catholics had certain characteristics that distinguished them from Protestants, both in the New World and in the Old. Whatever one may think of the quality of the literature on Irish-American history, it is a fecund source of hypotheses that are relevant to the present study.

According to the Irish-American literature, the Irish Catholics who issued forth from nineteenth-century Ireland were identified by four important socioeconomic characteristics.[17] First, "most of them had arrived penniless and had been 'immobilized' in the port where they landed."[18] Second, it is posited that the Irish Catholics were technologically backward. Lawrence McCaffrey states: "Lack of skills was far more important than a shortage of funds in determining the Irish-American decision to become city dwellers. Because manorialism and serfdom had not encouraged agrarian skills or knowledge, Irish peasants were among the most inefficient farmers in Europe and were not equipped for rural life in America."[19] Third, it is held that the Irish Catholics' historical experience had burned them so badly that they were phobic about certain forms of economic activity. "The Irish rejected the land for the land rejected them" was the way the most widely read of popular histories of the Irish-Americans put it.[20] And, fourth, it has frequently been argued that the communal nature of Irish-Catholic society meant that individual and isolated forms of livelihood were culturally interdicted. "The Irish temperament, unfitted for lonely life, shuddered at the prospect of a wilderness clearing without Irish fellowship."[21]

In 1985, Kerby A. Miller's *Emigrants and Exiles* appeared. It is the ne plus ultra of books in the tradition of Irish-American historiography and not merely because of its monumental size: nearly 700 pages. It captured both the Merle Curti Award in American Social History and the Saloutas Memorial Book Award in American Immigration History. Unlike virtually all of his predecessors, Miller writes about the Irish migration to America from the Irish end. That is, the story of the Irish in North America is an offstage event, that everyone is assumed to know about, and his study explains in detail the cultural background of those who left. Crucially, he mentions Protestants directly and, further, he exhibits an expertise in the history of the Irish homeland that few, if any, of his predecessors in American immigration history possessed.

The volume fits easily into the dominant mode of the Irish-American historical literature because of the way that Miller links the culture of the homeland to the behaviour of the emigrants overseas. Three of his observations are especially provocative. One of these is that "much evidence indicates that Catholics throughout Ireland, not just in the remote Irish-speaking areas, were much more reluctant to leave home than were their Protestant countrymen."[22] It is significant, because, if Catholics were markedly more attached to their homeland than were Protestants, and thus less willing to leave it, their behaviour in the new country might be hindered by their sense of exile. Miller's second controversial point ties into this, namely that, in contrast to the Protestants, emigration "posed severe social, cultural, and even psychological problems for many Catholics caught between individual necessity or ambition on the one hand and customs and obligations on the other."[23] And, third, Miller suggests that, in contrast to the English-language culture of the Protestants, Irish-Catholic culture was a handicap in dealing with the rapidly modernizing culture of the New World. "Traditionalist rural Catholics" in the emigration stream had an outlook on life that was "fatalistic and dependent and their religious faith was usually neither generalized nor internalized, but instead was almost inseparable from archaic customs and landmarks rooted in particular locales now thousands of miles behind them."[24] Miller postulates a "Catholic Irish propensity to avoid individual responsibility for innovative action such as emigration and to fall back on communally acceptable 'explanations' embedded in archaic historical and literary traditions and reinforced by modern Irish political rhetoric."[25] To the extent that the Irish language still was a significant component of the Irish-Catholic culture it undercut still further the Catholic's adaptability. "The semantic structure of the Irish language," Miller suggests, "itself reflected an Irish world view which emphasized dependence and passivity."[26] There was, then, "a distinctive Irish Catholic worldview rooted deeply in Irish history and culture," and "armed with a worldview so shaped, the Irish Catholic experienced the socioeconomic changes associated with the modern commercial and industrial revolution with certain psychological as well as political and economic disadvantages."[27]

One of the admirable characteristics of Kerby Miller's cultural observations of the differences between Irish Protestants and Catholics is that they can be empirically tested in several places in the world. Each of his points is a contrast between Catholics and Protestants and each is an indication of an impediment to Irish-Catholic success abroad as compared to the Irish-Protestant experience. If Miller's view of Irish culture is accurate – and, one may fairly add, if the historiography of Irish-America, of which this is the capstone, is valid – then the following four hypotheses, when tested in various overseas laboratories, would be confirmed:

Hypothesis no. 1: That, the Irish Catholics would be found to be a city people in their various New Worlds. More precisely, that in absolute terms, Irish Catholics would not settle in the rural worlds of North America or of Australasia. This would be the case because of the highly communal and familial nature of their culture in the homeland: they would huddle together abroad. Further, their technological backwardness and their traumatic experience with farming in the homeland would lead them to shun the agricultural sector.

Hypothesis no. 2: That, in comparison to Irish Protestants, this Catholic preference for city life and this abhorrence of agricultural activity would be especially marked. This would be because, according to the literature, the Protestant culture was more individualistic and less communal than was the Catholic and because the Protestants had not experienced the allegedly ennervating passivity of the Gaelic culture – such activity being inappropriate to the aggressive life of various New World frontiers.

Hypothesis no. 3: That, as compared to Irish Protestants, the Irish Catholics would have a markedly lower occupational profile in their various New Worlds. This would stem from their psychological, political, and economic disadvantages in the homeland.

Hypothesis no. 4: That, as compared to Irish Protestants, not only would Irish Catholics start lower on the occupational scale, but they would show significantly less rapid upward social mobility as the years passed. This would follow from the cultural handicaps they brought with them.

These hypotheses will be tested with a collection of several million pieces of systematically collected data, generated by the life course of hundreds and hundreds of thousands of individuals. If the hypotheses are confirmed, then it is highly probable that the cultural distinctions said to have existed between Irish Protestants and Irish Catholics were real, not just historians' vapourings.[28] If the verdict is "not proved" – that is, if the results are inconclusive – then one will have to look elsewhere for evidence; but if the hypotheses are directly disproved, then the interpretations of Irish history and society upon which they are based will have to be abandoned.

We have three potential laboratories in which to test our hypotheses: Great Britain, Australasia, and North America. These labs are not identical, but they need not be. All that is required is that Irish Catholics and Irish Protestants were given roughly equal economic opportunities in each place (effectively, that there was no penal legislation) and that good records have been kept of each individual's situation. Nor is it necessary that the sort of person who went to each of these three laboratories be the same. Indeed, recent research is beginning to indicate a certain degree of specialization as between the various countries that received the Irish.[29] But all that is necessary for the present purposes is that a significant body both of Protestants and Catholics went to each place. To the extent that each recipient country drew a slightly different sort of emigrant than did the others, this actually is to our advantage, for it gives us the possibility of testing our

Table 2
Irish Emigration to Great Britain, 1876-1920

Period	To Great Britain	As percentage of total of all Irish emigration including that to Great Britain (registrar general's tally)
1876–80	84,753	32.6
1881–90	70,786	9.2
1891–1900	27,961	6.4
1901–10	37,144	10.7
1911–20	15,864	10.4

Source: Emigration returns of the registrar general, as found in W.E. Vaughan and A.J. Fitzpatrick eds., *Irish Historical Population, 1821-1971* (Dublin: Royal Irish Academy, 1978), 264-5. See also, text, chapter 3, note 31

four hypotheses over a wider range of appropriate conditions.

The most striking characteristic of the emigration flow to Great Britain is its magnitude. Just after the Famine, an estimated three-quarters of a million Irish-born persons were estimated to have been living in Great Britain.[30] It is only after 1876, however, that one gains an accurate idea of the flow to Britain and these figures indicate that Ireland's traditional enemy was one of the most popular new homes for Erin's children. Table 2 provides the registrar general's tally of Irish migration for 1876 to 1920.[31] This material is tantalizing, for it is only part of a curve whose two ends, unseen, stretch on the one side all the way back to the mid-eighteenth century, and on the other side, to the present day. That the curve bulged high early in the nineteenth century can be inferred not only from the numbers of Irish-born living in Great Britain just after the Famine, but from the fact that whereas, in 1901, the Irish-born were only 1.3 percent of the general population, in 1861, they had been 3 percent.[32] That is, there must have been a massive post-Famine migration across the Irish Sea that has been largely uncharted by historians of the Irish diaspora. As for the modern end of the curve, we know that at present over 80 percent of Irish emigrants go to Great Britain.[33]

Frustratingly, we know very little about the Irish who emigrated to Great Britain in the last century. One of the few empirical investigations that casts light on this group, that done by David Fitzpatrick, shows that in the years 1876-1920 the emigrants to Great Britain tended to come from the northeast of Ireland. This does not mean that they were exclusively from Ulster, but rather that Ulster was over-represented. In these years, "the Irish in Britain tended to be products

of what passed in Ireland for an industrial economy, and their movement across the water may be regarded as circulation around the
larger British economy, of which the major Irish urban regions formed
a rather vulnerable part."[34] Further, Fitzpatrick notes that in this era,
1876–1920, the correlations between emigration to Great Britain and
Protestantism were even higher than the general correlation between
emigration and residency in the northeast.[35] This, of course, is not to
say that Ulster Protestants predominated, but that they were a larger
part of the emigrant flow to Great Britain than they were of the Irish
population at home.

Given this overrepresentation of the Protestants and of people from
Ulster in general in the flow to Great Britain, it is unfortunate that the
literature on the Irish in Great Britain had concentrated almost exclusively upon emigrant communities composed of persons who came
from classic rural peasant environments in the south of Ireland. Some
of these studies are of high quality – notably Lynn Lees's *Exiles of
Erin*,[36] – but they are misleading, albeit by accident. In practice, most
of the studies of the Irish in England focus their attention on ghettoized Irish-Catholic peasantry who collected together in several of the
larger English cities. These people are easily identified and easily studied, for the urban ghettos invariably supported the Catholic church,
often had some kind of ethnic news service, and inevitably generated
masses of civic and police records. Studying such communities is a
valid historical exercise.[37]

What is not valid is to lose sight of the larger context into which
these ghettoized Irish fit. Namely, that: (1) a larger, but unknown
proportion of Irish emigrants to Great Britain were not ghettoized but
were dispersed among the general population; (2) the proportion of
Protestants among the Irish emigrants to Great Britain was larger than
in the population at home; (3) among both Catholic and Protestant,
persons from the industrial north of Ireland were overrepresented,
which means that people who were not classic peasants, but who had
experienced life in a modernizing society, were overrepresented
among the Irish in Britain; and (4) to talk about "the Irish" in Great
Britain as being merely the Irish-born is a practice that distorts the
real situation, for it focuses exclusively upon the generation that had
the hardest lot in life. Certainly "the Irish" should be traced at least as
a two-generation ethnic group, and when that is done, considerable
upward social mobility is revealed.

Why is this context so frequently lost? Because of the weak British
data base. The British censuses did not make provision for enumerat-
ing the children or grandchildren of immigrants, so that all sense of
ethnic adaptation and mobility was lost. After surveying the literature

on the Irish in Great Britain, C.J. Houston and W.J. Smyth concluded that:

A basic weakness in almost all these studies is that the data employed refer only to first-generation immigrants, those actually born in Ireland.... These studies of the Irish are, in reality, studies of immigrants. Not unexpectedly, therefore, the geographical location of the Irish within cities tends to be associated with the slums of cellar and court dwellings and overcrowded tenements. Irishness and poverty appear to be virtually synonymous in these studies, and the location of the Irish community can be employed almost as a surrogate measure of the location of slums in the British Victorian cities.... Unfortunately, the relative success of the British-born generation in freeing itself from the immigrant slums cannot be traced from ethnic data that is defined solely by place of birth.[38]

The other fundamental weakness in the British data base (which, unfortunately, is directly reflected in the studies of the Irish in Great Britain) is that there never has been a British enumeration of the religious profession of the individuals in the country's population. This fact may surprise the reader who, being familiar with British history, knows that a religious "census" in 1851 created a great deal of controversy. That "census," however, was not an enumeration of what each individual espoused as his or her religion, but rather an aggregate recording of church attendance on a particular Sunday.[39] This did indeed reveal the relative strengths of the various religious denominations, but it does not tell the social historian what he would like to know: for instance, if the Irish ghetto in Lancashire was an integrated settlement of Irish Protestants and Catholics (and, if so, in what pattern), or was it a segregated settlement? And, given that among many of the Irish, identifying as Protestant or Catholic did not necessarily imply attendance at church but, rather, tribal identity, the church attendance figures become even less useful. In any case, the 1851 experiment caused so much trouble that the British never repeated it, so one really has no accurate information from British sources on the religious adhesion of the Irish in Great Britain.[40]

The lack of religious data and the absence of multigenerational information on the Irish in Great Britain explains why studies of the Irish in Britain have been virtually monopolized by a "community model." Rather than study emigrants from Ireland as a group that dispersed widely and, therefore, has to be studied equally widely, it is suggested that this community or that one was typical of the Irish in Great Britain. This, obviously, is to confuse a subset with a whole, one of the elementary logical fallacies that was cautioned against in chapter one. In fact, there is no study of the Irish in Great Britain that gives even the most elementary demographic profile of the group's characteristics in the nineteenth and early twentieth centuries: not their religion, not their general settlement pattern, not their intergenerational economic mobility. This is both a reproach and a frustration. It means that one of the most potentially valuable laboratories for studying Irish religious cleavages is closed, at least for the present scholarly generation.[41]

Fortunately, there is a laboratory that works: Australasia. If, because of the immense distances involved, New Zealand and Australia can be considered to be one laboratory, they should be thought of as one that has two distinct divisions in which slightly different sets of data are collected.

Take New Zealand first. Although the serious scholarly literature on the Irish in New Zealand is severely limited,[42] and although the demographic data are not as precise as one would like, the general gestalt is revealing.[43] Given below are the numbers of the Irish-born in New Zealand and the proportion that they formed of the overall population.[44]

Year	Numbers of Irish-born	Percentage of population
1878	43,748	10.6%
1886	51,408	8.9
1896	46,037	6.5
1901	43,524	5.6
1906	42,460	4.8
1911	40,958	4.1
1916	37,380	3.4
1921	34,419	2.8

These figures are quite late in the history of the Irish diaspora because the settlement of New Zealand itself was accomplished late in the history of the British empire. Neither from New Zealand nor from Irish sources can one directly determine the geographic or religious background of these Irish migrants, but recent research indicates that they probably were loaded towards the north of Ireland and, slightly, towards Protestantism.[45] That, of course, is a relative statement and in absolute numbers Catholics almost certainly predominated among the Irish migrants to New Zealand.

Although one cannot in New Zealand say that Irish equals Catholic, one can make with confidence the related (but not equivalent) identification – namely, that almost all Catholics were Irish. This is because there was very little migration to New Zealand from European Catholic countries and no marked migration there from the Catholic areas of Scotland. In 1896, 97.1 percent of New Zealand's population had been born in the British Isles or British empire and the figure for 1921 was 98.4 percent.[46] In this population, Ireland was the only significant source of Catholics. This means that one can use the census category of Catholicism to give a close approximation of the characteristics of Irish Catholics – always provided that one remembers that this is a multigenerational group which includes not only immigrants from Ireland and their children but, in some cases, their grandchildren as well.

Recall hypothesis no. 1, that because of their cultural characteristics, the Irish Catholics would settle in absolute numbers in cities, rather than in rural areas and, recall also hypothesis no. 2, that this would be particularly marked in comparison to Irish Protestants. In the context of these hypotheses, it is useful to compare the region of settlement of Roman Catholics in New Zealand with that of the general population (which was overwhelmingly Protestant) in the year 1916:[47]

Region	Percentage Distribution of Entire Population	Percentage Distribution of Catholics
Auckland	28.29%	29.05%
Hawke's Bay	4.98	4.90
Taranaki	5.11	5.24
Wellington	20.52	20.68
Marlborough	1.49	1.92
Nelson	4.40	3.89
Westland	1.29	3.78
Canterbury	16.39	14.51
Otago	12.08	10.35
Southland	5.45	5.68

This is strong circumstantial evidence that the Irish did not bunch, and, actually, that they distributed themselves the way everyone else did.

Still, it might be argued, that although the Catholics (who we are using as a surrogate for the Irish and their descendants) spread themselves across civic districts in a pattern virtually identical to that of the general population, they may have settled within those various districts in aberrant ways. Specifically, it is possible that they found their ways to urban centres. That is possible, in theory, but note the following profile for the year 1921:[48]

urban/rural breakdown of the entire population	56/44%
urban/rural breakdown of Roman Catholic population	57/43%

The Irish Catholics appear to have preferred to have been a city people (thus confirming hypothesis no. 1, seemingly). "Urban" was defined in the official statistics as including everyone who lived either in a city or a municipal borough, the latter sometimes having only a few hundred people, so whether these really were "city people" is a difficult point. In any case, the Irish were *not* more urban than the general population. The profile of the entire population considered by place of birth is illuminating:[49]

Urban/Rural group	*Urban/Rural Breakdown*
Entire population	56/44%
All foreign-born persons	62/38
English-born	64/36
Scottish-born	59/41
Irish-born (includes both Catholics and Protestants)	55/45
Native-born New Zealanders	54/46

Assuming that one is willing to accept these data,[50] then they lead us to the following observations. The first of these stems from the notable fact that the Irish Catholics (immigrants, and their descendants) had an urban/rural breakdown (57/43%) that was very close to that of the Irish immigrants (both Catholics and Protestants combined), namely 55/45%. Much the most probable explanation of these two interrelated pairs of numbers is that, in the immigrant generation, Irish Protestants and Irish Catholics settled in nearly identical residential patterns. Nevertheless, it is just barely conceivable that the apparent identity of the urban/rural breakdown of the Irish ethnic surrogate (the Catholics) and the entire Irish-born population is spurious. One is dealing with four cells, all of which are related, but on none of which do we have individual direct data:

Irish Protestants 2nd and 3rd generations	Irish Catholics: 2nd and 3rd generations
Irish-born Protestants:	Irish-born Catholics

What we know is that:

Irish-born, both Roman Catholic and Protestant = 55/45

And that:

	Irish Catholics 1st, 2nd, and 3rd generations = 57/43

The most likely situation is that all four cells are nearly identical. However, they could be different, and the conventional wisdom about Catholic-Protestant differences somewhat defended, *if* (a) the Irish-born Catholics were very heavily skewed towards urban life; and (b) the Irish-born Protestants were skewed equally in the opposite direction, towards rural settlement; and (c) the second and third generation of Irish Catholics were skewed strongly towards rural life and in just the right proportions to offset the urban skew of the first generation. Not only is all this inherently unlikely (would one seriously posit that a large number of Irish immigrants would settle in the cities of New Zealand and then raise their children to be farmers?), but the logic of the objection is self-defeating: to talk away the strong rural proclivities of the first generation of Irish Catholics in New Zealand one would have to suggest a strong rural propensity in the second and third generations. Thus, it is better to take these data at face value and to accept that in both the immigrant and in later generations, Irish Protestants and Irish Catholics settled in nearly identical patterns. This, of course, runs counter to hypothesis no 2.

A second, equally important observation is that although the Irish Catholics settled in absolute numbers more often in urban than in rural areas, nevertheless the number settling in the countryside was so large as to preclude the interpretation that the religion, communalism, or alleged technological backwardness of the Irish Catholics worked against their successfully making a life and a livelihood in a rural environment. This point is underscored by a comparative fact: that the Irish Catholics as an immigrant group can be inferred to have settled in rural areas more frequently than did the Scottish-born and much more frequently than did the English-born, groups that stemmed from Protestant cultures and from modernizing societies, and which no one has yet suggested suffered from a cultural or technological inability to deal with rural life.

When one turns to viewing the actual occupations of the population, the dead-centre normalcy of the Irish-Catholic males is striking. The profile for males in 1921 is given below (and once again, one is using Catholicism as a surrogate for the multi-generational Irish Catholic ethnic group):[51]

Occupational group	Percentage of Catholic males	Percentage of entire male population
professional	4.72%	4.78%
domestic service	2.13	1.43
commercial	6.94	9.39
transport and communications	9.97	8.45
industrial	14.38	15.82
primary producers (mostly farmers)	22.01	22.90
other	4.39	4.11
dependent upon others for livelihood (mostly children)	35.46	33.12
Total	100.00	100.00

There are thus some slight, teasing differences between the Irish Catholics as an ethnic group and the general population: such as the Irish being somewhat *under*represented in the industrial category, where the unskilled jobs were. But, in general, typicality is striking, and one notes that the largest group of Irish Catholics were primary producers – that is, farmers.

Although studies of female occupational profiles are not as revealing as those of males, because traditional occupational categories lump together all housewives, even though they frequently performed different jobs, these female data indicate that women of Irish-Catholic background were little different from the general population:[52]

Occupational group	Percentage of Catholic females	Percentage of entire female population
professional	4.78%	3.71%
domestic service	7.08	5.50
commercial	3.46	3.46

transport and communications	0.69	0.45
industrial	3.55	3.41
primary producers	1.57	1.54
other	3.22	3.53
dependents (children and housewives)	75.65	78.40
Total	100.00	100.00

Unfortunately, we have no surrogate for Irish Protestants that operates the way Catholicism works for Irish Catholics, so one cannot conclude anything directly about the comparative occupational profiles of those two groups. However, given that the Irish Catholics were typical of the New Zealand occupational distribution, it means that if either Irish group was economically deviant, it was not the Catholics, but the Protestants. That in itself is not a major conclusion, but it contains a mordant little irony, for the literature on Irish-Catholic economic behaviour always has postulated that they, not the Protestants, were the deviants.

New Zealand is not the centre of the universe, but that is irrelevant. *If* one accepts the canons of experimental design, then even this single, somewhat muddy case would be enough to make one question much of the accepted wisdom of the Irish diaspora studies.[53] Although the migrants to New Zealand were a small proportion of the entire Irish emigrant stream, Protestants and Catholics went there in significant numbers, and moreover, because of governmental assistance schemes, both groups were selected for migration by the same process. Thus, they were comparable groups. The New Zealand data directly disprove hypothesis no. 2, for Irish Protestants and Catholics can be inferred to have had identical settlement patterns. Hypothesis no. 1 is another and more complex matter. The hypothesis is confirmed that Irish Catholics are shown to have settled less often in rural than in urban areas, very broadly defined, but they did so less often than did other groups that are considered to have been culturally advantaged. Hence, the reasoning about cultural handicaps upon which hypothesis no. 1 is based appears invalid. As for hypotheses nos. 3 and 4, a Scotch verdict emerges. The Irish Catholics are shown not to have been economically disadvantaged in comparison to the general New Zealand population, but how they compared to Irish Protestants is unknown. Given that they did as well as did the general population, it is hard to accept that the Irish Catholics carried with them economic handicaps from the homeland.

Australia provides another clean historical laboratory and the data available there are more comprehensive and systematic than those generated in New Zealand. The greatest impediment to using Australia intelligently as a lab is the image of the Irish migrants to Australia as being a mélange of people from prison ships, of Irish rebels, of Ned Kelly, and of wild colonial boys. This misleadingly contumacious image of the Australian Irish is hard to combat, for only in the last year has there appeared a readable and reliable history of the Irish in Australia.[54] Although the use of parts of Australia as penal colonies is famous, for the Irish in numerical and cultural terms this was a phenomenon of second-level importance. Between 1788 and 1853 (when transportation to Australia's eastern colonies was abandoned), roughly 40,000 Irish persons were shipped directly from Ireland to penal exile in Australia, and another 8,000 Irish persons had been shipped from either Scotland or England.[55] This sixty-five year running-total of 48,000 compares with a total Irish-born population living in New South Wales in 1846 of 47,457,[56] and in Victoria in 1857 of 65,264,[57] which is to say that by mid-nineteenth century most of the Irish immigrants in Australia were free immigrants, not convicts. Further, even when dealing with the Irish prisoners, it is important not to accept the myth that most of them were what would today be called "political prisoners." Actually, over the years the total of political prisoners was less than 600, which is to say, about 1½ percent of the total of Irish convicts. Even if one adds to that number those who might be called "primitive rebels" against landlordism and economic exploitation, the total would only be one-fifth of the Irish convicts. Most of the Irish exiles were everyday criminals, mostly thieves. A significant minority, perhaps 10 percent, were Protestants.[58]

The convict stream among the Irish (and, indeed, among the entire population) was strongly diluted by a variety of governmental assisted-passage schemes, as well as by emigrants who paid their own way to Australia. From the later 1830s onwards, migrants from the British Isles flowed into New South Wales and into what was then called Port Phillip (later to become Victoria) in ever-growing numbers. From 1837–50, inclusive, over 52,000 British and Irish persons were assisted in settling in these two Australian colonies. Somewhat under 12,000 of this number were from Ireland.[59]

Unlike the case of North America and of Great Britain, Australia did not experience a great flood of migrants immediately consequent upon the Great Famine. Instead, the great surge came in the middle of the 1850s as part of the Australian gold rush.[60] As a group, Irish migrants to Australia were far from well-off financially, but they were not refugees from the Famine.

As in the case of New Zealand (and, as was the case in English-Canada – and was not the case in the United States) the Irish in

Australia in the second half of the nineteenth century and in the early twentieth century were not a "minority group." They were too large a portion of the population to be treated cavalierly. In New South Wales, for instance, in 1846 (the first census to give place-of-birth), the Irish-born were 25.4 percent of the total population and 37.4 percent of the immigrants.[61] In 1871, to take an all-Australia stance, the Irish-born were 24 percent of the foreign-born population.[62] Naturally, as the population of Australia came to consist mostly of persons born in that country, the Irish-born proportion of the total population dropped. But, as the following figures indicate, the Irish-born remained a fairly large segment of the foreign-born.[63]

Year	Total Population	Irish-born	Percentage of total population Irish-born	Austra-lian-born	Percentage of total population Austral-ian-born	Total foreign-born	Irish-born as percent-age of foreign-born
1891	3,174,392	226,949	7.1%	2,158,975	68.0%	1,015,417	22.4%
1901	3,772,891	184,085	4.9	2,908,303	77.1	864,588	21.3
1911	4,455,055	139,434	3.1	3,667,670	82.3	787,335	17.7

Even these figures understate the significance of the Irish in the population of Australia, for as the nation matured, the impact of any ethnic group rested not on its immigrants, but on the second and third generations. Here, unfortunately, the Australian data fail. There are no direct demographic data on ethnicity and one must fall back on indirect information. That, however, is not crippling. Employing quite simple, but reasonable, methods of redacting the census data, Charles Price of the Australian National University has produced the following estimates of the nonaboriginal population of Australia in the second half of the nineteenth century:[64]

Ethnicity	Percentage, 1861	Percentage, 1891
English	49.0%	48.8%
Irish	25.5	25.7
Scottish	14.3	14.0
Welsh	1.4	1.5
Channel Islands, etc.	0.2	0.3
Total British Isles	90.4	90.3

Given that the Irish were Australia's second largest ethnic group from mid-nineteenth century onwards – and Price's data show that as of 1978 they still were second largest[65] – the logical question is: how did they break down between Catholics and Protestants? One will recall that in the case of New Zealand, it was possible to use the

Catholic population as a quite accurate surrogate for the multigenerational Irish Catholic population because non-Irish Catholic migration to New Zealand was minimal. For Australia in the late nineteenth and early twentieth centuries (that is, before the era of large-scale slippage in religious adherence), the Catholic population can be used as a surrogate for Irish Catholicism but with some modifications. These are required because about 10 percent of the Australian population in the second half of the nineteenth century was of non-British Isles origin and a fair number of these people were Catholics. A reasonable approximation from Price's data is that in 1891 just under 4 percent (3.94 percent) of the population of Australia was Catholic, of non-Irish background.[66] This was at a time when Catholics were 22.5 percent of the total population (see Table 3), so that one could infer that persons of Irish-Catholic ethnicity comprised approximately 18.6 percent of the total population. Therefore, a reasonable revision of the ethnicity figures for Australia for 1891 would be as follows:

Ethnicity	Percentage
English	48.8%
Irish Catholic	18.6
Scottish	14.0
Irish Protestant	7.1
Welsh	1.5
Channel Islands, etc.	0.3
Total British Isles	90.3

This makes the points, first, that Irish Catholics were a very significant group in the general population and, second, that among the overall Irish ethnic group the Protestants were a very noticeable minority: about 28 percent in 1891. This second point must be made clearly because the single most influential article on the religious composition of the Irish in Australia is misleading. This is "The Irish in Victoria, 1851-91: A Demographic Essay," by Oliver MacDonagh and one hesitates to point this out because MacDonagh in other efforts has made major, indeed brilliant, contributions to Irish studies. This essay was given as a paper in 1969 and was published in 1971 and as such was a pioneering piece of Australian historical demography because it gave a clear tabulation of the available information on Irish settlement and related matters that was scattered quite inconveniently in various census reports. The problem arises in his analysis of the data. MacDonagh specified two variables and then tried to show their relationship. One of the variables was the percentage which the Irish-born comprised in the population of the several administrative districts of Victoria, and the second was the Roman-Catholic percentage of the

Table 3
Proportion of Catholics in Total Australian Population, 1851–1921

Year	New South Wales	Victoria	Commonwealth of Australia
1851	30.4		
1857		18.8	
1861	28.3	20.4	
1871	29.3	23.3	
1881	27.6	23.6	
1891	25.6	21.8	22.5
1901			22.7
1911			22.4
1921			21.6

Sources: compiled from Oliver MacDonagh, "The Irish in Victoria, 1851–91: a Demographic Essay," in T.D. Williams, ed., Historical Studies (Dublin: Gill and MacMillan, 1971) 8: 82–92; Walter Phillips, "Religious Profession and Practice in New South Wales, 1850–51: The Statistical Evidence," Historical Studies (Melbourne), vol. 15 (Oct. 1972), 381; Walter Phillips, "Statistics on Religious Affiliation in Australia, 1891–1961," Australian Historical Statistics No. 4 (Nov. 1981), 11.

population of the same districts. He then worked out a correlation (the type of correlation is unspecified) and found that in the years 1851, 1861, 1871, 1881, and 1891, the correlations were, respectively, .907, .943, .907, .897, and .879. From these he concluded that "the Catholic and Irish communities can be treated as substantially synonymous."[67] Here is what MacDonagh thought his study proved:

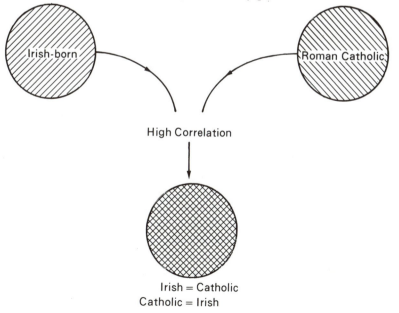

What he did not recognize was that there were two situations which, under certain circumstances could produce an equally high correlation, but which have very different meanings. One of these is the instance wherein all the Irish were Catholic but all the Catholics were not Irish.

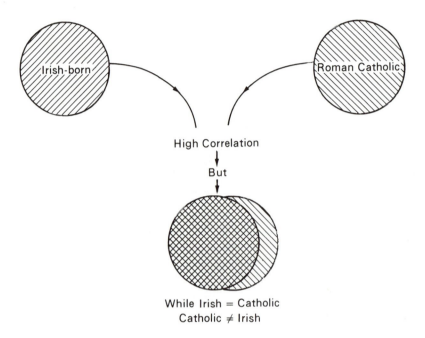

High Correlation

But

While Irish = Catholic
Catholic ≠ Irish

More damaging is the other possibility – namely, that there was a significant number of Irish who were not Catholic: (see next page).

The flaws here in the logic and experimental design are considerable and obvious. They are magnified by MacDonagh's having specified no null hypothesis, so not only does a high correlation not prove what he thought it proved,[68] but even a correlation of zero would not have disproved his suggestion that Irish and Catholic are two-way synonyms: if every Catholic was Irish and every Irish person was Catholic, one could still have a correlation of zero if these individuals were distributed so that in each civic district they were the same proportion of the population of that district as they were in the general population. In that case, no correlation would exist, although the identity would be perfect. This extreme case is unlikely to occur, of course, but it indicates another basic flaw in MacDonagh's work.

The sad part of this revisionist exercise is that a quick glance at readily available direct evidence would have prevented these mis-

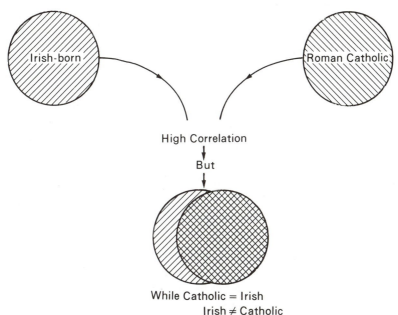

High Correlation
↓
But
↓

While Catholic = Irish
Irish ≠ Catholic

takes. The 1911 census of Australia provides a number of valuable cross-tabulations, among them tables on the relationship of place-of-birth and of religion. If one takes the population of the state of Victoria, one finds that of the 41,477 Irish-born persons, 28,552 were Catholics.[69] That is, Roman Catholics were 68.8 percent of the Irish immigrant population in the state of Victoria, and that is a long way from an identity of Catholicism and Irish birth.

One might argue that 1911 was too long after the time period studied by MacDonagh for the census data to be relevant, but in fact it was not. The Irish-born in Victoria were a long-settled group and in 1911 83.8 percent (34,759 of the 41,477 Irish-born) had been resident for twenty years or more,[70] which means that they were living in Victoria in the last of the years for which MacDonagh did his correlations. In sum, the real situation was as follows:

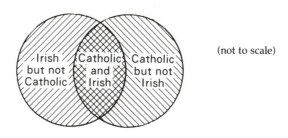

(not to scale)

that is: a large (but not entire) portion of Catholics was of Irish origin and most (but far from all) persons of Irish origin were Catholic. And that holds not just for Victoria, but for the entire Commonwealth.[71]

With that as background, let us examine the first of the four hypotheses that derive from the conventional literature about the cultural propensities of the people of the Irish diaspora. Hypothesis no. 1 was that the Irish Catholics, because of cultural disabilities, would be deposited in cities, like particulate matter in industrial soot. Immediately one runs into a surprise: historians of the Irish in Australia report nothing of the sort. David Fitzpatrick remarks in a statistical study of Irish emigrants worldwide, that:

In Australia, the diffusion of Irish expatriates throughout the population was remarkable. Those districts which gained local reputations as Irish enclaves, such as Shepparton or Belfast in Victoria and the Darling Downs in Queensland, were far less aberrant in terms of their proportions of Irish-born than were more "Irish" localities of Britain or America. Within the major Australian cities, also, the Irish were far more evenly distributed than folklore would suggest.[72]

A study of residential segregation in Melbourne and Sydney, 1861–91, revealed that at no time did either Catholics or Irish immigrants even approach the threshold of significant residential segregation.[73] Most importantly, as Patrick O'Farrell has noted, "in fact, from the beginning of Australian settlement the Irish exhibited a veritable obsession with the acquisition of land and livestock."[74] Oliver MacDonagh's data base (which, his correlational analysis aside, is quite solid) revealed that in Victoria in the second half of the nineteenth century the districts with the highest proportion of Irish-born persons were rural and agricultural in character.[75]

The 1911 census, the first conducted for the Commonwealth of Australia as a federal unit, is particularly interesting on this point. In 1911, there were 139,434 Irish-born persons in the country. Of these, almost 80 percent had been in Australia for at least twenty years,[76] which means that they had come to Australia as part of the great nineteenth-century Irish diaspora. In 1911, the census authorities tallied each person's place of residence and noted whether or not they lived in one of the six main cities or their suburbs: Sydney, Melbourne, Brisbane, Adelaide, Perth, and Hobart. By including in the tally the vast suburbs (parts of which still were bush), the authorities erred in the direction of classifying some predominantly rural areas as cities, but for our purposes that is all to the good, because any error will be in the direction of overemphasizing the city-bound nature of the Irish immigrants. Even so, only 41.6 percent of the Irish immigrants lived in metropolitan areas.[77] The smallest of these city-and-suburbs – Hobart and its suburbs – in 1911 had only 18,487 population, so even these city dwellers were not living in great urban concentrations.

In order to keep this in context, note that despite the legend of the pervasive Australian bush, the population of Australia at the turn of the last century was one of the most urbanized in the New World[78] – and even so, the Irish-born did not have strong urban proclivities. In comparison to the general run of immigrants, the Irish-born in 1911 were less urban:[79]

Group	Percentage living in metropolitan areas and suburbs
All immigrants	44.4%
Irish-born immigrants	41.6
Entire population	38.0
Native-born Australians	36.7

Viewing the settlement pattern of the Irish immigrants to Australia, David Fitzpatrick has remarked on "the particular readiness" with which the Irish settlers grasped the opportunities open to them, "as shown by their comparative concentration in agricultural districts." This propensity to settle in agricultural areas, he suggests, was in part the result of there being plenty of marriageable Irish women among the Irish immigrants and "still more influential, perhaps, was their predominantly rural background, which gave most Irish settlers knowledge of how to work the land not shared by their urban counterparts from England."[80]

Curious, is it not? – the dominant literature on the Irish diaspora (from which our four major hypotheses are drawn) posits that the Irish emigrants to various New Worlds would not settle in rural areas because their farming background in the Old World was a disadvantage to them, and here it is being suggested not only that they did not avoid rural areas, but that their agricultural background gave them an advantage in such places over other settlers.

It must be remembered that the information on the place of residence of Irish immigrants to Australia lumped together Catholics and Protestants. There is no convenient way to separate them out and this leaves open the possibility that (just maybe) the Irish-born Protes-

tants were overwhelmingly rural and, therefore, the Irish-born Catholics were metropolitan dwellers after all. There is nothing in the historical literature to suggest that this indeed is the case, but the arithmetic
is interesting. If 100 percent of the Irish-born Protestant immigrants
settled outside of the metropolitan regions, then, in 1911, the Irish-
born Catholics would in Australia have been 59 percent metropolitan
residents.[81]

Manifestly, that is a profitless exercise, particularly because indirect
evidence indicates that Irish-Catholic immigrants were mostly rural.
One can infer this by a chain of reasoning that begins with the Irish
Catholics as a multigenerational ethnic group (of which the immigrant
generation is the first). Entry into this cohort is best made through an
examination of the census data on Catholics in general. Given below
are the proportions of various populations that were living in cities
and suburbs:[82]

Group	Percentage in metropolitan areas and suburbs
Entire population	38.0%
All Christian denominations	37.9
Catholics	36.3

As mentioned earlier, unlike New Zealand, the Catholic population of
Australia cannot be taken as being entirely Irish, but the signal characteristic of European migration to Australia (from which non-Irish
Catholics would stem) was that the Europeans had very close to the
same urban/rural pattern as did the general population. In 1911, the
foreign-born Europeans were 35.4 percent metropolitan-and-suburbs
in their settlement[83] which is very close to the Catholic pattern as well.
This means that the Catholic pattern is not skewed by an inclusion of
a deviant band of Europeans Catholics and, therefore, that the Catholic urban/rural pattern can be taken as representative of the several
generations of Irish Catholics which it encompasses. Which is to say
that the Irish-Catholic immigrants, their children and grandchildren,
were not chiefly a city people, but a people of small villages and of the
countryside. A reasonable speculation would be that the first generation
Irish Catholics living in Australia in 1911 were slightly less rural than
were the second, third, and subsequent generations (simply because
that was the pattern for all ethnic groups), but not markedly so: neither
the Irish immigrants nor their descendants were a city people.[84]

❧

Hypothesis no. 2 – that the Irish Catholics in their several generations would be markedly more urban than Irish Protestants – is
impossible to examine directly. However, a notable intergroup similarity seems the only way to characterize the Australian data. Recall that
Catholics in the Australian population were 36.3 percent city dwellers
and that this was shown to be representative of Irish Catholics considered as a multigenerational group. This is remarkably close to the
settlement patterns of the four major denominations to which Irish-
Protestant immigrants and their descendants belonged:[85]

Denomination	Percentage in metropolitan areas and suburbs
Church of England	39.9%
Catholic	36.3
Presbyterian	34.6
Methodist	32.2

This implies (but certainly does not prove) that as a collective group
Irish Protestants probably acted in choice of residence the same way
as did Irish Catholics. There, for the moment one must stop, but to
someone who has been accustomed to the notion that the Irish were
almost inevitably deviant in their social and economic patterns, one
can only be struck by what David Fitzpatrick has called "the impression of normality among the Australian-Irish settlers."[86]

The occupational information collected by Australian officials is
revealing. At the end of our period of study, 1921, there was a valuable
Commonwealth-wide census that provides an effective summation of
the position of the Irish immigrants in their society. The 1921 census of
Australia revealed an Irish immigrant population that was long settled
and, if anything, better situated than were Scottish and English immigrants. Granted, the analytic categories used by the enumerators were
too coarse to be anything but crudely indicative, but it is interesting
to note that the Irish-born were stronger in the entrepreneurial
groups (employers and the self-employed) than were the Scots and
the English, and, for that matter, the Australian-born. Conversely,
they were more often unemployed, but that is to be expected: unem-
ployment is the occupational hazard of the entrepreneur. Certainly
this overrepresentation in entrepreneurial activities is exactly the
opposite of what one would expect if the Irish immigrants were, as
much of the literature of the Irish diaspora holds, unprepared to deal
with a fast-changing and modernizing economy.

Figure 7.
Occupations of Male Adults, by Place of Birth, Australia, 1921

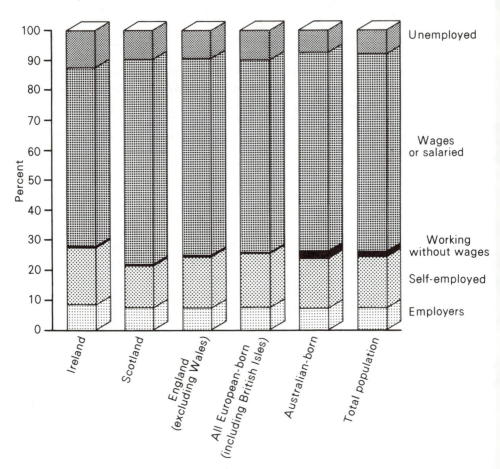

Source: See Appendix J

Patrick O'Farrell has studied emigrant correspondence, as has Kerby Miller, and they have come to opposite conclusions about the commercial and economic attitudes of Irish migrants. Whereas Miller perceives the emigrants' letters home as cries of pain from exiles and as evidence of the Irish migrants' inability to cope with the modern world, O'Farrell says that "what is remarkable about emigrant correspondence is not its piety, but its consistent satisfied worldliness. It is crammed with detailed reportage of material conditions, particularly catalogues of prices and wages. This fixation on material affairs was natural enough among people formerly poor who had now found relative affluence."[87]

This concern with the material world helped the Irish immigrants, Catholic and Protestant alike, to overcome whatever disadvantages they may initially have had, particularly if they had been in the early convict population.

What is remarkable about the bulk of the Irish emancipists is their relative prosperity. Somewhere between twenty percent and twenty-five percent of free Irishmen in the colony [of New South Wales] held land or livestock or both, and some were among the leading land-holders or flockmasters in their districts. Still others were well established in the middling areas of commerce. The 1828 census contradicts the traditional historical depiction of the early Irish as restricted to the bottom of the socio-economic scale. . . . This situation also points to a feature of colonial society which was to be the basis of Irish [Catholic] assimilation in Australia – that however hostile the Anglo-Saxon Protestant majority might appear, it was still possible for the Irish to make their way up in the Australian world, even from positions of the greatest disadvantage.[88]

This is not to say that the Irish, and especially the Irish Catholics, did not experience discrimination in their individual lives, but at a communal level it is clear that they overcame it. Admittedly, the Catholics were virtually locked out of certain occupational groups, but they were a large enough community, and sufficiently powerful, that they were able to practice discrimination against persons of other ethnic backgrounds and other religious faiths. So, what they lost by being locked out of (as was the case) dealerships in surgical instruments, they made up for by controlling portions of the lucrative drink business. (This brings to mind the assertion by a generous and broad-minded Cork publican that the only lasting effect of Ireland's penal laws was to lock the poor unfortunate Protestants out of the licensed trade.)

The census of New South Wales of 1901 is the first for any Australian state to provide cross-tabulations of occupation and place of birth and religious persuasion. It provides a valuable picture of the economic profile of the group of Irish migrants who, in the average case, had come to Australia in the 1860s and now were at their economic maturity. This material is presented in detail in Appendixes K and L (pp. 185-8).

The single most important point these appendixes convey is that among Irish immigrants and among Catholics generally (most, but not all of whom were Irish), agriculture was far-and-away the most popular occupation. Further, not only was it the most common choice of occupation in absolute terms, it was relatively more popular among Irish immigrants than it was among those from other countries:

Group	Percentage of males in agriculture
Entire population	37.3%
Born in Australia or New Zealand	38.2
Foreign-born:	
England and Wales	25.6
Scotland	28.9
Ireland	33.0

Source: Appendix K

These data make waste of the argument that Irish immigrants were too technologically backward to farm, or too given to communal living to stand pioneering loneliness.

Of course, the higher propensity of Irish immigrants to enter agriculture may have been chiefly a function of their having been in Australia longer in the usual case than had the English and the Scots immigrants, but if that is so, then it is hard to see how the following tally of farmers and ranchers by religious persuasion (a multigenerational set of categories) could have emerged:

Religious denomination	Percentage in agriculture
Entire population	37.3%
Anglican	33.9
Methodist	40.1
Presbyterian	36.8
Catholic	37.7

Source: Appendix L

If one accepted the basic tenets of the consensus-interpretation of the Irish diaspora that stem from the U.S. literature, namely that a group's taking up agricultural occupations in relatively low numbers is a sure sign of its being culturally handicapped, then one would be required to mourn the cultural handicaps of that traditionally privileged group, the Anglicans, who went into agriculture with less alacrity than did the Catholics.

On several matters, the Australian demographic data cast a direct, although not definitive, light upon possible differences between Irish Protestants and Catholics. Among these, the matter of relative levels of literacy is both puzzling and tantalizing. Throughout the English-speaking world, census data on literacy is notoriously difficult to interpret. Frequently it is unreliable (are individuals merely asked if they are literate or actually to prove it? – and at what level of competence?) Moreover, the standard way of discussing the matter among educationalists is misleading if adopted by social historians of modern societies. Educational policy makers almost always talk about *il*literacy rates, and for social planners trying to promote schooling this is sensible enough, for the eradication of illiteracy is in many ways like the stamping out of a social blight, and this method of speaking keeps attention focused on the malaise to be attacked: illiteracy. But for the social historian, use of illiteracy rates is deceptive, for it leads one to lose sight of the actual historical fact – namely, that most people are not illiterate in modern societies. Use of illiteracy statistics for comparing social groups is especially dangerous. For instance, if Group A is 0.1 percent illiterate and Group B is 0.2 percent illiterate, it is arithmetically true that Group B has twice the illiteracy rate of Group A. That statement, however, is virtually meaningless to the historian. For the historian the salient point is that Group A is 99.9 percent literate and Group B is 99.8 percent and that each of these figures indicates an extremely high degree of literacy.

With that as background, consider two intriguing sets of data. The first of these comes from the first census of an Australian state that allows accurate cross-tabulations of literacy and other factors, the New South Wales enumeration of 1901. If one considers children ages five to fifteen years of age, inclusive, who were able both to read and write, the results are as follows:[89]

Group	Percentage
Entire population	73.7%
Catholics	71.4
Anglicans	73.6
Various Presbyterians	75.7
Various Methodists	76.5

This is a surprisingly small degree of variation and, considering that Catholic schools were underfunded relative to the state schools attended by most Protestant children,[90] bespeaks virtual identity.

The second data set is from 1921 and is Australia-wide. If one considers the proportion of persons five years of age and over who could read and write, one discovers the following distribution:[91]

Group	Percentage
Entire population	92.8%
Australian-born	93.0
All European-born (including British Isles)	94.2
English-born (excluding Wales)	96.8
Scottish-born	97.9
Irish-born	92.8

Although these figures are all within a range of little more than 5 percentage points and all indicate a high degree of literacy, there is no denying that the Irish immigrants were somewhat less apt to be literate than were those from England or Scotland. (The reader will notice that the Irish immigrants, however, were as literate as most Australians and as literate as the Australian-born.) This, though, tells us nothing about the possible differences between Irish Protestants and Irish Catholics. Note, however: if one takes the 1901 New South Wales data as indicating that the Roman Catholics (among whom is included the entire Irish-Catholic ethnic group) had near average literacy, as compared to other multigenerational groups and, that the Irish immigrants had a somewhat lower literacy rate than did other immigrant groups, then, the most obvious explanation of these two phenomena is that the Protestants among the Irish immigrants were less apt to be literate than were the Catholics. By the lights of the conventional wisdom on religious persuasion and literature that is a very outré suggestion (and, admittedly, it is based on some rather tenuous reasoning) but it is worth investigation. It makes the point, however, that one should not assume a priori that merely because the literacy rate among the Irish immigrants was lower than among the English and Scots that it was the Catholics among the Irish who brought that rate down.

When one turns to matters of family structure, the material is equally tantalizing. If one looks at Catholics in the Commonwealth of Australia in 1911, one finds that this group (which included all persons of Irish-Catholic ethnicity, plus some non-Irish Catholics as well) had slightly larger families than did Protestants. Given below is the average issue of each woman who, by 1911, at any time had had a child.[92]

Group	Number of children
"Roman Catholic"*	4.14
"Catholic" (undefined)*	3.85
Anglican	3.82
Presbyterian	3.90
Methodist	4.10
Lutheran	4.87
All Christian denominations	3.95
Non-Christian	3.27
"Indefinite"	3.59
No Religion	3.13
Entire Population	3.93

At last it seems that we have a set of differences between Irish Catholics and everyone else, differences that can perhaps be causally ascribed to cultural factors. Except ... except that such differences in total family size could also be the result of different age structures among the various denominations, rather than of cultural causes. A religious group, most of whose married women were quite young, would have fewer children-per-woman than those loaded toward women of middle age whose families had reached nearly their full natural size. Thus, Figure 8 is illuminating, for it indicates that it was only in the age brackets thirty-five to sixty-four that Roman Catholics had slightly larger families – and then, at the very maximum period, ages fifty to fifty-four, only .37 children-per-woman higher than the national average. And, from age sixty-five onwards, the Roman-Catholic family was smaller. What this adds up to is a pattern that is no pattern: there is no regular or strong association between Roman Catholics and larger-than-national-average families.

---

*"Catholic (undefined)" and "Roman Catholic" can be taken to be the same denomination. On most issues it is possible to reprocess the census data so as to combine the categories, but in tabulating birth rates this is not possible. "Catholic (undefined)" comprised approximately 7 percent of the total of the two categories, so of the two figures, the Roman Catholic figure is the more revealing.

Figure 8
Religious Persuasion and Child-bearing, Australia, 1911

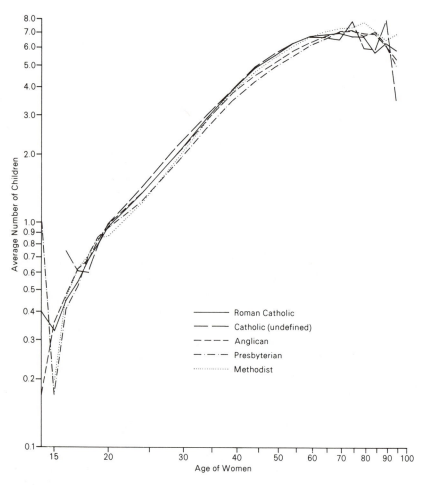

Source: See Appendix M

This fact is usefully juxtaposed to a set of 1911 data that seem to show that the Irish-born had a predilection for large families:[93]

Birthplace	Average issue of wife
Ireland	5.27
England	4.66
Wales	4.98

Scotland	4.90
United Kingdom as a whole	4.86
Europe, exclusive of United Kingdom	5.34
Australian-born	3.68
Entire population	3.93

Remember, however, that in 1911 the immigrants from the United Kingdom had been in Australia for a long time – most of them for over twenty years – and the age profile of the United Kingdom immigrants, therefore, was high. And highest of all was that of the Irish: 48.4 percent of the English-born population (both sexes combined) was over fifty years of age in 1911; the figures for the Welsh and the Scottish-born were, respectively, 48.7 percent and 51.5 percent. For the Irish, the figure was 62.19.[94] This points to the strong possibility that the seemingly high Irish family size had nothing to do with Irish cultural determinants and everything to do with the structure of the immigrant group. Unfortunately, age-specific fertility was calculated by the census takers only for immigrants from the United Kingdom as a whole and not for the Irish, English, Welsh, and Scottish-born separately. This is not fatal for the point at hand, however, for, considered as a whole, the United Kingdom immigrants had a family size far in excess of the national average and an age structure skewed towards middle- and old-age. Yet, the data in Figure 9 reveal that in *every* age category between twenty and ninety, the United Kingdom-born had a smaller number of children-per-wife than did both the native Australian-born and the Australian population considered as a whole. This leads one to conclude that the larger size of the family of United Kingdom emigrants was entirely a result of the structure of the age group – and, mutatis mutandis, this holds with an extremely high degree of probability for the emigrants from Ireland who, amongst the United Kingdom cohort, had the greatest age of all.

Thus, despite what the data at first glance seem to say, there is no demonstrable association either between Roman Catholicism and large family size or between being Irish-born and having a large family. The most logically compelling inference (although, certainly not the only possible one) is that *in this era* Irish-Catholic families were not significantly larger than were Irish-Protestant ones, either in the immigrant generation or later. One emphasizes "in this era" because one does not wish to gainsay the strong possibility that in various parts of the world it may be found that in the mid-twentieth century persons of Irish-Catholic background have had larger families (and probably, different familial ideologies), even when variables such as age and class are controlled. But, like Cormac O'Grada's work on the

Figure 9
Place of Birth and Child-bearing, Australia, 1911

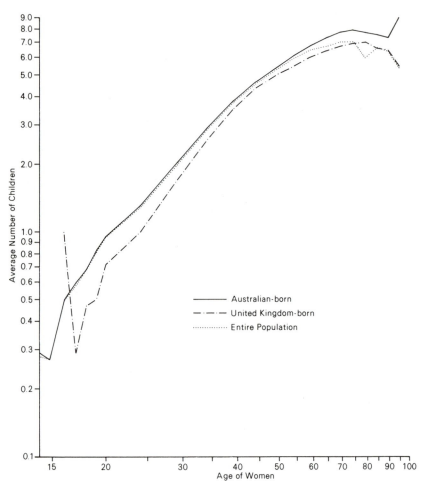

Source: See Appendix N

Ulster family structure in the first decade of the twentieth century, these data indicate that, in Australia, at least, it would be wrong to project present-day differences back into an earlier era.

One reason that it makes sense to suggest that the Irish-Protestant family was of the same size as the Irish-Catholic is that family structure is in large degree affected by occupational status of the major breadwinner,[95] and as argued earlier, it is highly probable that Irish Protestants and Irish Catholics had very similar profiles.

Demographic and social historians long have noted the apparent aversion to marriage among the Irish in the homeland, which existed from mid-nineteenth to mid-twentieth century, and was particularly strong among Catholics. Postponed marriage and celibacy rates in the Republic of Ireland were the highest in the world at mid-twentieth century, and it is worth inquiring whether or not this pattern existed in the people of the Irish diaspora earlier in the present century. Apparently yes. Given below are the percentages of the major Australian religious groups whose members in 1911, aged fifteen years of age and over, had never married:[96]

Denomination	Percentage never married
All Christian denominations	45.04%
All non-Catholic Christian denominations	45.05
Anglican	43.53
Presbyterian	45.67
Methodist	42.91
Catholic	49.83

Place of birth and marriage were related as follows:[97]

Place of birth	Percentage unmarried at time of census (15 years and over)
Total European (including British Isles)	41.17%
England	38.01
Wales	37.56
Scotland	42.00
Ireland	47.40

One might reasonably speculate that the Irish immigrants' marriage rate held the two subsets: relatively high aversion to marriage among Irish Catholics and less harsh aversion among Irish Protestants. This would tie into the fact that the multigenerational Roman-Catholic group (mostly, but not entirely Irish Catholics), had a relatively high aversion to marriage. These suggestions are speculative and are slightly dissonant with the tone of the present analysis, which is more empirical than speculative, but not only would these suggestions explain the available data, they tie into another area of family ideology where it appears there was a real, if small, difference between Irish Catholics and Irish Protestants: marriage breakdowns. Neither Protestants nor Catholics in Australia in the nineteenth and early twentieth centuries much practised divorce, which is hardly surprising considering that it was an expensive and difficult legal process. In 1911 the percentage of Catholic divorces to the total number of Catholic marriages was .289 percent and for the non-Catholic Christians the figure was .317 percent. Both figures are so small as to be negligible.[98] However, there was one noticeable phenomenon that can be directly associated with Irish Catholicism – namely, a relatively high incidence of husbands being absent from their families. Note:[99]

Denomination	Percentage of wives whose husbands were absent
Entire population	15.00%
Anglican	15.62
Presbyterian	14.03
Methodist	11.54
Catholic	17.63

Significantly, this held among the Irish-born population:[100]

Birthplace	Percentage of wives whose husbands were absent
Entire population	15.00%
Australia and New Zealand	16.57
England	15.99
Wales	15.43
Scotland	16.44
Ireland	20.40

This is a rare configuration in the Australian data: a characteristic that is associated both with Catholicism and with Irish birth. So, one can suggest that it is highly probable that in this matter there was a difference of significance between Irish Catholics and Irish Protestants and one that held for more than a single generation. Simply put, the Irish-Catholic husbands did not stick so close to the family hearth. Of course many, perhaps most, of the men tallied in these figures were absent from home because of the need to find work, but given that Irish Protestants and Catholics had similar occupational patterns, this should have affected both groups roughly equally. I suspect that what one is seeing here is the beginning of what became known in the Irish homeland in the mid-twentieth century as "the Liverpool divorce." It is only a hint, more a portent than a major phenomenon in itself. It points to a time beyond the chronological boundaries of this study, when Irish Protestants and Irish Catholics, the world over, developed radically different ways of ending unsuccessful marriages: the Protestants in the main came to effect legal separation and, outside of the Republic of Ireland, divorce. The Catholics either negotiated informal separation agreements or the husbands levanted.

In analyzing the Australian demographic data as they appertain to the Irish, one is dealing with tribal groups, at least in metaphor. One of the most salient criteria that early anthropologists used in delineating social patterns among various cultures was whether tribes were endogamous or exogamous. This is a very touchy subject with the Irish and it is impossible to obtain direct data on the actual incidence of "mixed marriages" in the homeland in the nineteenth and early twentieth centuries. Fortunately, the Australia material is revealing. Not that the religious authorities were at ease with the idea of intermarriage, far from it, but the data are quite good. Indeed, the Australian Catholic authorities, dominated by prelates and clergy of Irish background, strongly warned against such marriages. The following is taken from a pastoral letter of the archbishops and bishops of the province of Australia, 1869:

Seven years ago, the Archbishop and bishop who were then in this province addressed an earnest and affectionate warning to the faithful laity on the subject of mixed marriages. We are very sorry to be obliged to confess that the admonition has not had the effect, full effect, which we hoped for and which it ought to have had. The frequency of mixed marriages is a terrible blot upon the character of our Catholic community. It is sad to think with what facility Catholic parents consent to such irreligious connections: with how little caution they expose their young people to social intercourse, where passionate fancy and the thoughtlessness of youth are certain to entail the danger of mischievous alliances. It is in the main the fault of the parents more than the children, who hear so little warning against mixed marriages – so little denunciation and deprecation of their dangers and miseries . . .

The sad truth is, dearly beloved, that the indifferentism, which we have already stigmatised as the mother heresy and pestilence of our day, has reached us, and has been fostered by those peculiar conditions of our colonial society which we began by indicating. Every worldly motive is intensified, every spiritual object and responsibility is bedimmed and attenuated. Mixed

marriages are formed by those whose faith is partly suffocated by the un-
wholesome atmosphere of indifferentism, consciously or unconsciously, and
mixed marriages directly propogate indifferentism.[101]

Nearly hysterical in tone as the bishops' pastoral was, they had something to worry about. A study of the Catholic community in Victoria
(which was overwhelmingly Irish) showed that in the decade after
1851, between 33 percent and 50 percent of Catholic women married in
non-Catholic churches, a sure sign of a religiously mixed marriage. In
Catholic churches in the same period, one out of three Catholic
women married non-Catholic men.[102]

A somewhat less contentious form of "mixed marriage" was
between people of different ethnic groups, whatever the religious persuasion. In Victoria in 1870–2, 65.5 percent of Irish immigrant bride-
grooms married Irish immigrant wives. At the same time, 52.3 percent
of Irish immigrant brides were joining with an Irish immigrant husband.[103] In many of these cases, the non-Irish born partner may have
been a second-generation Australian of Irish ethnicity, but even these
data suggest that Irish immigrants were not locked into an immigrant
social world, but easily formed alliances outside of their own group.
The same pattern is shown in more comprehensive data for 1911.
Given below are the proportions of immigrants of various ethnic
groups who entered mixed marriages (recall here that most of these
immigrants would have arrived before 1901 and that their marriage in
the usual case had taken place before the end of Victoria's reign).[104]

Place of birth	Percentage of men with ethnically mixed marriage	Percentage of women with ethnically mixed marriage
England	61.40%	43.68%
Wales	79.41	70.28
Scotland	69.01	54.37
Ireland	56.43	52.48

Of course the definition of "mixed marriage" used here by the government officials exaggerates the degree of intermarriage. If, for example,
an English male immigrant married the daughter of English parents
who had emigrated to Australia before her birth, the marriage was
tabulated as mixed. (And, unfortunately, no detailed information on
such cross-generational marriages is available.) However, even from
these rudimentary data two important points emerge. The first is that,
in common with every other group from the British Isles, the Irish
immigrants usually married *outside* of their immediate immigrant

cohort. Second, the reason that the Irish had a lower rate of intermarriage (so defined) than did other British Isles groups (save English women) is that the Irish had a singular social advantage over those groups: alone among the immigrant groups in Australia of the period, the Irish had a nearly balanced population between men and women.[105] Irish men, therefore, had a much greater chance of finding a partner of similar background than did the men of the other immigrant groups.

This, though, is a sidelight. The Catholic bishops' definition of "mixed marriage" – as involving partners of differing religious faiths – is the more important. If one defines "mixed marriage" very widely, so as to include every case wherein someone married a spouse of another denomination (such as when a Presbyterian married a Methodist) then the proportion of mixed marriages in 1911 was as follows:[106]

Denomination	Percentage of men marrying outside of the faith	Percentage of women marrying outside of the faith
All religions	20.93%	20.93%
Anglican	18.79	17.66
Presbyterian	26.77	22.58
Methodist	15.03	17.78
"Roman Catholic" (excluding "Catholic undefined")	17.73	26.10

Further, if one considers as instances of "real" mixed marriages only instances of Catholics marrying Protestants or Protestants marrying Catholics, the results are very surprising. When one examines those married couples on whom we have information both on the husband's and the wife's religions (and when one excludes a small fraction of marriages that occurred outside the Christian faith) one finds that 17.66 percent of marriages involving a Catholic were mixed – that is, to a Protestant – but that marriages involving a Protestant were mixed in only 5.72 percent of the cases.[107] This situation goes against the traditional picture of the Catholic church being effective in inhibiting the occurrence of mixed marriages and may point to a quieter, but more more pervasive form of social control by the Protestant churches. It may, however, be simply an artifact of there having been many more Protestants than Catholics in Australian society, so that a simple epidemiological model explains things: that is, that Catholics, being more apt to be surrounded by Protestants than vice versa, contracted the "disease" of mixed marriage more often than did Protestants, who were more likely to be protected by enclaves of other Protestants.

These possibilities are not mutually exclusive, and both could apply simultaneously.

There remains, however, one set of relations in the data that are not yet explained, namely: (1) that as a group containing both Protestants and Catholics, the Irish immigrants married outside their immediate immigrant group less often than did people from elsewhere in the British Isles and (2) that the Catholics as a group had a higher rate of religiously mixed marriages than did the Protestants by a considerable degree. A future researcher might do well to test the hypothesis that one of the chief reasons for this configuration is that in the immigrant generation Irish Protestants and Irish Catholics married each other with a frequency that both sides found embarrassing and would like to forget.

⚜

The Australian case, and to a slightly lesser extent, the New Zealand one, are in direct conflict with much of the historical literature about the Irish diaspora, particularly the dominant wisdom that draws its inspiration from the Irish-American scholarship on the hibernian outflow. Hypothesis no. 1, that the Irish Catholics would be "city people" was contradicted strongly by the Australian data and, although most of the Irish Catholics in New Zealand lived in "urban" areas (as did almost every other group in the society) this was because the definition of urban included small municipalities of a few hundred souls. More important, hypothesis no. 2, that Irish Protestants and Irish Catholics would have different settlement patterns, was directly and overwhelmingly disproved in both cases. Hypotheses nos. 3 and 4, concerning the occupational profile and economic mobility of the two Irish groups were seriously, but not definitively, called into question. Although data on the Irish Protestants were elusive, the key discovery was that the occupational profile of the Irish Catholics was close to that of the general population and, crucially, the most common occupation was the pursuit of agriculture. The Irish Catholics who migrated to Australia and New Zealand would have been amazed to learn that they did not have the cultural or technical capabilities to farm in a New World.

These conclusions come from several hundreds of thousands of datum points and conflict with the impressionistic evidentiary base of much of the diaspora literature. The natural response to these data on the part of those who wish to defend the status quo is to discount the Antipodean experience entirely. The most promising way to do this is to note that the people who emigrated from Ireland to Australia and New Zealand for the most part were special in some way. Unlike those going to the United States, Canada, or Great Britain, most of the migrants to Australasia were selected by state officials and aided financially on their long journey. Leaving aside the double-edged fact that the early Irish convicts were negatively selected before receiving governmental travel grants of a particularly generous nature, it is true that the later nineteenth-century emigrants were selected for their good qualities. The real losers – the thugs, the crippled, the maimed of Irish society – were excluded from the various government assisted-passage schemes. The governmental system ran from 1831 until being virtually terminated in the 1890s.[108] Recent studies have suggested that in the late nineteenth century the Irish who migrated to Australia came from areas in Ireland affected not by direct privation, but by the spread of grazing agriculture and that they tended to be individuals who had held substantial and regular employment until led, by loss of economic status, to emigrate.[109] That granted, one should not conclude that the Irish migrants to Australia were predominantly middle class. They were not, as can be inferred from the analysis of their literacy: a study of the years 1853–5 and 1871 indicates that the Irish adult migrants to Australia were only marginally more apt to be literate than was the Irish home population.[110] The Irish emigrants to Australia and New Zealand were overwhelmingly the respectable poor, the hardworking rural peasantry, and the members of the middle class who, for whatever reason, had taken a drop in status and now, in Australia or New Zealand, expected to recoup their losses.

Any suggestion that the Australasian laboratory is not a suitable testing site because the migrants to Australia and New Zealand were of too high a social status is not only factually misconceived, but is also logically self-destructive. The basis for the four hypotheses that are being tested here is that the dominant historical literature posits a strong cultural chord running through the Roman-Catholic population, one which distinguishes it in behavioural terms from the Irish-Protestant population. To argue that the Australia and New Zealand data sets – which provide direct evidence of an identity of behaviour among Irish Protestants and Irish Catholics on crucial issues – reflect not Irish culture, but Irish social class configurations, is to surrender the central tenet of the dominant historiography, namely, that any major differences in Ireland between Catholics and Protestants are culturally determined. Thus, this defence of the conventional wisdom is no defence, but a complete surrender.

The rules of experimental design are not facultative, and one cannot toss out the results of an experiment merely because they are inconvenient.

CHAPTER FOUR

Seeming Contrarieties

If the available historical sources accurately reflected historical realities, then North America would have a mass of records that would permit one to use it as a single laboratory for testing the behaviour of the Irish emigrants and their descendants. Until well into the twentieth century, people moved easily back and forth across the border between the United States and Canada. But it was not until 1908 that the American government initiated a continuing and accurate count of entrants to the States from Canada.[1] This is unfortunate, because in the first half of the nineteenth century, until the mid-1840s, most migrants to North America from Ireland landed in Quebec City, Montreal, or St. John. A considerable proportion of those people found their way to the United States, sometimes in a few weeks, other times over years and over decades. How large this stream was cannot be determined, and contemporary estimates vary greatly. The highest plausible contemporary estimate was made in 1872 and this suggested that the U.S. immigration totals should be increased by 50 percent to allow for arrivals by way of Canada.[2] Most authorities made lower estimates but the signal point is that one should not conceive of two separate flows of Irish migrants, one from the homeland to Canada and one to the United States, but of a single North American pool. Not only were Canadian ports the place of disembarkation for many Irish migrants to the United States, there was a smaller, but significant, counterstream of individuals who shipped from Ireland to Philadelphia, Boston, or New York and then moved northward to Canada. This complex pattern was compounded in the second and third generations when, for example, a Nova Scotian of Irish parentage moved to Boston where his uncles and cousins had settled and, conversely, it was easy for a second-generation Irish person in Buffalo to move to Toronto and there settle in the Irish community.

Unhappily, although in the nineteenth and early twentieth centuries the North-American Irish were not divided by the U.S.-Canada border, the data we have on them are. That is ironic, but the real irony of the history of these Irish immigrants is that the country with the poorer data has produced most of the historical literature. Although the American demographic data on the Irish is extremely weak, there are nevertheless hundreds of studies of the Irish in the United States. The Canadian data are much more precise and have a much longer temporal run and yet until recently there has been only a handful of significant studies of the Irish in Canada. The superiority of the Canadian data are threefold. First, unlike the United States, various Canadian provincial censuses enumerated the Irish-born (as well as other nationalities, of course) in the years before the Famine. American data on foreign-born persons begins only in 1850, after the primary effect of the Great Famine had greatly influenced the character and magnitude of the Irish diaspora. This means that there is no baseline in the United States that will permit a systematic evaluation of the impact of the Famine upon the character of the Irish population in the United States. Second, various Canadian provincial governments and, after confederation, the federal government, asked information on the religious affiliation of each individual in the population. Direct data never have been collected in the United States, except for an ill-fated sample study conducted in 1957, which raised such a furore that its results were suppressed. For a religiously split ethnic group, such as the Irish, this is fatal, for it makes virtually impossible accurate descriptions of the religious fractions of the group and, of course makes impossible systematic examination of the differences between Irish Protestants and Irish Catholics. Third, in 1871, the Canadian census authorities introduced what today would be termed an ethnicity question. They asked each individual not only in what country he or she had been born, but what his or her national origin was in the Old World. Thus, a person might indicate, for example, that he was born in Canada, of Irish national origin. Shrewdly, the census authorities permitted each respondent to name only a single national origin, the one to which he or she felt primary allegiance. An ethnicity question, in one form or another, has been asked in every Canadian census since 1871 (with the unhappy exception of 1891 when noncomparable methods were used) and one has a valuable run of data on ethnicity that now stretches over a century. Equally important, the individual manuscript census forms have been preserved, so that scholars eventually will be able to make linkages of records and trace patterns of intergenerational mobility over two and three generations. In contrast, the U.S. enumeration did not ask an ethnicity question until 1970, much too late to help our understanding of the nineteenth-century Irish. The most one can do (and this from 1880 onwards) is chronicle the pattern of the first two generations of the Irish in America. The third generation, however, is lost in an undifferentiated lump the census officials called "native born of native parentage."[3]

Thus, although it is possible to do detailed local histories of specific bodies of Irish settlers in the United States – and there are scores of such studies, many of them admirable in quality – long-term studies of an entire population of Irish-descended people is possible only in Canada. This point may be resisted by historians of the Irish in the United States, but no amount of resistance will alter these fundamental facts: that for the United States there is no pre-Famine base-line, that there are no data that distinguish between Irish Protestants and Irish Catholics, and that, for the period we are here studying, there is no set of data on Irish ethnicity, but only on the first two generations, and then only for quite a late period.

In fact, the four hypotheses specified for testing in our several laboratories cannot be tested in the United States at all, for the weakness of the U.S. data, particularly the total absence of direct religious information, precludes our running tests at the requisite level of reliability. (The paradox here is striking and an interesting commentary on the historical profession: the hypotheses about the Irish which dominate the literature on the Irish diaspora cannot be demonstrated or· critically examined in the very nation for which they were articulated.)

The necessity of using Canada as our primary North American laboratory would hold even if only evidentiary considerations were involved. There is more to it than that, however. Unlike the United States, nativism in Canada was weak.[4] Granted, there were anti-Catholic attitudes in Canada, but not close to the mob violence and systematic discrimination that the Irish Catholics encountered in the United States.[5] Therefore, as a laboratory for testing hypotheses about the differences between Irish Catholics and Irish Protestants, the Canadian site is much cleaner and much more apt to give accurate results. If it were shown that in the U.S. on the basis of systematic evidence (which, sadly, does not exist) the Irish Catholics were disadvantaged, one still would not know if their inhibited behaviour was the result of cultural inheritances from the homeland or from the discriminatory structure of the American republic.[6]

What were the salient characteristics of the Irish migration into British North America? The direction and velocity of the flux of Irish

Figure 10
Canadian Proportion of Irish Migration to North America, 1825-71

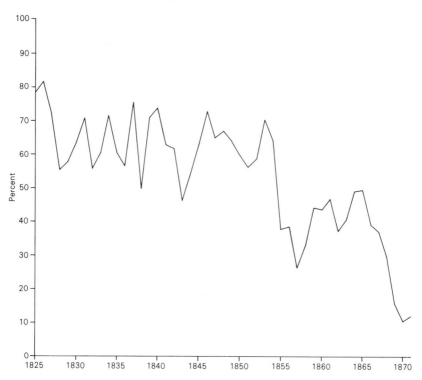

Source: See Appendixes O and P

migrants to North America are found in Figure 6, in chapter three and in Appendix I. One of the most important characteristics of the flow to Canada is that, despite the twentieth-century image of Canada as being mostly English and Scottish in its heritage, during the crucial formative years of the nineteenth century, the Irish formed the largest constituent element in English-speaking society. The Irish immigrants comprised most of the flow from the British Isles from 1825 (when statistics first became available) until the mid-1850s: they exceed the number of Scottish and English immigrants combined. After the mid-1850s, the number of Irish immigrants dropped, but it was not until the late 1860s that the immigrants from England and Wales came to outnumber the Irish immigrants in most years. During the 1870s and '80s, Scottish immigration finally came to equal that of the Irish, but it was not until the 1890s that Scottish newcomers consistently outnumbered the Irish. As the Irish migrants had children of their own, and sometimes grandchildren, the multigenerational Irish ethnic cohort expanded quickly. When, in 1871, the first Dominion census ascertained the national background of the entire Canadian population, the Irish were found to be the largest English-language ethnic group:[7]

Ethnic Group	Percentage of total population
French	31.1%
Irish	24.3
English	20.3
Scottish	15.8
All others combined	8.5
Total	100.0%

Religiously, Catholics comprised the largest single denomination among the nineteenth-century Irish in Canada. A large-sample study of the Irish ethnic population showed that 38 percent was Roman Catholic. The next largest group of Irish-Canadians were Anglicans, who represented somewhat under 23 percent of the total ethnic population.[8] Since the Protestant Irish outnumbered the Catholics by nearly 2:1, Catholicism and hibernicity cannot by any stretch of the imagination be equated. Nevertheless, the Irish Catholics were a sufficiently large group to permit one to study them as a distinct subgroup. One can gather several hundred thousand data points on their behaviour in the nineteenth century and compare their pattern to that which emerges from similar data on Canadian Protestants of Irish extraction.

The Irish-born and their children spread throughout the four original provinces of the Dominion of Canada (Ontario, Quebec, Nova Scotia and New Brunswick) and, later, into the Canadian west. (Also, they long had been a significant presence in Newfoundland, but since Newfoundland stayed outside of the confederation until the mid-twentieth century, the Newfoundland Irish are not part of the Canadian data base in the nineteenth century.) Despite this dispersal, the focus of the Irish experience in Canada in the last century was Ontario. For the Irish, Ontario was the agora of their life, the place where most of them engaged the world of North American culture and commerce. That Ontario was indeed the pivot is shown by two sets of facts. The first of these is the percentage distribution of persons of Irish ethnicity who lived in Ontario:[9]

Year	Percentage of Canadian-Irish living in Ontario
1871	66.1%
1881	65.5
1891	N/A
1901	63.2
1911	57.2
1921	53.3

The other fact is that in Ontario, persons of Irish ethnicity were invariably a larger proportion of the population than they were in other provinces. In 1871 persons of Irish descent comprised 34.5 percent of the Ontario population, and though, with the shrinkage of Irish immigration, this figure had declined to 20.1 percent in 1921, it still was larger than for any other provincial jurisdiction.[10] This emphasis upon the primacy of Ontario is not meant to obviate the importance of the other provincial Irish populations, but it is necessary to emphasize Ontario's historical predominance in this matter because the present day emphasis upon Canadian regionalism can too easily distort historical realities.

With that as background, one can now examine the four major hypotheses concerning the differences between the behaviour of Irish Catholics and Protestants. On the question of settlement patterns, the Canadian data are particularly telling. Table 4 indicates the percentage of persons of Irish extraction who resided in rural areas. The data indicate that, as a group, persons of Irish descent settled in rural areas in proportions virtually identical with those of the general Canadian population. To carry the observation back before Confederation, one must go to the provincial censuses and the Ontario enumerations of 1851 and 1861 are especially important. In 1851, 14.0 percent of the Irish-born people living in Ontario now lived in cities and in 1861 the corresponding figure was 13.6 percent. These two provincial censuses, taken after the Great Famine had deposited its thousands on North American shores, give lie to the notion that the Irish immigrant, and particularly the Famine migrants, were inevitably city people. Even if one expands the definition of urban to include all incorporated towns and villages (the average size of which was 2,111 in 1851 and 1,957 in 1861), one finds that the Irish immigrants were overwhelmingly settled in the countryside.[11]

It is possible, of course, that there was a sharp disjuncture between

Table 4

Persons of Irish Ethnicity Living in Rural Areas: Canada, 1871–1931

As percentage of total Irish population in area

Year	Ontario	Quebec	Nova Scotia	New Brunswick	Canada
1871	77.8	63.9	81.2	73.1	75.3
1881	70.4	58.6	73.2	72.6	69.7
1901	58.4	48.7	60.3	66.3	60.0
1911	51.2	43.6	49.4	63.1	52.8
1921	45.7	38.8	46.9	62.1	49.2
1931	42.8	29.9	45.0	59.6	45.3

Year	Percentage of total Canadian population living in rural areas
1871	79.6
1881	74.3
1901	62.5
1911	54.6
1921	50.5
1931	46.3

Source: D.H. Akenson, *Being Had: Historians, Evidence, and the Irish in North America* (Toronto: P.D. Meany, 1985), 85

the Catholics and the Protestants which the overall figures obscured. Perhaps the Catholics settled in towns or cities and the Protestants, the larger group, in the countryside. The 1871 census provides an opportunity for tabulating the residences of the approximately 560,000 persons of Irish ethnicity living in Ontario (and this was roughly two-thirds of the entire Canadian Irish population). The Catholics were distributed as follows:[12]

Residence	Percentage
Cities (average size: 26,517)	14.7%
Towns and villages (average size: 2,148)	19.0
Countryside and hamlets	66.3
	100.0%

Here, as in the case of the Irish in Australia, one has compelling mass-data disproof of the hypothesis that the cultural inheritance of the Irish Catholics predisposed them to be a city people in the New Worlds to which they journeyed.

Compelling as this is, one must enter a caveat. Although in absolute numbers the Irish Catholics were predisposed to become rural in settlement, they were relatively less so inclined than were the Irish Protestants, or so it appears. Persons of Irish Protestant ethnicity in 1871 were distributed as follows:[13]

Residence	Percentage
Cities	6.9%
Towns and villages	9.9
Countryside and hamlets	82.2
	100.0%

This opens the way to three possible explanations: (1) that, indeed as compared to Irish Protestants, the Irish Catholics were in some ways culturally handicapped when it came to dealing with rural environments; (2) that there were structural impediments in the Canadian social and economic structure that made it harder for Irish Catholics to enter farming and rural occupations than for Irish Protestants; or (3) that some other factor, which has yet to come to light, will be found to explain this situation.

Light is thrown upon this matter and also upon the other hypotheses concerning comparative occupational structure and economic mobility in the remarkable work of A. Gordon Darroch and Michael D. Ornstein, both of York University, Ontario. Using the original manuscript census material for nineteenth-century Canada, they have constructed a data base that, on matters of ethnicity, religion, occupation, and social class, is unmatched, either in quality of their input data or in the sophistication of their analysis, by anything else yet attempted in the English-speaking world. There is nothing in the work of American scholars of nineteenth-century social and ethnic history to rival their work, the only drawback of which is that Darroch and Ornstein have presented their material with such modesty as to be misleading. One of their studies consists of nothing less than a virtual retabulation from original manuscript sources of the 1871 Dominion of Canada census. This is done so as to allow the posing and answering of many questions that did not occur to the nineteenth-century census officials. In particular, the nineteenth-century censuses are notoriously frustrating in that they contain data on several important variables but they do not provide cross-tabulations of these items. For instance, no cross-tabulation was made of the relationship of occupation and ethnicity until the 1931 census, even though information on both items was collected from 1871 onward. To overcome these difficulties, Darroch and Ornstein drew off from the 1871 Dominion of Canada census a random group of 10,000 cases of male heads of household, on each of whom there was available, direct or indirectly derivable, data on several dozen characteristics. Anyone who has done much quantitative work will realize that this is a very large number of random cases and that it yields hundreds of thousands of data points.[14]

When examining the economic behaviour of Irish Catholics, Darroch and Ornstein found intriguing "the seeming lack of a very distinctive occupational distribution of the Irish-Catholic population.... It is common in commenting on the nineteenth century to suggest that the Irish Catholics were predominantly urban, proletarianized, and a largely impoverished population. Yet, in a national perspective, the proportion of farmers among Irish Catholics is only ten percent lower than the national average."[15] With restrained irony, Darroch and Ornstein note: "The difference between more conventional interpretations of the class position of Irish Catholics and this national view would appear to result from exclusion from prior studies of the rural farm and nonfarm population."[16]

Among persons of Irish-Catholic ethnicity in Canada, farming was by far the most frequent occupation: 44.3 percent of the adult males. It was, however, lower than the proportion of Irish Protestants who were farmers: Protestant proportions ranged between 51.8 percent and 65.3 percent, depending on the specific Protestant denomination, and the average was 58.3 percent.

If one lumps together labourers (including farm workers), servants, and semiskilled labourers, one finds that 29.7 percent of persons of Irish-Catholic background were so engaged, compared to 19.2 percent of persons of the entire population and 15.5 percent of persons of Irish-Protestant ancestry. Thus, once again, one has a two-fold set of observations, namely that in absolute terms "it is misleading to refer to a national pattern of Irish urban proletarianization."[17] and, yet, in relative terms, Irish Catholics were more likely to be labourers than were Irish Protestants.

If farmers and labourers can be thought of as two legs of the socioeconomic tripod in nineteenth-century Canada, the third leg consisted of the bourgeoisie and artisan groups. In these groups the "data show that the proportions of the Irish Catholics and of the total labour force are virtually identical for bourgeois occupations, merchants, manufacturers, dealers, shopkeepers, and for the proportion in professional occupations as well as in artisanal work."[18] Most significantly, in the privileged "bourgeois" sector, the proportional representation of Irish Catholics and Irish Protestants was virtually identical: 26.0 percent of the Irish Catholics were in bourgeois occupations and 26.2 percent of the Irish Protestants.

Given the proportional equality of Irish Catholics and Irish Protestants in bourgeois occupations, it seems that the real difference between the two groups was that the Protestants tilted somewhat towards farming (which, recall, was the largest Catholic occupation too) and the Catholics slightly towards labouring. But these may not be real differences of economic status. The available data do not sort out farmers by size of their property or by productivity. That a farmer trying to eke out a living on one of the thin pockets of soil on the precambrian shield actually was any better off than was an agricultural labourer in one of the more fertile regions of southern Ontario is far from clear.

Some of the questions raised by Darroch and Ornstein's pioneering work on the 1871 Dominion of Canada census was answered by their second major study. They linked a large body of data from central Ontario from the censuses of 1861 and 1871. Unlike the earlier nationwide study which dealt with ethnicity as a multigenerational phenomenon, this research focused on the immigrant generation. It assayed the extremely difficult task of tracing, through census records, the changing life patterns of a large body of specific individuals. As in virtually all Victorian census-based studies, the research necessarily concentrated on males, because the Victorian censuses lumped most women together in a single undifferentiated occupational group. Darroch and Ornstein transcribed the individual records of roughly 100,000 persons and found that 65,000 of these records could be linked between the years 1861 and 1871. From this set, 10,000 males, whose occupations were known, were randomly drawn off. The result was the first study of social mobility in nineteenth-century North America that has an adequate data base and a reliable mode of analysis.[19]

To interpret this monumental study, one must remind oneself once again of the need for two levels of interpretation: noting fundamental patterns of behaviour of any group as shown in absolute numbers and the secondary relative comparison of that group to any other. The most salient conclusion of the study was that:

Following the pathfinding work of Pentland, many nineteenth century Canadian historians have posited a split labour market in the crucial period between 1850 and 1870. According to this view, the period saw the creation of a landless proletariat, essential to the transformation of the country from an agricultural and commercial to an industrial and capitalist economy. This nascent group was identified along ethnic lines, English and Scottish workers gaining the skilled, and the Irish workers the unskilled jobs.... An examination of the 1861 and 1871 censuses in south-central Ontario, however, suggests that immigrant Catholic and Protestant Irish were not concentrated in low-paid industrial work, but in agriculture.[20]

A related, crucial point was that the overall occupation shift was *not*, as is usually thought, from farming into industrial occupations, but from labouring *into* farming. The shift out of agriculture came later in the century and to project it back into the first three-quarters of the nineteenth century leads to anachronism and confusion.

Both Irish-Catholic immigrants and Irish-Protestant immigrants preferred farming to any other occupation (as was shown to be the case with the entire multigenerational Irish ethnic group in 1871). As in the instance of the entire ethnic group, Irish-Catholic immigrants were less apt to be farmers than were Irish-Protestant immigrants: 47.2 percent of the Irish-Protestant immigrants in 1861 and 57.8 percent in 1871, compared to figures for the Irish-Catholic immigrants, respectively, of 27.6 percent and 35.8 percent. (Notice here that both groups were moving increasingly into farming over this ten-year period, the Catholics at a somewhat faster rate, calculated on the basis of the percentage increase from the original base for each group.) If one takes entry into farming as being upward occupational mobility (and this is reasonable; labourers who became farm owners usually had taken a step up in the world), then one has an interesting pattern:

that the Irish-Protestant immigrants in both census years were better off, but that the Irish-Catholic immigrants had a slightly greater upward occupational mobility. In every one of the bourgeois and skilled artisanal occupations, the Irish-Catholic proportions increased faster than did the Irish-Protestant.[21]

The question now becomes: were the differential characteristics that one finds associated with Irish Catholicism in the Darroch and Ornstein data merely associative or were they causally connected to something in the Irish-Catholic culture? That one is dealing with something other than straightforward cultural determinism is suggested by the fact that, "indeed, Irish [immigrant] Catholics were as likely to be farmers in 1871 as were [immigrant] men of English origin"[22] and the English were a group that was neither Catholic nor economically disadvantaged. Possibly what these groups, the English- and Irish-Catholic immigrants, had in common was that, considered as a group, they had arrived relatively late on the scene in central Canada as compared to the Americans (loyalist and post-loyalists) and the Irish Protestants. Recall here that the Irish Catholics were relatively overrepresented in the cities of Ontario of 1871. The same held true in 1881 for the English-born. (The English, as a group, had come later than the Irish Catholics, so the comparison between 1871 on one hand and 1881 on the other is justified.) In 1881 English immigrants comprised 7.2 percent of the total population of Ontario, but twice as large a proportion – 14.1 percent – of the total population of the five major cities.[23] Which is to say that the relative underrepresentation of both the English and the Irish Catholics in rural areas and in farming (as compared to Irish Protestants) well might be a function not of cultural factors but simply of length of residence in the New World. As Darroch and Ornstein's study shows, the difference in occupational profiles between various ethnic groups diminishes over time. Therefore, what appears at first to be a culturally determined ethnic stratigraphy is nothing of the sort, but merely a spectrum of peoples who are distinguished in the New World chiefly by the timing of their arrival.

One of the bigger problems in dealing with the relative difference between Irish Catholics and Irish Protestants is that the norm-deviation distinction is potentially misleading. Almost universally, the mindset in North American studies unquestionably accepts the assumption that it was the Irish Catholics, not the Irish Protestants, who were deviants from the norm. Given that both groups show a pattern of occupational mobility from labouring into farming (Darroch and Ornstein's data are totally convincing on this matter) and that from 1861 to 1871 the Irish Catholics moved into farming at a slightly higher rate than did Irish Protestants, one has the task of explaining why, in the base year of 1861, the Catholics started out with a smaller proportion of farm owners than did Protestants. Another way of phrasing this is to suggest that prior to 1861 the Irish-Protestant immigrants seemed quicker at getting into farming than were the Irish-Catholic immigrants. Maybe the Irish-Protestant immigrants arrived richer and maybe they had been in Ontario longer, but there is another suggestion that fits more closely with the available nonquantitative evidence. Specifically, in Ontario, the Irish Protestants possessed a strong institutional network in the form of the Loyal Orange Order. This society was strong in both urban and rural environments and catered to all Protestants, including English and Scottish persons. Its greatest benefit, however, was to the Irish-Protestant immigrant, for it gave him access to information about land markets throughout the province, provided access to minor government officials who could help him in the purchase or patenting of farm land and, once he was settled in a rural area, provided introductions to sources of credit and entry into local social life.[24] There was no Irish-Catholic equivalent of this network, so it is possible that the real case was not that the Irish Catholics were abnormally slow in moving into the countryside, but that the Irish Protestants, because of their unique institutional affiliations, were abnormally quick.

In discussing large groups of people, one is trying to develop meaningful generalizations and of necessity one loses the sense of the myriad and fascinating smaller patterns that lie beneath the surface of generalization. Community studies can help one's appreciation of these matters. For instance, one needs to be reminded of the historical reality of the small minority of Irish Catholics in Canada who were trapped in urban ghettos,[25] just as one needs to be reminded of,those equally atypical rural communities where the Irish Protestants formed the lower class and the Irish Catholics formed the economic elite.[26] In the future, one wishes to be able to observe the range of economic status that is hidden behind the single census category of "farmer."[27] Always, such individual studies must be set against the large context of provincial and national patterns. To do otherwise is to abandon historical inquiry and to engage in mere antiquarianism.

Undeniably, the Canadian case is complex, but that is the way it should be: one of the iron laws of historiography is that the richer the data are, the more complex the story to tell. The Canadian data can be read in various ways, but my judgment is that the conclusions dictated are as follows. First, there is no doubt that the Irish Catholics (like the Irish Protestants) settled overwhelmingly in rural areas and that their most frequent occupation was farming. This directly disproves hypothesis no. 1. Second, the verdict on hypothesis no. 2 is mixed. Although Irish Catholics settled less often in rural areas than did Irish Protestants and were engaged in agriculture somewhat less often, this seems to have had little to do with the cultural disposition of either group, but to be either a function of length of residence, or, equally likely, and more important, of the institutional advantages that the Irish Protestants enjoyed. Third, it is clear that the Irish-Catholic immigrants in 1861 and 1871 had a lower occupational profile than did the Irish Protestants, and this would tend to confirm hypothesis no. 3, except for a fourth fact: that the Irish-Catholic immigrants' rate of occupational advance was greater than that of the Irish Protestants (thus disproving hypothesis no. 4). Obviously one cannot use the lower occupational profile of the Catholic immigrants to confirm the suggestion of hypothesis no. 3 that Irish-Catholic immigrants had psychological, political, and economic disadvantages in dealing with the modern world, unless one is willing to infer that their greater rate of occupational mobility shows that they had psychological, political, and economic advantages in dealing with the modern world. Manifestly, these are contradictory notions. The data can be covered by simply suggesting: that (a) Irish Catholics started off in the base year below Irish Protestants because they arrived a bit later than the Irish Protestants and did not have the Orange Order to help them into farming, and (b) that the Irish Catholics rose faster because they were starting from a lower base. That takes care of the phenomenon efficiently and does not involve any reference to putative cultural determinants. Given the general convergence over time of the Irish-Protestant and the Irish-Catholic profiles, one cannot argue that there was any significant handicap stemming from Irish-Catholic culture.

Although the Canadian data base on matters of ethnicity, religion, and occupation in the nineteenth century is the most precise in the English-speaking world, and although its implications are obvious for nineteenth-century United States' history, it is inevitable that there will be strenuous attempts to wall it off from the general discussion of Irish-Catholic cultural propensities and especially to keep its implications from impinging on the history of the Irish in the United States. One form of wall building is to suggest that the Canadian case be ignored because, as David Fitzpatrick has correctly shown, towards the end of the nineteenth century those Irish emigrants who chose Canada (and, also, those choosing Australia) were "rather more likely then emigrants to the United States to diverge from stereotypes by claiming higher occupational status or travelling in family groups."[28] That is true enough, but the situation holds true only quite late in the

Irish diaspora and certainly not before the 1860s. Indeed, "the reverse probably applied during the Famine period when the criteria for assistance to Australia and the cheapness of tickets to Canada tended to draw those who were unskilled and unattached to colonial ports."[29] As Oliver MacDonagh noted of the Famine emigrants, the Canadian emigrants were more apt to be impaired by sickness: "The mortality was much lower among direct emigrants to the United States, largely because the restrictive legislation rushed through the New York and Massachusetts legislatures in the spring [of 1847] forced American fares upward and induced masters to change their destinations to St. John and Quebec."[30] In support of the comparability of the Irish emigrant to Canada and to the United States before the end of the nineteenth century, one can point to the fact that labourers comprised 81.4 percent of the emigrants to the United States in 1857 and 84.1 percent to Canada in the same year, which, given the limits of the data collection in those years, is virtual identity.[31] Ten years later, this had changed somewhat: in 1866 labourers were 85.4 percent of the U.S.-bound migration and 66.2 percent of the Canadian-bound,[32] but the great bulk of the population that was delineated on the Canadian census of 1851, '61, and '71, and which was analyzed earlier in this chapter, had arrived in the era before there was any significant socioeconomic distinction between Irish migrants to Canada and to the United States.

A second objection, less apt to be clearly articulated than the first one but for that very reason more dangerous, is that the Canadian case is not useful because the Irish who migrated to Canada were, in some vague way, too Protestant. This is not so much a rational argument as an ingrained habit of mind among historians of the Irish in America who usually wall off the Irish Protestants into some non-Irish category: calling the Irish Presbyterians "Scotch-Irish" is the usual method, while the Anglo-Irish are simply ignored altogether. When clearly articulated, the reason why this method of proceeding is unacceptable is obvious: merely renaming or ignoring the Irish Protestants does not make them disappear. That they were a significant part of the Irish diaspora has been clearly established. To act as if the only Irish immigrants and the only descendants of Irish immigrants who existed in the United States were Irish Catholics is to assume the existence of a phenomenon, a completely efficient filter that kept Irish Protestants out of the United States. This is so unlikely as to be risible.

A third, and much more reasonable objection is that, in a twofold way, the Irish Catholics and the Irish Protestants in Canada (as in Australia and New Zealand) were more privileged than were those in the United States. In Canada, the Irish, both Protestant and Catholic, were a "charter group." English Canada was a much younger society than was the United States and the Irish immigrants, if not quite founding people, were close. Thus, this objection is based on fact and so too is another one, namely that the Irish formed a much larger proportion of the population of Canada in the nineteenth century than they did of the United States and thus were harder to push around. If one considers the situation in 1870 for persons born outside of the administrative unit of their residence (state or province), "the percentage of Irish were eleven in Great Britain, thirteen for the United States, twenty-four for Australia and thirty-three for Canada. If internal migration were excluded, these proportions would of course be higher."[33] There is a prima facie (and, I think, provable) case that the Irish in Canada (and in Australia and New Zealand) faced less discrimination and were by virtue of their numbers harder to take advantage of than were those who migrated to the United States. This is another way of saying that the American republic visited ethnic and religious discrimination upon its Irish newcomers rather more severely than did the various British colonies – but what is the import of noting that probability? Certainly it should not thereby be concluded that the United States is a better laboratory than is Canada to test hypotheses about the cultural background of the Irish emigrants. Quite the opposite. To the extent that there is a lack of comparability, it argues for discounting the American, not the Canadian, case.

Earlier it was pointed out that there are no systematic American demographic data on religion that could be related to other information, such as place of residence and occupation, and, further, that the U.S. data on ethnicity in the nineteenth century are severely limited. Were one dealing with any other nation, one would simply note that, unhappily, the country had to be ignored because of the absence of reliable systematic information. One must be less abrupt than this, however, because such a large proportion of the Irish diaspora settled in the United States and also because there is a formidably large literature on what is usually called "Irish-American" history. Although the absence of American data on the religious affiliation of the Irish makes it impossible to advance our analysis of the nature and degree of religiously determined cultural propensities of the Irish, one owes the reader a brief discussion of why much (indeed, most) of the historical literature on the Irish in nineteenth-century America is unintentionally, but thoroughly, misleading.

All but a very few of the studies of the Irish in the United States in the nineteenth and early twentieth centuries fall into two categories:

specialized local studies, almost all of which deal with urban Irish-Catholic settlement, and attempts at a synthesis for the general reader.[34] Typically, the local studies take as their backdrop the same outlook (albeit with a more sophisticated vocabulary) as do the works of syntheses. This viewpoint was cleanly summarized by the journalist William V. Shannon who posed as the central phenomenon: "The history of the Irish in America is founded on a paradox. The Irish were a rural people in Ireland and became a city people in the United States."[35]

Without using Shannon's lapidary formulation, most scholars have accepted the idea that the proletarianization in the city of the Irish immigrant and his descendants was the primary character of nineteenth-century Irish-American history.[36] A very large literature has emerged and much of it is devoted to an explication of this phenomenon – that the Irish became a city people.

This is a demonstrably false premise, certainly for the nineteenth century, the era of the greatest Irish migration to the United States. If one considers all the Irish immigrants from 1820 through 1975 and even if one accepts without correction the notoriously low underestimates for the pre-1841 era, it still holds true that slightly over half of the Irish migration to the United States was completed by 1870.[37] In that year, the U.S. census figures show that only 44.5 percent of the Irish immigrants lived in cities, and even that greatly overstates the Irish propensity to live in cities[38] because the data come only from the migrant generation and not from the entire ethnic group. For every Irish immigrant living in the U.S. in 1870 there was, roughly, one person of Irish parentage who had been born in the United States:[39] that is, whose parents had come to America in the previous generation, some before the Famine. That earlier generation had arrived in the U.S. when the country was markedly more rural than it was in 1870,[40] so the likelihood of their settling in cities was less than that of the 1870 group. Even those who were stranded in cities, cut off from the promise of American westward expansion, frequently saved enough resources so that their children could fully engage the opportunities that the mobility of American life and its expanding frontier provided. These factors hold even more strongly for the third generation of Irish people living in the United States in 1870 (almost all of whom would have traced their roots back to the pre-Famine era) and who, by the third generation, had escaped any direct handicaps of their poverty in Ireland.[41]

Historians of these Irish Americans have not willfully misled their readers, but, rather, themselves have been unwittingly misled by their viewing the Irish in America through a lens that is marred with sev-

eral waves of parallax-causing imperfections. Although the great bulk
of the nineteenth-century Irish migration to America was completed
by 1870 (and, perforce, the majority of the multigeneration Irish group
in America looked to roots in the New World that were found in the
first two-thirds of the century), reasonably accurate information on
the Irish migrants to the United States does not become available until
after 1870, and even then it is sketchy. For example, trustworthy material on where the immigrants came from in Ireland was not collected
until 1876.[42] And useful information on the second generation in
America began to be collected in 1880. The irony is that one begins to
find details about the Irish in America which, if incomplete, are at least
systematic, just at the point when most of their migration is done and
just when they are becoming a very small part of the foreign migration
to America.[43]

That would not be fatal – under proper circumstances, one can take
the points of a reclinate curve and project them backwards – but this
quantum increase in the quality and quantity of the information on
the Irish immigrants occurred at almost the same time that a major
shift was occurring in the character of the Irish migration to the
United States. From the mid-1870s onwards, the Irish immigrants in
general became quite different from those who came earlier and by
projecting the characteristics of this late-arriving minority upon the
historical experience of the earlier-arriving majority of Irish immigrants, American historians have extrapolated from a false base. David
Noel Doyle has argued that the shift in the character of the Irish
migration to the United States in the 1870s produced a "gulf" between
what he calls "the old and new Irish-Americans."[44] By the 1870s, Famine and post-Famine immigrants from Ireland and their children had
by and large made good, finding niches of modest success in American society, but the influx of later Irish immigrants, particularly in the
depressions of 1873–7 and 1893–7, was of another level entirely: people
pauperized and seemingly with little upward mobility over time.
Thus, there emerged an extremely wide occupation and status distribution among the Irish, moreso than for any other ethnic group. This
ranged from a "quasi-establishment" of very well-off Irish merchants,
politicians, and governmental officials all the way down to a large
group of out and out paupers. As Doyle demonstrates, this disjuncture cannot be explained solely in terms of intergenerational mobility.
It makes sense only if one postulates that "major and unstudied
changes in the background of continuing Irish migration are at least
equally important and perhaps moreso."[45]

The shift that Doyle hypothesizes should not be overstated – one of
the noteworthy features of Irish migration was that every country

sent migrants to every major destination overseas – but if it is taken as meaning that there was a shift in the balance of where the migrants to the United States came from in Ireland and the balance of their occupational skills and backgrounds in the homeland, then it makes sense of some otherwise puzzling pieces of data. Specifically, Doyle's suggestion helps one to understand where the results of David Fitzpatrick's analysis of aggregate emigrant data fits. His research showed that in the period 1876–95, the immigrant to the U.S. "tended to come from counties which might be termed 'backward.' These counties had many Irish-speakers, few Protestants, large agricultural populations, and low valuation per capita."[46] And, from the year 1903 (when statistical data become very good) onwards, the data reveal a marked contrast between the regional origin of emigrants to Canada and to the United States. "There is some evidence that emigrants from Ireland to Canada were less likely that those to the U.S.A. to be labourers or servants, more likely to belong to the lower middle classes or to be farmers."[47] Yet, as discussed earlier, it also has been shown that at least through the 1850s (the end of the Great Famine migration) the Irish emigrants to Canada contained as high a proportion of labourers as did the emigrants to America. Further, in the Famine era, the stricter level of U.S. regulations meant that, if anything, the U.S. received a lower proportion of heavily disadvantaged Irish as immigrants.

Doyle's hypothesis permits harmonization of these seemingly conflicting pieces of data in a simple, elegant fashion: that from the Famine through, roughly, the 1860s, there was no significant differentiation along occupational or geographic lines within the North American immigrant pool of those who settled in Canada and the United States. In contrast, from the mid-1870s, the "new" Irish migration to North American became increasingly (but not entirely) speciated by geographic region and social background, with persons from the more backward parts of Ireland, people with fewer commercial and technical skills, migrating to the United States, and more able and skilled persons and those from the more developed parts of the country, going to Canada.[48] Under Doyle's hypothesis, two sorts of shifts in the character of the Irish migration to America are implied (and again, these are relative shifts, not black-and-white changes). The first of these is that the locus of the U.S.-bound migration in the homeland shifted from the south of Ireland (Munster, and particularly County Cork had been the great source of migration to the U.S.) to the west, the province of Connacht.[49] Simultaneously, a greater proportion of economically bereft landless labourers entered the flow, people who had not held farm tenancies of their own, and who had not operated

commercial enterprises, but who instead had been in the most insecure and least technically demanding position in the Irish economy.
These people were the extrusion of the "class collapse" of the Irish
countryside, the product of the long decline of Irish agricultural
labourers that had begun in the 1840s and reached its final spasms in
the days of the land war of the 1870s.[50] So, historians in studying a
post-1870s migration strongly tinctured by the introduction of a growing proportion of these western and landless migrants, without realiz-
ing that these people were markedly different from the pre-1870s
migrants, have viewed the earlier migrants through a distorted lens.

The parallax has been doubled, indeed tripled, by two other imperfections. One of these is that historians of the Irish in America have
assimilated into their picture of the cultural characteristics of the Irish
immigrants to the U.S. in the last quarter of the nineteenth century,
patterns of behaviour that had nothing to do with immigrants being
Irish. It is correctly pointed out that the Irish immigrants of the last
quarter of the nineteenth century did not settle very often in rural
areas and this fact frequently leads to a long chain of explanation of
how this behaviour was determined by uniquely Irish cultural characteristics. That is silly. From the 1870s onward, the entire U.S. society,
including descendants of long-settled American families, was moving
out of rural areas. As David Ward remarks, "it would appear that
before about 1870 opportunities in the West for urban as well as agricultural employment competed with local urban centres within the
areas of emigration. Thereafter, however, the proportion of long-dis-
tance movements within the total internal migration declined and
even newly settled areas began to experience the effect of the cityward
movement."[51] That is, with the western frontier filling up, long-settled
Americans as well as new immigrants, began to move to cities. "The
large proportion of 'new immigrants' from abroad with urban destinations was probably no greater than among native-born Americans
who migrated [within the U.S.] after about 1875. In some areas, a large
segment of the latter were the children of immigrants who had settled
on the land earlier in the century."[52] Although it is true that the Irish
among the 'new' immigrants were somewhat more apt to settle in
cities than was the norm, this difference was one of degree only. For
example, the Dillingham Commission found that in 1890, 44.1 percent
of the total immigrants to the United States were living in cities with
over 25,000 population. The percentage of Irish immigrants was 56.0
percent, higher than the average, but lower than the percentage of
Italians, Russians, or Poles.[53] Thus, one need not posit any unique
cultural characteristics compelling the "new" Irish immigrant of the

late nineteenth century to live in cities, merely that, like most groups in American society, the Irish immigrants recognized that opportunities were better in the city than in the countryside.

The other problem with the lens by which the Irish in America usually have been viewed is that, while collecting data on the "new" Irish immigrants of the late nineteenth century, historians have forgotten that there is a big blind spot in their viewing apparatus. It consists of nothing less than a demographically invisible majority of persons of Irish ethnicity. Between 1820 and 1850 there had been at minimum 1.04 million Irish migrants to the United States (the sources are very murky about the precise number, and it probably is an underestimate).[54] By 1880, when usable data on both first- and second-generation individuals become available, many of these people not only had children, but grandchildren who had been born in America. Although the U.S. census authorities never collected information in the nineteenth century on more than the first two generations, as time went on, a larger and larger proportion of the resident Irish ethnic group was third and fourth generation: yet no information was collected upon them. They were simply labelled as being native Americans of "native white stock." Most of the studies of "the Irish" that have been conducted with a nationwide data base have employed data from the period 1890–1920 and have studied only two generations.[55] Although one can argue about what the precise "multiplier" might be between the earlier arrivals from Ireland and the first- and second-generation Irish persons whose lives in the 1890–1920 era have been heavily studied, it is manifest that during this period there were more persons of third and later generations of Irish stock than there were immigrants and their children. Yet generalizations about the Irish as an ethnic group – and especially about their long-term economic mobility – have excluded this majority of people of Irish descent from the data base.[56]

Therefore, for the purposes of the present study, one must bypass the United States and the American data. This conclusion can only be reached with great regret, for the U.S. was potentially the richest and most spacious laboratory in which one could have tested hypotheses about the cultural differences between Irish Protestants and Irish Catholics. Unhappily, not only is there no direct data on the religious persuasion of the Irish settlers and their descendants in America, but the historical literature, while containing many admirable local studies, is fundamentally misled in its assumptions. One cannot accept on faith (and, necessarily in the American case, without data) the prevailing postulate that the Irish Catholics were predisposed by their cultural backwardness, technological inflexibility, and strong communal affiliations to be ghettoized in America.

Elsewhere, I have speculated upon the reasons why the historians of the Irish in North America have been able to maintain a set of beliefs that is so far out of synchronization with reality.[57] Here, the remaining question is: will they change significantly their beliefs in the face of a new examination of the evidence? Only slowly, one suspects, and with great reluctance. Whatever the weakness of its evidentiary base, the standard viewpoint on the Irish in America is an economic and sociological reality of its own. Indeed, it is a small industry. There is too much investment in the existing set of beliefs to permit quick change. As Thomas Kuhn's study of paradigmatic shifts in scientific work has shown, scholars are rarely convinced by new data or new arguments to make major changes in their own viewpoints. Instead, new ideas and more accurate evidence triumph only because, eventually, a new generation grows up to supplant the old.[58]

That noted, one should hark back to one tiny little fact about the Irish in America, namely, that in 1870 even the Irish immigrants (much less the second and third generations) were not city people. That is a small fact, but it can be ignored only by employing the same excuse that the chambermaid made to her priest about her recently-born child. "But, Father, it's such a *wee* thing."

CHAPTER FIVE

Keeping Separate: Boundary Maintenance Systems

Leopold Bloom had two definitions of a nation, each applicable here. "A nation?" says Bloom. "A nation is the same people living in the same place." Slightly later, he added, "or also living in different places."[1]

The several million data points that have been analyzed in the preceding chapters point in a clear, albeit complex, fashion to this conclusion: that in a fundamental sense, the nineteenth-century Irish indeed were a nation. In the Irish homeland, despite a mass of folk beliefs about the differences between Protestants and Catholics, there was found to be no empirically verifiable evidence that cultural factors caused a differentiation between the two religions on major social and economic axes. Neither in family structure, nor in economic behaviour, nor the treatment of women was there any compelling evidence for major differences, and, in some instances, there was positive evidence of fundamental similarities. What differences there were in these matters were much more plausibly ascribed to class than to culture.

By adopting Bloom's dictum that a nation can live in different places, the analysis of behaviour of the Irish-derived populations in New Zealand, Australia, and Canada showed not only that there were no major behaviour differences between Catholics and Protestants that stemmed from cultural factors, but that there was strong positive evidence for actual and demonstrable similarity and, indeed, near identity. When systematically tested in various laboratories, the behaviour of Irish Protestants and Irish Catholics was fundamentally the same.

Though simply stated, that fact is no small matter. It changes profoundly the way one views nineteenth- and early twentieth-century Irish social history and raises an entirely new set of questions. One of the most important of these is: how was it possible to keep apart two such similar groups of people? Why did they not blur together? How could they be so sharply delineated from each other?

Instead of responding to these questions by plunging into a filigree of Catholic-Protestant theological differences, or dealing with the psychology of Irish nationalism, or the motives behind the internal colonialism of Irish life, let us proceed slowly and first examine the *mechanisms* that permitted Ireland to operate as a largely segregated society. Later, the social psychology of that segregation will be approached.

The most important mechanism by which Irish Catholics and Irish Protestants kept themselves separate from each other have involved social and religious institutions. However, in viewing the historical situation, it is important not to portray the institutions as being independent agents that somehow forced the Irish people to act in ways in which they otherwise were not inclined. This caution is necessary because the most important Irish institutions assumed a nomothetic character – this is particularly true of the churches and of educational institutions – and when religious and educational authorities made pronouncements they frequently did so with a force and certitude that made their institutions seem to be independent law makers. Actually, church and educational authorities only articulated what the mass of the people already believed. Religious and educational institutions crystalized in social practice what the Irish people believed to be the proper relationship between persons of differing Christian denominations. The institutional structures, therefore, were the mechanisms whereby the Irish-Catholic and Irish-Protestant people, by their own volition, kept themselves apart from one another.

The two social practices which were most important were, first, the enforcement of denominational endogamy and, second, the segregation to a high degree of the youth of each "tribe" from those of the other.

The study of patterns of intermarriage between distinct tribal groups has been a staple of anthropological work since the earliest days of that discipline. One of the standards of the field is Sir James Frazer's study, *Totemism and Exogamy*, the first volume of which was published in 1887. The work eventually ran to four volumes (published as a unit in 1910) and a coda that appeared in 1937.[2] Among the several concerns of Frazer's rambling classic was how it came to be that certain groups which he regarded as primitive (he studied mostly Australian aboriginals) enforced a system of restraints on marriage that was, in fact, genetically intelligent. He described myriad patterns of exogamy (that is, the social practice of groups that required marriage outside the immediate tribal group) and he attempted to show how systems of symbol, particularly totems, were often used to express and to reinforce the marriage rules.

Despite the criticism that his work justifiably engendered, Frazer's fundamental point is well-taken and is directly applicable to nineteenth- and early twentieth-century Irish society: that there is an interplay between the symbols and belief system of a distinct group of people and the rules they develop concerning the choice of marriage partners. In Ireland, the interesting historical point is that a system of exogamy operated simultaneously with a larger system of endogamy. That is, each of the Christian denominations enforced a set of rules (usually called the "prohibited degrees") concerning how closely one could be related in blood to another person and still be eligible for marriage. This was a system of exogamy and the rules are probably most familiar to readers by way of Victorian novels, wherein the limits of cousins marrying each other, or the infamous deceased-wife's-sister problem, often pops up. But surrounding this system of exogamy was a larger, more pervasive system of endogamy: a set of civil laws, religious codes, and social customs that severely inhibited the intermarriage of Protestants and Catholics.

This system was remarkably strong in the period covered by the present study, and persons familiar with present-day Irish life must be reminded that the inhibitions on religious intermarriage in the present day are a pale shadow of past restrictions. In our own time (since, roughly, the early 1960s), impediments to intermarriage between Catholics and Protestants in the south of Ireland have been reduced drastically. Largely because of the sharp decline in the Protestant population of the Irish Republic since independence in 1922, the remaining Protestant youths have had their chances of finding suitable Protestant marriage partners sharply reduced and thus nowadays frequently marry Catholics, perhaps in as high a proportion as one-fifth of all Protestant marriages.[3] That, though, is a recent phenomenon, and should not be projected backwards in time.

Similarly, it would be a mistake to adopt a romantic view of nineteenth-century denominational intermarriage, in the relatively infrequent cases that it occurred. One sometimes hears talk of the good old days when allegedly it was understood that in a Protestant-Catholic marriage, the boys would follow the father's religion and the girls the mother's. In rare instances that may have happened, but only in the case of couples of very strong character who were able to withstand the disapproval of both the priest and the rector, and, probably, of most of their own families and relations. Of course, in this matter, as in virtually every Irish social practice, within the national pattern there was a great deal of local variation. Interfaith marriages were more apt to be socially acceptable in locales in which one group was in a strong majority than in areas where the two rival sides were more closely economically and numerically balanced (such as was the case in much of Ulster and in the '98-ravaged parts of Wexford and Wicklow).

The Irish phrase for religious intermarriage is "mixed marriage" and it is not an innocent term. Even moreso in the past than at the present time, the phrase is more than merely descriptive; it is one of implicit opprobrium. In the mind that created this coinage, anything mixed partook of baseness of nature. This impurity was of a profane character (in Emile Durkheim's sense), as distinct from the purity of a proper marriage.

Laws inhibiting mixed marriages were written in broad strokes on the eighteenth-century Irish statute books and in this form were intended to protect Protestants against the pollution of Popery. These inhibitory statutes were of two sorts: those that affected the "consumers" of mixed marriages (the couples intending to marry) and those inhibiting the "producers" (the clergy who officiated at such unions). In the first category, any Protestant who married a Roman Catholic came under the rigours of the entire anti-Catholic penal code which meant, among other things, that he could not hold land in fee simple or on a long lease. A separate provision applied to Protestant women who held estates in their own right. In the event of marrying a Catholic, they were at once deprived of their inheritance, which passed on to the nearest heir of the Protestant faith.[4] The direct impact upon marriageable couples of these provisions was reduced and eventually removed by a series of "Catholic relief acts" of 1778, 1782, and 1793. The statutes against those who celebrated such unions lasted longer, however. An early eighteenth-century law had made it a capital offence for a Catholic priest to officiate at a marriage between a Protestant and a Catholic and, in fact, one priest was executed under this law in the year 1726. In 1793, the penalty for celebrating such a union was changed to a fine of £500. Between 1820 and 1832, six Catholic priests were convicted of celebrating mixed marriages. The statute was repealed in 1833. It was not until 1870, however, that an act of 1745 which had rendered null and void any mixed marriage celebrated by a Catholic priest was repealed.[5] As is the case of the entire anti-Catholic penal code, both the intent and the efficacy of the legal taboos against religious exogamy is uncertain and, probably, ultimately unknowable. It is a matter of some debate whether or not W.E.H. Lecky was right in holding that the penal code "was directed less against the Catholic religion than against the property and industry of its professors,"[6] but he is undeniably correct in asserting that one result of the code was that "the division of classes was made as deep as possible and every precaution was taken to perpetuate and to embitter it."[7]

Although the officials of the Catholic church deeply and justifiably resented the penal code of the eighteenth century, they agreed in principle with the fundamental assumptions of the code's inhibition of interfaith marriages. Such marriages, they thought, were unnatural and, even if tolerable under certain circumstances, were of a base, second quality. John Thomas Troy, bishop of Ossory (and later archbishop of Dublin) wrote in 1780 to one of his coreligionists that marriages between Protestants and Catholics were "unlawful, wicked and dangerous."[8] In fact, he elsewhere noted that he did not wish to see the penal laws against mixed marriages repealed, because they deterred Catholics from entering into such unions.[9] The abhorrence of interfaith marriages was shared in kind, if not perhaps to the same degree, by most of the Catholic prelates and clergy. Even Daniel Murray, archbishop of Dublin and one of the least judgmental of Irish-Catholic bishops, was strongly opposed to such unions and stated in 1825 that he believed that they should be permitted only on condition that the children of the marriage be raised Roman Catholic.[10]

The Council of Trent of 1563 had decreed that marriages which were not celebrated by a Catholic priest were invalid and that meant, implicitly, that the church would accept denominational intermarriage only if the new union came under its hegemony. Because the Catholic church in Ireland was under siege from the sixteenth through the eighteenth centuries, the decrees were promulgated unevenly throughout the country, and thus, the intermarriage rules varied by locality. The Trent decrees were published in Ulster in the late sixteenth century and in some parts of the Province of Tuam in 1685, but were not published in the rest of the Province of Tuam until 1745 and not in the Province of Cashel until 1785. In the rest of Ireland, it was only in 1827 that the canon laws on such marriages were made uniform.[11]

Given the stipulation of the Council of Trent, one would have thought that the Irish-Catholic church would have been unambiguously negative on the question of whether or not Protestant marriages were valid: the Trent decrees required a Catholic priest to be in charge of any valid ceremony. However, it would have been risking a clash with the civil authorities to require a Catholic priest to be present at *all* marriages as a precondition of their legality. So, rather than take this politically suicidal position, the Catholic authorities recognized as valid non-Catholic marriages. This brought them to the interesting point of what to do about mixed marriages celebrated by a Protestant minister, a particularly vexing point, given that the death penalty was in effect in much of the eighteenth century for a Catholic priest who conducted such a ceremony. The Catholic church's way out of this dilemma was the "Dutch precedent." In 1741, it had been ruled that in the Netherlands, where at the time the civil law required a Calvinist pastor to officiate at all marriages, a mixed marriage was valid even if a Catholic priest was not present. The Irish bishops saw that this precedent got them out of their difficulties, and, after their strenuous appeals to Rome, in 1785 the Vatican authorities extended the Dutch precedent to all parts of Ireland, including those already covered by the Tridentine decrees.[12] So, although the church might frown heavily upon mixed marriages, especially those conducted by a Protestant clergyman, both parties in the union were still expected to fulfill the same moral obligations as if they had been married by a Catholic priest: that is what entering a valid marriage entailed.

If the church's canon law permitted plenty of scope for the exercise of discretion by local parish priests, as the nineteenth century progressed, clerical attitudes hardened, and from roughly mid-century onward, mixed marriages were a staple item of pastoral denunciation by the prelates and clergy. The evils of intermarriage were the particular concern of the century's mightiest churchman, Paul Cullen, consecutively archbishop of Armagh (1849–52) and of Dublin (1852–78). The synod of Thurles, convened by Cullen, came out unequivocally against mixed marriages.[13] It is diagnostic of the Irish scheme of values that the bishops were much more concerned about interdenominational marriages than were those of the United States and of England who, in some circumstances, actually favoured them.[14]

Whatever softness and ambiguity remained in the Catholic position on interfaith marriages was removed in 1908. That year saw what Owen Dudley Edwards has called, "the outlawry of mixed marriages."[15] This was not a response to any stimulus from Protestants in Irish society or to an increase in interfaith marriage, but was the result of an increasingly aggressive tone on the part of the Vatican authorities that had been gaining force since the middle of the nineteenth century. The Sacred Congregation of Propaganda drafted a decree on marriages in 1907 which Pius X promulgated to come into effect on 19 April 1908. This *Ne Temere* decree required that to be valid under Catholic canon law, all interfaith marriages now had to be celebrated by a Roman Catholic priest: the Dutch precedent was cancelled. Further, the non-Catholic party was required to sign a contract which in its Irish form contained four points: (1) that there would be no interference with the religion of the Catholic partner; (2) that the Catholic party would endeavor in every way to bring the non-Catholic to the True Faith; (3) that all children of the marriage would be baptized Catholic and be educated in Catholic schools; and (4) that the couple would not either before or after the Catholic marriage ceremony present themselves for a similar ceremony before the minister of any other religion.[16] Even when these conditions were agreed to, the interfaith marriage was conducted by the priest in a service that was determinedly second class. Under a papal decision of 1858, these marriages took place in a side chapel and without a nuptial mass and consequently without the nuptial blessing of the mass.[17] One observer has described the tone of such interfaith marriage services in Ireland as being conducted in a "degrading atmosphere."[18] Although there may be disagreements with that observation, there can be no doubt that, in general, the Irish-Catholic clergy carefully orchestrated services so as to contrast the flawed marriage with the more perfect union of two Catholics. The *Ne Temere* decree greatly offended Irish Protestants because of its imperialistic tone, but the clergy and bishops enforced it among the Catholic population with enthusiasm, and the requirements of the decree were accepted by the Catholic population without significant complaint. That is not surprising, for the Sacred Congregation of Propaganda had framed exactly the kind of canonical decree that would fit Irish-Catholic society.[19]

If, in the nineteenth and early twentieth centuries, the Protestant churches were less overt in their condemnation of interfaith marriages than was the Catholic church, that does not mean individual Protestant rectors and ministers did not counsel their young people against interfaith marriages. Protestant fear of mixed marriage was especially strong after the *Ne Temere* decree came into force. If more diffusely expressed than was the Catholic position, the Protestant churches nevertheless were very effective in enforcing their inhibitions of these marriages. After observing rural communities in parts of Ulster for several years, one social scientist concluded that "intermarriage is so rare that they can be considered as two endogamous societies."[20] Actually, that judgment would have held up for most parts of Ireland for the entire period 1815–1922.

This degree of nuptial segregation could not have occurred without the full consent of the Irish people of both faiths. The various civil and canonical inhibitions on interfaith marriages were an articulation of generally (if not quite universally) held beliefs about how the Irish social universe should operate. Of course, to state this fact leaves unresolved the cause-and-effect question, of how it all began, but that question is essentially unresolvable. One has here a perfect causal circle: the Irish people favoured marital segregation of the two major faiths, and thus embraced religious regulations that helped minimize the chance of interfaith marriages, and this minimization in turn yielded a population that favoured marital segregation; and so on and on.

It is possible to discuss the Irish inhibitions on religious interfaith marriage as being analogous to inhibitions in other societies on racial intermarriage. Owen Dudley Edwards has suggested that:

Marriage itself has always been seen as the key to any resolution of a segregated society. It has been rightly acknowledged that inter-racial marriage is the most outstanding witness that can be given against racial discrimination. . . . The prohibition of inter-racial marriage is therefore a fundamental article to the maintenance of *apartheid* in any state, and stood on the statute books for that end in many American states, northern and southern, in the last century, and so stands in South Africa in this.[21]

This analogy, however, misses the crucial point that both groups, Protestant and Catholic, have disapproved of intermarriage. In nineteenth- and twentieth-century Ireland, one is not dealing with the attempt of an hegemonous group to keep itself pure of contamination by another undergroup, but with a mutually agreed decision to keep apart. Thus, instead of imposed apartheid, it is more accurate to think of the Irish as having developed mutually acceptable boundary maintenance systems.

The purpose of these systems (of which the inhibitions on intermarriage were central) was to control the limbic regions of society, to keep under control those border areas where, unless controlled, confusing ambiguities would arise. Recognition of the character and understanding of the mechanics of the Irish boundary maintenance system is a necessary prerequisite to any analysis of the divergent belief systems accepted by Irish Catholics and Irish Protestants in the nineteenth and early twentieth centuries. Only by keeping themselves segregated in family life and by separating the young was it possible for the two groups to develop and perpetuate entirely incompatible social cosmologies and grossly inaccurate views of each other.

Educational institutions have long been a matter of central concern in Irish society and understandably so, for if children are raised together it is very difficult for them to develop totally incompatible world views and to come to believe that their religious opposites are fundamentally different sorts of human beings. And, of course, if Catholic and Protestant children grow up attending the same schools, the chances of interfaith marriages will be increased and that is societally unacceptable.

The nineteenth-century word used in Ireland for integrated education was "mixed" schooling and, like "mixed" marriage, it was a term of opprobrium. There was no nineteenth-century term for segregated schooling, although the term "denominational" education was used by Catholic authorities to describe a system of Catholic schools (and, by exclusion, implicitly to recognize that there would be an all-Protestant system, if there was an all-Catholic one).

Behind the good-bad duality involved in the mixed-denominational distinction was a fear that if children attended religiously integrated schools they would come under pressure to give up their faith. Both Protestants and Catholics worried about this, although the Catholic authorities were more articulate on the matter, largely because in the first one-third of the nineteenth century, Protestant proselytizers had tried to use elementary schools to spread Protestant beliefs.[22] Fears, though, were not limited to the elementary level. Edward Maginn, coadjutor bishop of Derry, wrote to Paul Cullen in 1848 that he had

... never yet known a Catholic youth to have spent any time in Trinity College who did not return home shipwrecked in faith and moral, wholly profligate. In faith latitudinarian, Protestants in morals are no less so. The very best of them would in the eyes of our Catholic ethics be considered anything but a safe companion ... I doubt whether Paganism in its filthiest lycees, where Venus and Bacchus were deified and recommended to gentle youths as objects worthy of divine worship, exhibits ... anything more detestable than our Dublin, Edinburgh and Oxford stews.[23]

The Catholic opposition to mixed education was somewhat muted before the 1840s but then, roughly coincident with Pius IX's enthronement as Pope in 1846, there occurred a hardening of the church's views.[24] When a system of religiously neutral university colleges was proposed by the United Kingdom government in the mid-1840s, the Catholic bishops at first split on the matter and, then, the majority having become convinced that these would be "Godless colleges," the bench accepted with alacrity Rome's rulings in 1847 and 1848 condemning the efforts at integrated university education.[25] When, at mid-century, Paul Cullen became dominant in the Irish hierarchy, the evils of nondenominational (that is, of religiously integrated) education became a major focus of his administration. As Emmet Larkin has noted, "in thus making the education question the great objective end in the subjective battle for the faith, and subordinating the other themes in the synodical address [of the Synod of Thurles of 1850], to that objective end, Cullen was, in effect, setting the political goals and priorities for the Irish Church for the next thirty years."[26]

No less than the Catholic leaders, the religious and lay authorities of the Established Church worried about the dangers of integrated schooling. For them, the concern focused almost entirely on the elementary educational situation: the Anglicans had their own network of secondary schools and Trinity College, Dublin, which accepted Catholic students, was firmly in Anglican hands, so only primary schooling was worrisome. The real problem was what to do with the hundreds of thousands of Irish-Protestant children, the offspring of small farms, of small town shopkeepers, or urban artisans. These were children who would not be rising up the social ladder to attend secondary school, much less Trinity, but they needed strong schooling in their faith, and this in many parts of Ireland was difficult, for the Protestants were, in places, a very thin minority. The answer was propounded' in 1838: the Church Education Society. Backed by most of the Church of Ireland hierarchy and by a collection of lay nobility and gentry, this society's goal was to prevent Protestant children (and, most especially, those of the Established Church) from being swept up in the "national schools" which the government had initiated in 1831. The motives behind the Established Church's educational initiative were complex, but one was to avoid Protestant children being placed in the difficult role of being a small minority in largely Catholic national schools – a situation that would prevail in much of Ireland if Protestants and Catholics went to school together. At its peak, in 1848, the Church Education Society had over 120,000 pupils on its rolls. Over one-third of these were Roman Catholics, but because the schools were run by clergy and laity of the Established Church, this degree of religious mixing was acceptable to Anglican authorities. Things turned sour, however, because running such a large network was very expensive and the Established Church was under continual attack in the mid-nineteenth century for its being a privileged minority church. After undergoing rigorous reforms directed by the United Kingdom parliament, the Church of Ireland did not have money to support adequately elementary education. The church's own system therefore declined, and by 1870 (when church disestablishment occurred), was down to 52,000 pupils and was headed for oblivion.[27]

While the actions and pronouncements of bishops and secular spokesmen for the churches were of importance, they would not obscure the crucial fact that the education of their children was a matter of central concern to the great majority of the Irish people of both faiths. And this fact must be underscored as far as Roman Catholic parents were concerned. It is one of the unexamined clichés of international educational historiography that Protestantism, and in particular, Scottish Presbyterianism, implied a much higher commitment to attainment of literacy and numeracy than did Roman Catholicism. Such observations do not take into account the matter of social class within a given nation or differing levels of economic development of entire countries, in those instances when international comparisons are being made. As applied to Ireland, the undeniable fact is that indeed Presbyterians had the highest literacy rate, Anglicans a close second, and Catholics a distinct third,[28] and this is sometimes taken to indicate a greater avidity for education amongst the Protestants than amongst the Catholics. Actually, all the various percentages indicate is that the Presbyterians were more concentrated in the middle classes than was any other group. The Established Church had a much broader social base: it enrolled the overwhelming majority of the upper classes, but the Established Church also encompassed most of the Protestant urban working class and the rural Protestant cottiers and agricultural labourers. The Catholics were more heavily concentrated in the cottier and labouring classes than either the Anglican or the Presbyterian; since access to education of all forms, even elementary education, depended to a considerable extent on the parents' ability to pay (both directly in school fees and, indirectly, in foregone child labour), one cannot posit relative indifference to education on the part of Roman Catholic parents.

Indeed, if one examines the actions of Catholic parents on education as far back as the mid-eighteenth century, one finds a remarkable willingness on their part to sacrifice for their children's schooling, haphazard though that training may have been. From 1695 to 1782 there were statutes on the Irish books that inhibited Catholic education. These ranged from early laws that provided for fines (in the first instance) for any Catholic who kept a school and (in the second instance) for imprisonment to stronger penalties in later acts for people who sent their children abroad for a Catholic education. Also, the general penal provision against Catholic priests hurt Catholic education, for the local priest frequently was the chief promoter of popular schools.

Crucially, the Catholic people responded instinctively to this situation: they realized that their cultural identity in part hinged on their acquiring and preserving at least a few shards of formal education and hence there emerged in penal times the "hedge schools," illegal day schools taught by itinerant school masters for the few coppers the parents could provide. These schools should not be romanticized – the education they gave was wildly idiosyncratic – but their existence, and the fact that they continued (in the form of "pay schools") even after the penal code was abolished is direct evidence of what counted in Irish-Catholic culture. The Irish peasantry, one of the poorest groups in Europe, was supporting in the 1820s out of its own scant resources schools that contained 300,000 to 400,000 children.[29]

Given, then, that schooling was a matter of intense concern not only to clergy, bishops, and lay leaders of the Irish religious groups, but also to the generality of the people, it is worth understanding how the state system of elementary education, which most of the nation's children attended from mid-century onward, started out as an integrated system and, under the pressure of Irish social life, became a segregated one.

In 1831, Edward Stanley, chief secretary of Ireland, established a state system of elementary education. Stanley was an important educational visionary, but many of the components from which he formed the system were largely pre-existent in Irish life. He put together from bits and pieces that had been formed in the 1820s – by royal commissions, governmental practice, episcopal demands, and so on – a system that worked as follows. A board of unpaid commissioners of both faiths was set up to allocate state funds for elementary education to be made to schools under their direct supervision. These men, "the commissioners of national education in Ireland" were gentlemanly amateurs and the everyday chores were performed for them by professional civil servants. The national education commissioners paid the salaries of all school teachers, made grants towards books and buildings, and defined the secular curriculum of the schools. At the local level, control rested in the hands of school managers who hired and fired the teachers and determined the details of each school's operation.

What was most original about Stanley's state system of elementary education was that it was intended to be nondenominational – not secular, nondenominational – and that it was to be religiously integrated. Seemingly, the Dublin authorities had taken to heart the minority viewpoint of James Doyle, Catholic bishop of Kildare and Leighlin who, in 1830 had stated:

I do not see how any man, wishing well to the public peace, and who looks to Ireland as his country, can think that peace can ever be permanently established, or the prosperity of the country ever well secured, if children are separated, at the commencement of life, on account of their religious opinions. I do not know any measures which would prepare the way for a better feeling in Ireland than uniting children at an early age and bringing them up in the same school, leading them to commune with one another and to form those little intimacies and friendships which often subsist through life.[30]

For religious integration to work in the "national schools," three practices were enjoined. The first of these was that at local levels, control of each school should be shared, if at all possible, by individuals of the two major faiths. The commissioners of national education were to look with "peculiar favour" upon applications for financial aid stemming jointly from Protestants and Catholics. That, automatically, would prevent the schools from becoming the fiefs of any one set of clerics. Second, it was intended that Catholic and Protestant children would be taught in the same school. Third, because religion was such a sensitive matter in Ireland, a clear and inviolable line was to be drawn between literary education and religious instruction. During "ordinary school hours," when children of both faiths were being schooled together, no sectarian religious teaching was to be allowed, although it could be given on a separate day of the week or after school hours as long as this was arranged in advance.

Lord Stanley's formula was visionary, well-intended, and, indeed, was typical of the decent and idealistic naivete with which English liberals so often approached Ireland. And as was often (actually, almost always) the case with outsiders' solutions to Irish problems, it ran headlong into the doleful realities of Irish life. To begin with, the commissioners of national education were under political pressure to begin and to expand their system as quickly as possible, so they did not press hard for fulfillment of the requirement that schools should be jointly controlled by Protestants and Catholics. In practice, they granted aid to anyone of good character and of local social standing, and the result was that of 4,795 schools in operation in 1852, only 175 were under ecumenical control. Which is to say: local management arrangements came under sectarian control. Further, because there was no tradition of local government in Ireland comparable to the English tradition, Irish laymen (and especially Roman Catholics) looked to their religious leaders for guidance in civic matters. Thus, it was the Catholic clergy who came forward to take charge of the local schools. Of 4,547 national schools in operation in 1850, 3,418 were under clerical managership. By and large, Catholic national schools were under priestly control, while Protestant schools were under the shared control of lay leaders and a local clergyman.

Second, despite the original intention of keeping religious and "literary instruction" (the contemporary term for secular instruction) separate, the commissioners of national education created a series of school books for literary instruction that contained a large amount of moralizing, as well as the rudiments of Bible history. These texts, if read in a proper context were neutral as between Christian denominations (both the Protestant and Catholic archbishops of Dublin had approved each book, as had a representative of the Presbyterian church), but when put into a school that was controlled by a manager or managress of a single denomination and who inevitably appointed teachers of their own persuasion, they inevitably were given a sectarian gloss. Therefore, the theoretical line between religious and literary education disappeared in practice.

Under these circumstances, the idealistic intention of mixing children of both faiths in elementary schools was a chimera. Truly religiously neutral schools existed only in the rarest of instances, and, understandably, parents were reluctant to send their children to schools run by the other faith. The inevitable result of all of these factors is that in 1862 (to take the first year for which statistics are available), 53.5 percent of the national schools had a mixed attendance. Most of the mixed schools were in Ulster, but even this percentage was artificially high: a school was counted as mixed if even a single Protestant child attended a Catholic school or vice versa. Even by this definition, the number of integrated schools was down to 35.6 percent in 1900. Just how little real integration was taking place is indicated by data for the year 1870: of the Catholic children in integrated schools, just under 90 percent were in schools run by Catholic authorities and staffed entirely by Catholic teachers. Only the odd Protestant child on the rolls made them, technically, "mixed schools."[31]

Unlike the state system of elementary education, the network of academic secondary institutions did not need to be restructured to fit the realities of Irish life, for they were denominational foundations from their beginnings. When, in 1878, the United Kingdom government began paying financial aid to "intermediate education" it was funding an avowedly denominational network of schools and made no pretense of encouraging integration.[32]

One of the curious things about nineteenth-century Irish education was that although by the 1850s the nation's schools at all levels were under denominational control and, in the case of Catholic institutions, under clerical control, and, further, although the institutions were religiously segregated and becoming moreso each year, nevertheless the Irish-Catholic bishops acted as if the opposite were the case. Archbishop Cullen warned a meeting of the Catholic Defence Association in 1851 that "the present efforts of the government were simply yet another example of a basic conspiracy to destroy the faith of Irish Catholics and that the key to success of that plot from the government's point of view was to acquire control over education in Ireland."[33] The Catholic bishops of Ireland in a joint pastoral of June 1856 warned their people of sinister efforts being made by the commissioners of national education to undermine the faith of Catholic children.[34] In another joint pastoral, issued in 1875, the bishops stated that "the control of the State over education in this country has been enlarged in some degree perilous to liberty."[35]

Such statements could be cited by the score. Their peculiar aspect is that they bear no apparent relationship to historical reality: the documentary evidence overwhelmingly establishes that the commissioners of national education had broken in the face of the realities of Irish life and that at all levels, from mid-nineteenth century onwards, Ireland had a de facto denominational school system.

What might facilely be described as collective paranoia on the part of the Irish-Catholic authorities was part of a larger, less unreal concern, as Emmet Larkin notes. If, in practical terms, the Catholic authorities wanted nothing less than a system of denominational education at all levels under which the state would pay for everything and they would themselves control almost everything, they were attacking the state for a considered reason. "The real enemy," says Larkin, "was not necessarily the state, but the liberal virus, to which the modern secular state seemed to be particularly prone."[36]

This view of the state as dangerously infected, explains why, in the early twentieth century, the Catholic bishops could act in good conscience while seeming to reduce the educational opportunities of Irish-Catholic children. There were three impediments to the efficient delivery of educational services to Irish children in the early twentieth century. First, many of the elementary schools were too small to be efficient: a large number of schools had only one teacher and had few educational supplies, no heating, and no sanitary facilities. Second, the proportion of children attending school regularly was low. Third, there was little provision for the involvement of local citizenry in the schools, since the control was shared by Dublin Castle authorities and by nonelected local school managers. The financial cognate of this lack of citizen involvement was that there never had been any provisions made for helping to finance local schools through the local rates.

When governmental authorities tried to move on these three problems, the Catholic authorities successfully fought against them. The bishops opposed the amalgamation of small schools because that opened the possibility of increased religious integration, and, equally, in areas where now there were separate boys' and girls' schools, these institutions might be joined together: coeducation of the sexes was believed to be a cause of sexual immorality. Further, mergers, even if they did not involve either integration or coeducation, often would mean that the boundaries of a local Catholic parish and of a school district no longer would coincide, and this would reduce the efficiency of the local priest in overseeing the morals and religious beliefs of his flock. So successful was the Catholic church in fighting the educational bureaucracy on this matter, that in 1904 (on the eve of the amalgamation program) the average number in daily attendance in Irish elementary schools was fifty-six; the corresponding figure for 1919 had risen only to sixty-one.

On the matter of large-scale absenteeism of Irish children, the problem was that the Irish Compulsory Attendance Act of 1892 applied only to urban areas and even then, the most important municipal corporations (Dublin, Cork, Limerick, and Waterford), under church guidance refused to cooperate. The Catholic bishops opposed both the existence of compulsory attendance laws and their extension, as an infringement of parental rights, so, in introducing and attempting to extend compulsory attendance laws, the state was abridging one of the church's prerogatives. The church successfully defended its ramparts so that no improvement of consequence was possible. In 1918, the last year for which reliable statistics are available for United Ireland, 68.9 percent of the children on the rolls were in daily attendance. In Scotland, where an enforceable school attendance act was in effect, even in the storm-swept Orkney Islands, where attendance was lowest in the entire nation, 83 percent of the children attended school every day.[37]

As for the involvement of local citizens in education, in 1907, and again in 1919–20, the Catholic authorities were able to block no fewer than four separate bills that had been introduced into the United Kingdom parliament with the intention of injecting a degree of lay influence into the educational system at the local level.[38]

From these actions, one should not conclude that the Catholic authorities had suddenly gone antipathetic to education. Far from it. But they perceived the three-faced vice of liberalism in each of the solutions to educational problems. These faces were: liberalism in the general sense of the belief that the state had a right to interfere in matters, such as education, that the Catholic church regarded as solely its own concern; liberalism in the specific constitutional guise of English liberalism, which postulated that the involvement of as large a group as possible of the citizenry in governmental affairs was "democratic" and thus desirable, and that such democracy improved the quality of government; and liberalism in the narrow sense of the English Liberal party which at this time was pressing in United Kingdom-wide matters for increased participation at the local level in civil matters by the general public.

Significantly, Irish Protestants, and particularly those in Ulster, supported these "liberal" measures even if they were not generally attracted to the English Liberal party. Protestants were particularly keen on having local schools become eligible for local tax revenues and also strongly favoured involving lay citizens more directly in school management. They were bitterly frustrated by the Catholic hierarchy's successful opposition. The result of the differences concerning education between Protestants and Catholics was that now not only were the schools effectively segregated institutions, but the Protestants and Catholics assumed directly polar ideological positions concerning schooling. The segregation of Irish children, the one faith from the other, came to be paralleled by a refusal of their respective leaders to make any contact with the other side on questions of educational policy. Yet, though Catholic and Protestant leaders barracked each other about educational matters, in the schools nothing significant changed either structurally or attitudinally. Both sides still believed that children of the two major faiths should be schooled only with their own kind and under the guiding hand of teachers of their own sort and that these teachers, in their turn, should be under the auspices of a Catholic priest or of a Protestant board of governors.

If one wishes to test this assertion, that fundamental attitudes remained the same, one has only to turn to two natural test cases: the north and south of Ireland after the Partition Act of 1920 and the Anglo-Irish treaty of 1922. In the Irish Free State and its successor, the Republic of Ireland, pre-independence precedents were followed with a slavishness that made observers wonder if, indeed, there had been an Irish revolution. In this overwhelmingly Catholic state, the schools became more segregated than ever, and their denominational character more sharply pronounced.[39] In the Protestant-dominated north of Ireland, educational change came more quickly. (In education, as in other areas, one of the paradoxes of Irish life has been that the counterrevolutionary unionist state has been more disposed to make radical changes than has been the revolutionary state in the south.) The government of Northern Ireland quickly improved the school attendance rate and arranged for local rate aid for education and made provisions for more local citizen involvement in education. These measures did not please the Catholic hieriarchy, but, the Northern Ireland government continued to pay for the great majority of the expenses of the Catholic schools. The interesting development in Northern Ireland was that under the aegis of Charles Stewart Henry Vane-Tempest-

Stewart, the seventh marquis of Londonderry, minister of education and peer of long Irish ancestry and of too-long residence in England, a quixotic attempt at reintroducing Lord Stanley's system of 1831 was assayed. Lord Londonderry tried to make Northern Ireland's non-Catholic elementary schools truly nondenominational, and thus, he hoped, eventually to make them attractive to Catholics as well as Protestants. Under his plan, sectarian religious instruction was to be banned and teachers were to be appointed without regard to their religious affiliation. The Londonderry Act of 1923 was a complex measure and many of its provisions were effective, but by 1930 a combination of the Orange Order and the Protestant clergy had forced severe modifications in its idealistic central features. The schools of Northern Ireland remained either Protestant or Catholic, and, like those of the south, were more segregated than ever.[40]

A shrewd commentator on the behaviour of the Anglican communion in the Irish Republic has made an observation that would apply to all Irish denominations and would apply equally well in the nineteenth as the twentieth century:

Next to the church, the other major cornerstone of the Church of Ireland community was its segregated system of education. At an early age, children occasionally developed friendships with neighbouring Catholics, but to the relief of most parents the beginning of school usually weaned them from these unfortunate tendencies. As they went their separate ways, they were imbued with the unthinking prejudices and historical memories of their own tradition, and when they emerged from the educational system, not a few found that they could never be completely comfortable with "the other side." In its heyday, this deeply divisive system extended from primary school through to university.[41]

Irish taboos on interfaith marriages and the practice of religiously segregating the young while they were being taught how the history, economics, and social processes of the world worked, constituted a social mortmain. Of course, as commentators frequently have noticed, there were other differences in social patterns between the two major denominations – how they spent Sunday, what sports they played and so on – but these matters were tertiary and were derivative from the two main systems of boundary maintenance: religious endogamy and segregated education. These two social practices were not cosmetic and temporary. They were at the very centre of Irish life and they were as permanent as any pattern of human social behaviour can be.

As a mortmain, these practices set fundamental limits on what was and what was not possible in Irish society. Above all, they facilitated the Irish pattern of religious segregation, without requiring a geographic separation of the two faiths. Sometimes, as in Belfast and Derry, one-faith ghettos emerged, but such enclaves were not necessary to the maintenance of the Irish social system. Protestants and Catholics could live side by side, as they frequently did, and still live in completely separate worlds. Ultimately, these two separate worlds, were worlds of the mind.

Systems of Belief

Milton Rokeach began his now classic *The Open and Closed Mind* with the following story from a Polish shtetl:

One day there came to visit the town Rabbi a man and wife who were in dispute over a marital problem. In accord with tradition, the Rabbi was to hear both sides of the argument and then decide who was right. He first heard the husband's side of the story, and, when he was finished, the Rabbi said to him: "You are right." Then he heard the wife's side of the story. "You are right," the Rabbi said. When they both left, the Rabbi's wife stepped from her hiding place behind the draperies. She had overheard everything. "But how could they both be right?" she asked. The Rabbi answered, "You are right."[1]

Systems of belief are like that. They are complex interworkings of attitudes, faiths, accurate and inaccurate empirical observations, which – if they are viable – have not so much a defensible logic, but to their adherents, a satisfying psychologic – and they permit their adherents to hold without disquiet beliefs that are rationally incompatible with each other.

In Ireland in the nineteenth and early twentieth centuries there were two over-arching psychologics, two complex networks of ideology, faith, social practice, and economic arithmetic, so strong that it is fair to call them "cosmologies." Undeniably, there were a thousand local variations and, among the Protestants, denominational striations of beliefs, but each of these variations fell clearly into one camp or the other, Protestant or Catholic. Although the Catholic and Protestant cosmologies differed on many matters, they had this in common: for their adherents, they worked. The systems of belief explained adequately in intellectual terms and, more important, satisfyingly in emotional ways, how the world operated. Like medieval walled fortresses, both of these systems of belief were closed. The two cosmologies covered every aspect of life and each facet of belief was tied protectively to every other component. One can be impressed, to take an instance, by the wry way in which the divine and the merely historical are joined in the old Orange joke:

"I've never heard of King Billy," the Catholic farmer remarked to his Orange neighbour.
"Och, away and read your Bible, man!" was the reply.

The obverse side of the coin was that one's opponents in the present day were automatically assumed guilty of moral evil: "In 1865 Archbishop Cullen not only boasted that he himself had never dined with a Protestant, but also identified Catholics who did mix socially with Protestants as persons uniformly hostile to the changes which he was attempting to bring about in the Irish church."[2]

In one of his more expansive moments, Friedrich Engels wrote to Sigismund Borkheim that "however simple the Irish problem may be, it is nevertheless the result of a long historical struggle and hence it has to be studied. A manual explaining it all in about two hours does not exist."[3] "Simple?" Perhaps: but Engels wrote that comment in 1872 and still no manual exists setting down Ireland's social physics and one suspects that the task would be rather harder than Engels thought. *If* one were to engage in the singular feat of intellectual compression that Engels suggested, the explication of Irish society in about two hours, one would honour the following cautions about potential errors. In the first place, one would avoid the seduction of the Irish taste for aperçu and for epigram. Everyone wants to be Oscar Wilde, so it sometimes seems. Although it is easy to draw facile and witty contrasts between the belief systems of Catholics and Protestants, these almost invariably are better literature than history. Real life rarely follows the mordancies of John Pentland Mahaffy. Second, one would do well to avoid drawing up a cultural taxonomy of differences in the cosmologies of the two main religious groups. The danger of giving in to the temptation to become a cultural Linneaus is that the passion for cultural morphology often leads one to forget that some things are more important than others and that many small details, while fascinating, are relatively trivial.

Third, one would accept that culture is historically important. This emphasis upon the validity of culture as an historical concept would not be necessary (especially not when dealing with Ireland) except that among present-day historians of Europe and of the British Isles there are two strong schools, ideologically opposed to each other, which share a denigration of culture. One of these groups consists of Cliometricians and other quantitatively oriented economic historians whose intellectual base is classical economic theory. In their explanatory system, culture is a variable that is invoked only as a residual factor. It usually is employed when nothing else will explain deviation from proper ("rational") behaviour. Under these rubrics, the fact that most Irishmen of the nineteenth century ascribed to religion factors which (as earlier chapters of this book demonstrate) are more accurately ascribable to other causes, is regrettable, but not very important: in effect, it means only that the nineteenth-century Irish people did not run their personal regression equations properly.

The other group that frequently denies, or heavily denigrates, the significance of culture in determining historical action consists of hard-shell Marxists, sometimes called structural Marxists, who lay emphasis upon economic causation to the exclusion of almost all else. Engels wrote to a friend in 1890 that, "Marx and I are ourselves to blame for the fact that young writers sometimes lay more stress on the economic side than is due to it. . . . Unfortunately, however, it happens only too often that people think they have fully understood a theory and can apply it without more ado from the moment they have mastered its main principles, and these even not always correctly."[4]

Given then, that one is dealing necessarily with culture, in Ireland perforce one is dealing with religion. This would lead one to a recognition that the word "religion" means two different things. It applies to the practices, beliefs, and organizations that are associated with formal religion and with its invariable accompaniment, informal superstition and magic. And, simultaneously, "religion" is the name by which the Irish people have called their tribal differences. Religion was one of the single most important ways by which nineteenth- and early twentieth-century Irishmen defined themselves. It mattered not if an individual entered his church only to be baptized and to be buried, the life he lived between those two signal events was, in the eyes of those with whom he dealt, the life of either a Protestant or of a Catholic. Religion in Ireland explained not only the way of God to man, but many of the relationships of man with his fellow man.

Finally, one would not become weighted down with pessimism. The only flaw in the late F.S.L. Lyons' Ford Lectures of 1978, published as *Culture and Anarchy in Ireland, 1890–1939* was his depressed sense of the social costs of Ireland's two separate belief systems. Lyons wrote that whereas Matthew Arnold:

saw culture as a unifying force in a fragmented society and as a barrier against anarchy, my thesis is that in Ireland culture – or rather the diversity of cultures – has been a force that has worked against the evolution of a homogenous society and in doing so has been an agent of anarchy rather than of unity. By anarchy I do not mean simply the collapse of law and order, frequent as this has been in one part or other of Ireland over the centuries. I mean rather that the co-existence of several cultures, related yet distinct, has made it difficult, if not impossible, for Irishmen to have a coherent view of themselves in relation to each other and to the outside world.[5]

It is easy for anyone sensitive to Irish history to be saddened by much that one sees. One feels, for instance, the anguish of Protestants who, in the 1830s, felt themselves persecuted:

For some years ... our people are beaten at fairs and markets and exposed at all times to the open hostility, as well as the secret enmity of the native and Popish population, insomuch that it would be impossible, even had they no other evils to contend against, for them to remain in the country. There is nothing more common, during the last few years than for some Roman Catholic who sees a Protestant possessor of a farm that would be a desirable acquisition, to resolve to make it his own; and in order to effect his object, a system of annoyance and persecution is resorted to, a threatening notice is put on his house, his family is insulted, himself beaten at the fair or returning from market, and his life made so uncomfortable, and, as he thinks, so insecure that he proposes to free himself from all by emigrating. ... In such a state of existence – for it can scarcely be called society – it ceases to be a problem why the Protestants of the lower orders are so eagerly rushing to our shores for the purpose of emigration; the truth is – and there is no use in either hiding it or trifling with it – there is no peace, no security, no happiness for Protestants of the lower orders in the very centre of a savage and hostile people, who civilisation has never tamed, and whose ferocious habits and turbulent tempers have never been chained down with effect by government of the country.[6]

With less anguish, but with equal force, the notable French observer of Ireland, L. Paul-Dubois, put the corresponding Catholic case:

Haunted by the memory of the Penal laws, they are but gradually freeing themselves from the idea that the Protestant is master of Ireland and that they are his slaves, that he is a free man and they are helots; if they attack members of the Ascendancy party of the English colony, it is rather on account of their tyranny and their privileges than on account of their religion.[7]

Pain is rightly felt, but to see the fundamental character of the Irish cultures, as Lyons did, as productive of anarchy rather than of order is to confuse product with by-product, to mix up substance and accident. In modern times, the Irish have had no single cultural system, but neither have they had anarchy. Undeniably, there were moments of horrific social friction between the two groups (who can forget the civil war surrounding the '98 uprising in Wexford, or the Belfast pogroms or the burning out of Protestant farmers during the early days of the Free State?) but to focus on such instances misses what culture, and particularly Irish culture, is all about: systems of conceptualization and attitude that have explained with remarkable efficiency to the Irish Catholic and the Irish Protestant how the world operates and what the right thing to do is in any given situation. These systems of belief and social prescription, Catholic and Protestant, have existed in the same time and the same place with each other. But they have overlapped without interpenetrating, like radio waves of close, but distinct, frequencies. This puts one in mind of John Hewitt's affirmation:

> I write for my own kind
> I do not pitch my voice
> that every phrase be heard
> by those who have no choice:
> their quality of mind
> must be withdrawn and still,
> as moth that answers moth
> across a roaring hill.[8]

That is the farthest thing from anarchy, and it is the embodiment of how each of the two main Irish cultural systems has operated.

Although here we certainly are not engaged in formulating the two-hour manual of the simplicities of Irish history that Friedrich Engels wanted, the five cautions just mentioned are well taken for any discussion of Irish belief systems. If the two main Irish belief systems of the nineteenth and early twentieth centuries were hermetic in the sense that – like Hewitt's moths communicating across a roaring hill – the two groups talked not to each other, but through each other, their two world views nevertheless had a great deal in common. Both Protestants and Catholics in Ireland were resolutely, indeed heroically, pre-modern. To begin with, each group believed that the world was governed by spiritual forces. This invisible world sometimes was conceived of as a set of impersonal transcendant forces; sometimes it was understood in abstract theological terms; other times as a set of forces that could affect a person directly and individually. But always the visible world was perceived as being ultimately subordinate to the invisible. Given that the visible and the invisible worlds interacted, this was a two-way process. The hand of God or the long spoon of the devil could touch anyone, that is, could impinge on the empirical reality of everyday life. Reciprocally, by acting in an appropriate fashion in the visible world, individuals could (through prayer or magic) change things in the invisible world, garner the favour of the gods as it were and, in turn, thereby influence events in the present world. A good deal was made by nineteenth-century Irish Protestants about their not being as superstitious and as addicted to magic as were the Catholics, but in fact they were every bit as given to supernaturalism as were their opposite numbers.

In the premodern world view shared by both Irish Catholics and Irish Protestants, it was clearly laid down that the world and human life had a purpose. Teleology, not anomie, prevailed, and if the world and human life had purpose, then so did individual life. Nineteenth-century Irishmen of either faith would have been utterly bewildered by the suggestion that randomness characterized human society. To them, each human event fit into a purposive scheme that, although only partly revealed to mankind, had its origins in the invisible world. Therefore, in Irish life one often had tragedy and frequently had comedy, but rarely was there the modern sense of meaninglessness.

Similarly, both groups believed that the world was a moral order, although they disagreed strongly about the details. Highly charged feelings of right and wrong pervaded each belief system. If, in practice, each group could be quite forgiving of the lapses of their own coreligionists (one is reminded of Daniel O'Connell's dictum that sins against faith were worse than sins against morals)[9] this was not moral subjectivism, but forgiveness.[10]

Irish history being the protean subject that it is, one is on occasion allowed to change metaphors: here let us replace John Hewitt's gossamer moth with a more prosaic item and suggest that the foundations upon which Irish Catholics and Irish Protestants constructed their separate edifices of belief were elements held in common. These were belief in the prepotency of spiritual forces (religious, magical, or, in some cases, "national"), belief in human experience as purposive, and belief in the world as moral order.

They had more in common than this. As the buildings of the mind rose higher, one notes that though they were facing in different directions, the two edifices shared a common wall. Long ago, Emile Durkheim drew attention to the fact that in all religious-derived belief systems, whether simple or complex, there was one notable characteristic. "They presuppose a classification of all things, real and ideal, of which men think, into two cases or opposed camps, generally designated by two distinct terms which are translated well enough by the words *profane* and *sacred*."[11] Though Catholic and Protestant beliefs were not simply mirror images of each other, much of what was sacred to Protestants was profane to Catholics and vice versa. There is a vast nineteenth- and early twentieth-century polemical literature on these matters, ranging from religious topics, such as contrasting use of the scriptures, baptism, absolution from sins, to contrasting views of politics and national identity. The key here is that both groups were virtually Manichean in their habit of thinking in sharp contrasts, of turning almost everything into good versus evil, light against darkness, them and us. This dualism was so sharp and the force behind it so electric, that it is easy to forget that the Irish Protestants and Irish Catholics needed each other. Much of each group's conception of the world depended not only on a positive affirmation of their own characteristics, but on negative denunciation of the other sides' – we're not like that other lot! Each group, then, had a mansion of the mind, walled off from the other side, but not independent of it.[12]

Many nineteenth- and early twentieth-century Irishmen tried to understand the differences between Protestants and Catholics not by dealing with culture, but by invoking race. Racial thinking was the common coin of the English-speaking world of the nineteenth century. This stemmed naturally from the colonial expansion into Africa, Australasia, and North America, where settlers encountered aboriginal people who, if admittedly human, were to the "civilized" eye very different sorts of humans. The inevitable tendency to ascribe to race what actually were cultural differences between human societies was reinforced in the later part of the century by Darwinian biology. Once it had been established that change and, particularly, speciation, occurred in the animal kingdom, it was only a small step to assuming that the same thing happened to human populations. So, a pseudo-science developed that involved measuring the physical differences among various human groups and then ascribing aspects of their collective cultural level to these various racial causes.

Within the British Isles, there were two dominant schools of racial thinking. These may be denominated "Anglo-Saxonism" and "Celticism." As L.P. Curtis, Jr. convincingly has argued, Celticism was "an ethnocentric form of nationalism with a strong measure of race consciousness."[13] It was both a response to the Anglo-Saxonism of the English racial thinkers and a virtual replication of that English model. In the Victorian era, both Celticism and Anglo-Saxonism held that there were very deep and inevitably clashing characteristics between the modern Celts and the modern Anglo-Saxons. Inevitably, each side propounded complex explanations of its own superiority.[14] Within Ireland, this kind of racial thinking fit perfectly with the sacred-profane disjuncture in the Irish mindset. Celticists in Ireland became as devoted to racial purity and racial exclusivism as were Anglo-Saxonists in England. Thus, there arose the phenomenon of "Irish race" conventions that brought together Irish-Catholic emigrants from all over the world, individuals who believed, among other things, that they were held together by a common genetic inheritance.

The problems with racial thinking are obvious. In our own time, the evidentiary bases by which cultural characteristics have been tied to racial factors have been shown to be so weak as to be either valueless or, at most, of tertiary consequence. More important, the human costs of such thinking, whether in the Third Reich or in present-day South Africa, have been shown to involve a price too high for a civilized society to bear.

As A.T.Q. Stewart notes concerning Irish racialism, "the theory of a racial distinction between planter and 'gael,' though it still dominates Irish thinking on the subject, can no longer be sustained."[15] Why does racialist thinking still find its place in the way that historians and other scholars deal with Irish culture? Part of the reason lies in terminology. One of the greatest imperialistic coups of the nineteenth century was affected not by the British navy but by Ireland's Catholic politicians: they captured the term "Irish" for themselves and their co-religionists. If, in 1782, one had told Henry Grattan, the Protestant patriot who brought about the "constitution of 1782," and who claimed, proudly, "I am now to address a free people . . . Ireland is now a nation," that he was not Irish, he would have guffawed. That idea would have been universally recognized as preposterous. Yet, as J.C. Beckett notes, by the time of Grattan's death in 1820, a change was occurring. One of the Beresfords, a family of Anglo-Irish power brokers, said in that year, "When I was a boy, the 'Irish people' meant the Protestants; now it means the Roman Catholics."[16] The hegemony of this new meaning took most of the nineteenth century to effect fully, but its triumph was sure. Daniel O'Connell, whose words were listened to in person by more Irish people than any other person of the nineteenth century, frequently used the phrase "Catholic Ireland."[17] Theoretically, one could have both "Catholic Ireland" and "Protestant Ireland," but this is not how the sacred-profane mindset works. Instead, an equation developed of Catholic = Irish and, perforce, non-Catholic = non-Irish. The operation of this mechanism and its tie to racialist thinking is illustrated by the evidence of one Catholic priest before a parliamentary commission in 1825. He was asked to explain the meaning of "Sassenach," a word frequently used in Ireland in his time. He explained: "The true meaning of it is Englishman. There is no Irish term for Protestant. They first knew a Protestant in the person of the Englishman and therefore they have identified it with him."[18] At a popular level, the refusal to see the possibility of Protestants as being Irishmen, of a particular sort, is understandable. If adopted by historians of Ireland, however, it means that a subset of Irish people, the Catholics, are studied as if they were the whole nation. And, strangely, the more given to present-day Irish nationalism an observer of the Irish past is – that is, the more committed to the ideal of a single, unpartitioned Ireland – the more apt he or she is to write the Irish Protestants out of the national history, as not being really Irish.[19]

One of the most interesting aspects of the sacred-profane mindset as it operates in Ireland has been the way that the form of Gaelic spoken in Ireland – called "Irish" – was tied into racial ways of thinking. "Celticism ... might equally well be labelled Gaelicism," Perry Curtis adjudged, so central was it to the emerging Celtic racialism.[20] The matter is particularly fascinating because, first, language by definition is a cultural artifact, not a racial phenomenon, and therefore tying it to race takes some very adept prestidigitation; and, second, despite the prescriptions of linguistic nationalists, the desirability of replacing the Irish language with the English language was one of the few things on which the overwhelming majority of the Irish people, Catholic and Protestant, agreed in nineteenth-century Ireland.

Exactly when the people of Ireland gave up the Gaelic language can be argued, but the causes for it are not in doubt. "The essential reason for the decline of Gaelic was the popular – more precisely, the Catholic popular – will," Oliver MacDonagh states.[21] "By 1800," the late Maureen Wall suggested, "Irish had ceased to be the language spoken in the homes of all those who had already achieved success in the world, or who aspired to improve or even maintain their position politically, socially, or economically."[22] At one time it was fashionable to explain the Irish people's rejection of the Irish language as a result of the three-pronged attack by the Irish national school system (which, until the early twentieth century did not permit a bilingual program), to the activities of Daniel O'Connell (the liberator made his speeches in English and showed no concern for preserving the language of the people), and to the Catholic church (whose priests for the most part showed a marked preference for English). Such suggestions miss the point that the Irish peasantry was shrewd enough to read the economic signs of the times. Britain, the most economically advanced nation in the world in the eighteenth and the first half of the nineteenth centuries, and Ireland's nearest neighbour, operated in English. Mastery of that tongue obviously was a prerequisite for breaking into that economy, whether as a day labourer in Lancashire or as a small merchant in Ireland itself. Moreover, the other country which loomed increasingly large in the mind of the Irish, the United States (and to a lesser extent, Canada, Australia, and New Zealand) required an ability to speak English. So, with a rational and a prudent calculus, the speakers of Gaelic in Ireland chose to learn English.

"It seems clear that the Gaelic language was in rapid decline from, at latest, 1750," Oliver MacDonagh observes and suggests that by 1801 only about half the Irish population was monolingual Irish-speaking.[23] Maureen Wall believed that the decline was later and that the Gaelic language "continued to be the language of the majority of the population of rural Ireland from the Treaty of Limerick until the Famine."[24] The available data suggest that MacDonagh, rather than Wall, is correct and that the decline of Gaelic in Ireland, though continuous throughout the nineteenth century, was largely completed before the age of O'Connell, of national schools, and of renascent Irish Catholicism. Figure 11 clearly indicates that by 1851 (the first date for which there are systematic data) the Gaelic tongue in Ireland was understood by less than one-quarter of the population, that at most the monolingual Irish speakers were less than one-twentieth of the population, and that even these proportions declined continually with each passing decade. Here one has one of those cultural areas wherein, during the nineteenth century, the majority of the Protestant and Catholic populations were not becoming more differentiated, but more and more alike. Certainly there were regional variations in the speed with which English became dominant, but undeniably a cultural convergence between Protestant and Catholic linguistic systems was taking place.

Yet, it is at this point that there arose one of those litmus items that distinguished Catholic from Protestant belief systems. Although by the late nineteenth century, the English language was the native language (that is, the language spoken most often and with most facility) of the overwhelming majority of the people of Ireland, the hibernian form of Gaelic came to be adopted as a symbol of Celtic (and, therefore, Catholic) purity. This process was especially ironic, because it was begun by Protestants of British stock. The early workers for the preservation of the Gaelic-language culture were Protestant scholars,

Figure 11
Irish Linguistic Preferences, 1851–1911

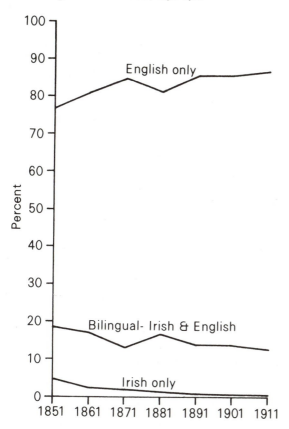

Source: See Appendix Q

men of letters such as George Petrie, Samuel Ferguson, and Standish O'Grady.[25] Preservation and revival of Gaelic culture did not become part of the mindset of those who believed in the existence of the Irish "race" until very late in the nineteenth century. When that occurred, the Gaelic language assumed the role of a racial icon and movement to revive it took the form of an attack upon English-language culture. There were a few Protestants associated with the Gaelic language revival, the best known being Douglas Hyde and Ernest Blythe, but these were rare, indeed very rare, exceptions. The movement, though cultural in form, had its militant undertones, as is well indicated by the prize offered by Patrick Pearse in 1914 to the boys of his school. For making "a genuine effort to speak Irish," the prize was a rifle.[26]

Crucially, in the early twentieth century, the language revivalists stopped talking about the Gaelic language and began pressing for the revival of the *Irish* language. The parallel to the way in which the word "Irish" gradually was taken over by the "Celtic" population of Ireland in the nineteenth century is obvious. One now was completely in a world of polar opposites: the English language and the English people were presented as the antithesis of the Irish language and the Irish people. Never mind that the native language of most Irish people was now English. This terminological coup – turning Gaelic into Irish – virtually precluded rational discussion of the language issue. After all, how could any Irishman be "anti-Irish?" The bulk of the Protestant people had little contact with the Gaelic language, either in its historical or its revived form, and they allowed this semantic coup to occur with nearly complete indifference. Granted, a few waxed splenetic. Some, like John Pentland Mahaffy, speaking before the Endowed Schools Commission of 1879, were merely patronizing:

Chairman: Now Celtic is of course a very interesting study from a philological point of view.

Mahaffy: Yes.

Chairman: In your opinion, viewing it as a living language, has it any educational value?

Mahaffy: None.

Mahaffy: (later, qualifying his previous answer). It is sometimes useful to a man fishing for salmon or shooting grouse in the west. I have often found a few words very serviceable.[27]

What was emerging in early twentieth-century Ireland was virtually a direct translation of the German (and, especially, the Prussian) doctrine of nationhood, which defined a nation in racial and linguistic terms. The German dogma was that the German language was special, because it was best suited to the German race. Similarly, it was posited that the Irish language was particularly noble and was the tongue best suited to the Irish race. Although the bulk of the Catholic population may have had doubts about this doctrine, it was an article of faith of the revolutionary political elite and thus, when the constitution of Saorstat Eireann came into effect in 1922, article four provided that the national language was Irish, although English was recognized as "an" official language. Thus, even though in linguistic terms the everyday cultural systems of Protestants and Catholics were becoming more and more alike, as more and more people converted to the use of English as their first language, the vocabulary in which they discussed language (English versus Irish) and attitudes towards the proper place of Gaelic in the society and political culture became even more differentiated.

"If religion be the opium of the people, the Irish were addicts," asserts Patrick O'Farrell, and he is right.[28] Although many of the political leaders of nineteenth- and twentieth-century nationalism adopted concepts of racial causality and ideas of linguistic purity in their world view, religion itself remained the most important component of the two Irish systems of belief. Even observers who view religion as a regrettable form of false consciousness, admit that the Irish were remarkably intense in seeking their gods. This was markedly so from mid-nineteenth century onwards, and although it was Catholic religiosity that drew the most frequent comments from visitors to Ireland, the Irish Protestants were very devout as well and certainly, as a group, were much more religiously sensitive than was the Protestant population of Great Britain.[29] "Religion was the central fact of Irish life," writes David Miller, a leading authority on nineteenth- and twentieth-century Irish history.[30] Contemporary observers frequently tied this religiosity to race. "Few race characteristics are so profoundly marked as is the intensity of religious feeling in the Celtic races and above all, in the Irish race," was the observation of the pioneering French sociologist, L. Paul-Dubois.[31]

One of the most interesting topics of discussion in recent Irish social history is the question of why the Irish, Catholic and Protestant, became so religious. Concerning the Catholics, the seminal item of scholarship is Emmet Larkin's essay of 1972, "the Devotional Revolution in Ireland, 1850–75."[32] This essay suggest that the Catholics were not particularly religious before the Great Famine, but that the Famine began a quarter-century-long process of growing religious adhesion. In that period, Larkin argues, the Irish Catholics were losing their cultural identity and becoming fervently devoted to their church allowed them to substitute a viable symbolic system for the dying world of Gaelic culture. (This, note, was before the attempts to revive Gaelic culture became widespread.) Larkin summarizes this process as being part of a group "identity crisis," which is the psychospeak of the 1960s, but not necessary wrong for that. David Miller, who has done the most sophisticated quantitative studies of Irish religious behaviour in the nineteenth century, confirmed that the levels of Catholic religious practice were not very high before mid-century – roughly one-third to four-tenths attended church regularly in the 1830s – and, strikingly, that attendance was much higher in English-speaking than in Irish-speaking areas. As Miller notes, this runs

counter to the romantic notion that the Gaelic culture was the back-
bone of the Irish Catholic church and it reinforces Larkin's position
that growing adhesion to Catholic practice was largely a function of
the replacement of a traditional Gaelic culture, with a quickly modernizing world view that involved English-language culture.[33]

These formulations have held up well under critical scrutiny. One
can debate the extent to which the ground had been prepared for the
post-Famine shift in Catholic religious patterns by events and trends
begun before the Famine,[34] and one can argue about the degree
(though not the fact) that the agricultural bourgeoisie were the lead
sector in introducing the new Catholic religiosity in much of Ireland[35]
but the basic case is clear: taking the entire span of time 1815–1920, the
Catholics of Ireland were becoming more intense about their religion
and this intensity greatly increased after mid-nineteenth century. The
first stage of intensification of religion involved the Catholic church's
repairing the rents in its organizational fabric that had been caused by
the eighteenth-century penal laws, and also involved gaining the
intense devotion of the bourgeois classes, particularly the farming
elite. The second stage, which began with the Famine, involved the
rapid extension of Cullenite ultramontane control over the organization and, simultaneously, the massive devotional revolution on the
part of the lower classes.[36]

This revolution was deep and pervasive and, like all such changes,
left behavioural evidence of what were deep spiritual developments.
At the simplest level, one can summarize and confirm this process by
noting a striking change: in 1834–5, there was one priest to every 2,987
Catholics;[37] by 1850, this ratio was one to 2,000; by 1870, it was one to
1,250.[38] The process continued. (By the 1960s, the ratio of one priest to
558 Catholics was reached.)[39]

Within the major Protestant denominations, a similar increase in
religious intensity occurred, although the mechanisms and timing
were different.[40] With the Presbyterians, one cannot be excessively
precise in defining the fulcrum of their religious intensification – there
is no equivalent of the Catholic situation marked by the concurrent
arrival of the Great Famine and Paul Cullen – but from the 1820s
onwards, there was a quickening of Irish Presbyterianism, centred of
course in Ulster. David Miller traced this quickening to the process of
"modernisation" which began in Ulster in the late eighteenth century
and which eventually changed the entire economic and social structure of the north. Thus, just as the Irish-Catholic peasantry responded
to the traumatic changes in their world by becoming hyper-religious,
so too did the Presbyterians. The two leading characteristics of the
Presbyterians' decades-long religious rejuvenation were, at first, a set

of intranicine splits and reunions which released an enormous amount of religious energy[41] and, second, a growing infusion of evangelicalism in all but the most rationalistic of Presbyterian congregations. This climaxed in the Great Revival of 1859, an event of earthquake-like proportions that, strangely, has been little studied by Irish historians. This evangelicalism, as Miller notes, was characterized by an emphasis on both prophecy and conversion.[42] For the individual believer, the combination of the eschatalogical and the conversional produced an emotionally rending epiphany. Believers came through the experience with a heightened awareness of the differences between the lost and the found, saved and unsaved, between salvation and damnation, all of which fit perfectly a society that was already predisposed to see things in terms of the sacred-profane disjuncture and in which the social order had two distinct groups, caused by fundamental religious cleavage.

A secondary, often overlooked, aspect of the Presbyterians' increasing religiosity was that it tied into a gentling of social life. The Presbyterian small farmer and linen weaver of the early nineteenth century had been the possessors of a lively, but very rough, indigenous culture. By 1870, their descendants were less often publicly disorderly, less given to recreational fighting, and more apt to have "soirées" in the parish hall than to attend punch-dances at the crossroads or taverns.[43] This joining of embourgeoisment and increasing religious devotion was the same phenomenon that was occurring in the Catholic community.

For adherents of the Church of Ireland, the intensification of religious devotion throughout the nineteenth century was, if anything, sharper than amongst the Presbyterians and Catholics. This point is often overlooked by Irish historians, in part because until the disestablishment of 1870 the Church of Ireland had its share of dead-level functionaries who had been foisted on it by the civil state and, in part, because the Anglican communion placed a premium upon public decorousness in its religious behaviour, so that the intensity of devotion is more difficult for an outsider to assay. Good taste, the Anglicans believed, was not incompatible with religious devotion. The Church of Ireland communion experienced a three-stage evolution during the nineteenth century and each successive stage increased the level of religious commitment amongst the clergy and laity. The Established Church had entered the nineteenth century as a markedly corrupt and inefficient religious institution. During the first three decades of the nineteenth century, the Church of Ireland underwent considerable internal reform – sinecure benefices were reduced, nonresidence among clergymen was limited, and new churches were erected. In common with the Presbyterians, the Anglican communion was considerably influenced by evangelicalism, particularly in the 1820s. The Anglicans had their own form of evangelicalism, which placed less emphasis upon conversion than did the other Protestant denominations, and greater emphasis upon regular performance of religious duties. This tendency also led to attempts to increase the Established Church's influence by way of schools and missions, some of which were aimed at converting Catholic children and were greatly resented by the Catholic authorities.

In the second stage, which covered roughly the years 1830–70, the Church of Ireland frequently was attacked by outsiders, because it was a minority church, supported by privilege granted by parliament. Therefore, a series of reductions to the church establishment was legislated, but paradoxically, these actually resulted in the Church of Ireland becoming more efficient. This occurred in part because the internal standards of administration improved greatly and also because the Anglican population, feeling threatened, drew closer together. Gradually, the Church of Ireland was transformed from being a nest of patronage appointments, to being an institution with a rich devotional life.

The third, capstone, phase occurred after 1870, the year in which the Church of Ireland was disestablished and cast upon its own resources. No longer having any special privilege in Irish society, it now was a voluntary church, just like all the others in Ireland. Given the stark choice of living or dying on its own merits, the church survived remarkably. The laity came forth with money and assumed greater influence in its day-to-day management. They were bonded closer to their church than ever they had been in the days of establishment. All the outward empirical measures of spiritual devotion – money given, sittings at services, numbers of communicants – rose.[44]

Thus, during the nineteenth century, both the Protestants and the Catholic people of Ireland became more and more religious. The institutional embodiment of their religious life became stronger in each case and, equally important, the emotional commitment to their beliefs became more intense. A shrewd observer of the American Catholic history has pointed out that, common conceptions aside, Roman-Catholic revivalism is fundamentally the same as Protestant revivalism. Each is a religion of the heart that overshadows the role of reason in one's personal orientation towards God. Granted, the symbols of piety invoked by each faith has been different – the crucifix, and the sacred heart for Catholics, the holy spirit and the Bible for Protestants[45] – but, as the nineteenth and early twentieth centuries passed, it was increasingly common for both Protestant and Catholic laity to have had a direct experience of the numinous.

Not that the official religion of the churches fully absorbed the religious energy of the Irish people. Despite the marked decline in the indigenous culture of Ireland throughout the nineteenth century, both Protestants and Catholics had a rich extraofficial religious life in the form of belief in spirits, magic, and omens. These parts of the two Irish cosmologies did not interfere in any way with the sacred-profane mindset and, indeed, in the case of curses, oaths, and maledictions, simply provided a dollop of venom and vitriol when dealing with one's enemies.[46]

One of the startling things about Irish religious beliefs is that each denomination was convinced that it was being persecuted. As just mentioned, the Church of Ireland spent the first seventy years of the nineteenth century as an Established Church and during that time was under varying degrees of siege. The Presbyterians, until the disestablishment of the Church of Ireland, felt that they were being discriminated against and, with long memories, harkened back to the eighteenth-century penal code, many of whose provisions had, in theory at least, applied to them as well as to the Catholics. And the Catholics had a rich tradition of persecution and martyrdom, one lovingly preserved in the church's iconography and sacred poetry. Paul Cullen, the most influential churchman in modern Irish history, was a particularly clear example of the persecution mentality. For example, while still rector of the Irish college in Rome, on the eve of his becoming archbishop of Armagh, Cullen wrote: "I think Englishmen and English money are moving the people here. Parsons and other black Protestants who are here are all delighted with the hope of seeing the Pope's temporal power destroyed or curtailed."[47] "Black Protestant" was a common nineteenth-century idiom, not Cullen's own coinage, and the phrase is all the more telling because of that. Its Manicheanism, its black-and-white distinctions between them and us, ran through Irish society, from top to bottom.

It is but a small step from perceiving one's own religious history as a morality tale of the survival of one's own faith under evil persecution, to viewing one's own secular history as being enobled and the other side's as being polluted. It is a commonplace to note that in Irish history Protestant victories were Catholic defeats, and vice versa and, to a considerable degree, this is true. For example, the victories memorialized in "The Sash," the quintessential Orange song – Derry, Aughrim, Enniskillen, and the Boyne – are all instances of Protestant victory (or, at least heroism) in the face of Catholic assault and conversely they fit into Catholic mythology as occasions of lamentation. King William III of Orange, the man on the white horse in Protestant iconography (again, notice the thinking: white against black) serves simultaneously as the equivalent of a Protestant secular saint and as a demon figure in Catholic history. He usually is juxtaposed with the figure of the tragic Catholic hero, Patrick Sarsfield who, following the Treaty of Limerick in 1691, went into exile and finally died, mortally wounded in battle on the continent of Europe in 1693.

Similarly, what was perceived during most of the nineteenth century as Catholic Ireland's greatest problem – the political union of Great Britain and Ireland of 1801 – was for most Protestants not a problem but a much needed answer, in this case an answer to the question of how to avoid being swallowed up by the Catholic majority. Thus, for the two religious groups, the meaning of nineteenth-century Ireland's most important political event, the union, was diametrically opposite.[48]

But simply to suggest that the Protestant and Catholic views of history were characterized by mirror logic would be an oversimplification, for they were not opposed at all points. One should remember that Protestants and Catholics thought alike about the importance of history.[49] To each side, history was useful. It was not a mere collection of distant facts, but a living set of symbols that had a direct relevance to the present. Taken together, Irish Catholics and Irish Protestants were among the most historically aware of European peoples. Both sides were given to genealogical thinking in an extreme form, so that events hundreds of years in the past become, through immediate links in the genealogical chain, an event of the present day.[50]

The other way in which the mirror image analogy is strained is that sometimes one group incorporated an historical event into its own cosmology, while the other side ignored it. The Great Famine is a case in point. Although the Famine fell hardest on the Irish Catholics, who were strongly overrepresented in the very poorest levels of society, it profoundly affected Protestants too. They underwent privation in many instances, and, more commonly, economic distress and, frequently, were virtually forced to emigrate. The Protestants, however, developed no collective mythology about the Famine, save for an attenuated tradition concerning how selfless some of their clergy had been in serving Protestant and Catholic poor alike, and how generous many Protestant landlords had been in supporting relief efforts.

In contrast, the Famine was built into the Catholic sense of history. The initial Catholic folk-interpretation of the Famine was in terms of supernatural judgment. Studies of the Irish folk tradition have shown that the commonplace reaction was to interpret the Famine as some form of divine punishment by the Christian God for the people's sins. Alternatively, it was commonplace to explain events by invoking the action of non-Christian spirits who, in some way, had been vexed and therefore attacked the Irish people. Whether interpreted in a Christian or a non-Christian form of supernaturalism, the Famine to the Irish people was "beyond indignation" and was perceived as an event of cosmic significance, not as a merely human conspiracy against the Irish people. In a brilliant analysis of the changing place of the Famine in Irish-Catholic history, Patrick O'Farrell has shown that this national folk memory was replaced by a "contrivance," a synthetic substitute that was, in its domestic form, anti-Protestant and in its external visage, anti-British. The great touchstone in this transformation was John Mitchell's *The Last Conquest of Ireland (Perhaps)*, published in 1860, and its long shadow has fallen across almost everything written about the Famine since then. Mitchell reinterpreted the common people's cosmic tragedy as a British conspiracy. Even the governmental relief efforts (quite unprecedented in scale in Europe in their own time) were presented as part of a plan to exterminate the Irish (meaning Catholic) people. Incompetence reinforced barbarism in the official relief actions, Mitchell argued, and, he was nothing it not acerbic in his denunciations. As O'Farrell points out, Mitchell's book was a remarkable artistic success. It was great propaganda, but very bad history. Mitchell's successors in interpreting the Great Famine not only attacked the British government, but added a vitriolic anti-Protestant element. Relief efforts by Protestant churches and voluntary groups were reinterpreted as "souperism," and the agencies themselves were defined as proselytizers. Thus, what had been perceived by those who experienced it as a total and overwhelming tragedy, one too deep to be trivialized with hatred, later became a simple proposition: Protestant Irishmen and British government officials had tried to exterminate the Irish people and those whom they could not destroy they tried to seduce from the True Faith with soup and damnable heresies.[51]

Because virtually everything in Irish life in the nineteenth and twentieth centuries could readily be interpreted under the dichotomous cast of mind of the two major Irish belief systems, it was natural that concepts of national allegiance would follow the same lines. And, since the two world views each hinged on formal religion for their primary concepts of sacred and profane, it was inevitable that the lines of national identity would follow the contours of religious identity. Strikingly, it is on this issue of national identity that one encounters one of the most extreme examples of the capacity of any strong cosmology to entertain radically inconsistent positions at the same time, just the way the rabbi did in Milton Rokeach's introductory fable. It is historically demonstrable that during the course of the nineteenth century, the sense of Irish nationality came to be largely, although not entirely, a concept embraced by Catholics and rejected by Protestants. Protestants, though willing under some circumstances to be labelled Irish, thought of themselves as Irish and something more: as part of a cultural commonwealth that embraced the British Isles and, perforce, the second British empire. At a behavioural level, in Irish parliamentary elections from the mid-1820s onwards, the Catholics voted one way, Protestants another. The electoral results are the closest thing one has in the last century to a set of nationwide polls on national identity and the results were unmistakable: Protestant and Catholic allegiances were sharply distinct.

Yet, among the politically articulate Catholic population, one encounters, from the 1820s onwards, two conflicting viewpoints: (a) that the Irish nation is the Catholic nation and (b) that Irish nationalism really has nothing at all to do with religion and instead is a political and constitutional movement that is open to all true Irishmen, whatever their religion. And, simultaneously, among the politically articulate Protestant population, there developed a parallel set of self-conflicting views: (a) that unionism (to use a convenient label) was not a religious movement, but was a political and constitutional movement open to anyone who was truly loyal to the Crown and to the British connection and (b) that one could not really trust the Catholics to be loyal to the Crown or the British connection. So strong was each belief system that their mutual internal inconsistencies neither brought down nor, indeed, even threatened to breach the integrity of either system. If one reads through the reports of political speeches that are given with admirable fulsomeness in the provincial newspapers, one easily finds instances in a single speech of the maintenance of these self-conflicting viewpoints. (Daniel O'Connell was particularly good at encompassing contradictory views in historical rhetoric; on the other side, James Craig was noteworthy.)

However compelling the rhetoric of political leaders, a psychological mechanism, an instrument of rationalization, was needed to help the ordinary person to harmonize these beliefs and to keep on believing them once the political meeting had dispersed and the words of the politicians ceased to sound. And here Protestants and Catholics worked identically in adopting a psychological syllogism that, stripped to its essentials, worked as follows:

1 We (being Catholic or Protestant) note with proper pride that only persons of the right sort adopt our concept of national identity;

2 We are not bigoted or exclusive, for we are open to anyone who sincerely holds our beliefs; and

3 The fact that our political group is almost exclusively Catholic (or, Protestant as the case may be) is accounted for by the fact that the leaders of the other side are bigoted and mislead their decent followers so that they do not see that their best interest is in joining us, which, of course, we would not really trust them to do, given the sort of people they are at heart.

That covers all the possibilities: in politics and nationality it allows both sides to be religiously exclusive, while at the same time to pretend not to be.[52]

In the era with which we are dealing, concepts of national identity were in continual evolution for both groups and one could at considerable length embroider upon the details of each group's self-concept. Instead, it is better to let their actions themselves speak for the Irish people. Their refusal to adopt a single national identity resulted, in the years 1920–2, in Ireland's being partitioned, the Protestant north from the Catholic south. This was, I believe, a tragedy, but it was a natural consequence of the intersection of constitutional change with the polarized mindsets of the Irish people. Since then, in nationalist rhetoric, partition frequently has been trivialized and made a matter of British conspiracy and of Protestant self-seeking, in much the same way that the Great Famine was reduced from tragedy to mere conspiracy. That is not merely callow, but it misses the point that the partition of Ireland was just an outward and visible sign of the partition of the Irish people, one sort from the other, that long had existed in their hearts and minds.

Yet, if the two incompatible belief systems eventually rent asunder Ireland as a geopolitical unit, these cosmologies simultaneously had a quite opposite effect: they kept the social order from fragmenting completely. One of the most common and most mistaken assessments of Irish society in the nineteenth and early twentieth centuries (one that holds even for journalistic assessments of present-day Irish life) is that it was a fragile society, just on the brink of chaos. In fact, though there were times of great national stress, and frequently sharp local tensions,[53] Ireland was a less volatile and less dangerous place to live in than were most contemporary large cities in the United States. In many ways, the social fabric has been stronger than for most European nations (it is France and Italy, not Ireland, that have had all those revolutions). One can argue that it is *because* of – not in spite of – the character of the two Irish belief systems, Protestant and Catholic, that the two tribal groups have managed to coexist. Their respective beliefs have been an analgesic and have limited the pathology of Irish communal rivalries so that a low grade fever, rather than a terminal illness, has prevailed.

By being self-enclosed and self-referential, the two major Irish cosmologies gave the two separate groups a secure knowledge of how the world ran. So strong was each belief system that in local societies individual Catholics and Protestants could cooperate effectively on small matters (a phenomenon frequently noted in the historical literature), without undercutting their respective sets of beliefs. There was room in each system for the honourable exception, the Protestant who turned nationalist, the Catholic who voted unionist, and for the everyday good neighbour. On divisive matters, Protestants and Catholics lived in different mental worlds and on occasions (as in 1920–2), these worlds collided disastrously. The sacred-profane disjuncture in each group's way of thinking was a wonderfully effective psychological safety device. When one learned that the other side was acting in a wrong (that is, profane) manner, that confirmed one's own world view of what was right (sacred) and that was comforting. Up to a certain point, the other side's bad behaviour made one more secure, and a sense of security generally reduces the chances of tertiary conflict.

Necessarily, both world views, Protestant and Catholic, were myth-making machines. They had to be, for facts and perceptions had to be bent to fit the pre-existent mental categories. Therefore, when either group made an observation or a generalization about the other side, they were more concerned with its credibility within their own system than with its necessarily being accurate or verifiable by an unbiased witness. And that is where matters have become difficult for historians: so many of the observations that Protestants made about Catholics and Catholics made about Protestants were inaccurate; they become highly plausible, however, if one uses as a reference point not some external and verifiable standard of observation, but instead adopts the assumptions and blinders of one or other of the belief systems held by the contemporary Irish themselves. Although the conclusions drawn by both sides about the impact of religious loyalties and cultural commitments upon the way the other group acted in economic life or behaved in familial and social matters cannot be taken at face value (any more than can self-referential observations about how "we" do things and why), Irish historians frequently have acted as if such contemporary testimony consisted of valid independent observations. Because almost all contemporary Irish social observation was formed from within one of the two main Irish cosmologies, it must be sharply redacted before it is historically useful. This prescription is easy to state, but is more than ordinarily difficult for Irish historians as a group to carry out, because the overwhelming majority of professional historians of Ireland are themselves residents of Ireland or are of Irish heritage living in North America or Australasia, and perforce tied in varying degrees to one of the two main Irish mindsets. The writing of history inevitably is an imperfect science, but we can limit our errors. In the field of Irish history, one of the main errors that will disappear through a more considered appraisal of the available evidence is the belief that there was a causal connection between Roman Catholicism and technological inflexibility and economic backwardness.

Sigmund Freud described the mechanisms whereby closely related groups – the Spanish and Portuguese for example – were engaged in constant ridicule or attack on each other as the "narcissism of small differences," and this description fits Irish Catholics and Irish Protestants in the nineteenth and early twentieth centuries. Freud saw that the antipathy expressed towards strangers and their institutions called forth the same kind of attachments within a group as do more positive forms of social relationship. Such group narcissism, Freud felt, was relatively (although not entirely) harmless, for it was a convenient way to satisfy the inclination to aggression by directing it outside one's own group and simultaneously to make it a source of cohesion between members of a given community.[54]

Certainly, each Irish group gave to the other adequate opportunities for fulsome self-love. In imaginatively calendaring the ways in which they differed, one from another, in dwelling on details too minor to matter but too delicious to forget, they kept alive, by the great god of contrast, their own sharp and treasured self-definitions.

Appendixes

Irish Religious Distributions, 1834

Diocese	Anglican	%	Roman Catholic	%	Presby-terian	%	Other Protestant Dissenters	%	Total
Province of Armagh									
Armagh	103,012	21	309,447	62	84,837	17	3,340	1	500,636
Clogher	104,359	26	260,241	65	34,623	9	26	–	399,249
Derry	50,350	14	196,614	54	118,339	32	1,738	–	367,041
Down	27,662	15	58,405	31	98,961	52	3,530	2	188,558
Connor	66,888	18	95,545	26	193,261	53	5,924	2	361,618
Dromore	41,737	22	76,275	41	69,264	37	933	–	188,209
Kilmore	46,879	16	240,593	81	8,736	3	97	–	296,305
Meath	25,626	6	377,562	93	672	–	199	–	404,059
Raphoe	33,507	16	145,385	70	28,914	14	24	–	207,830
Total	500,020	17	1,760,067	60	637,607	22	15,811	1	2,913,505
Province of Dublin									
Dublin	106,599	21	391,006	78	2,290	–	2,082	–	501,977
Kildare	13,907	10	120,056	89	9	–	384	–	134,356
Ferns	24,672	12	172,789	87	19	–	300	–	197,780
Leighlin	20,391	11	169,982	89	191	–	288	–	190,852
Ossory	12,361	6	209,848	94	8	–	108	–	222,325
Total	177,930	14	1,063,681	85	2,517	–	3,162	–	1,247,290
Province of Cashel									
Cashel	6,178	3	196,256	97	62	–	26	–	202,522
Emly	1,246	1	97,115	99	1	–	1	–	98,363
Cloyne	13,866	4	328,402	96	14	–	195	–	342,477
Cork	35,220	10	303,984	89	510	–	871	–	340,594
Ross	5,988	6	102,308	94	–	–	2	–	108,298
Killaloe	19,149	5	359,585	95	16	–	326	–	379,076
Kilfenora	235	1	36,166	99	4	–	–	–	36,405
Limerick	11,122	4	246,302	96	85	–	191	–	257,700
Ardfert & Aghadoe	7,529	2	297,131	98	–	–	27	–	304,687
Waterford	5,301	11	43,371	88	110	–	433	1	49,215
Lismore	5,970	3	209,720	97	164	–	382	–	216,236
Total	111,813	5	2,220,340	95	966	–	2,454	–	2,335,573
Province of Tuam									
Tuam	9,619	2	467,970	98	367	–	65	–	478,021
Ardagh	17,702	8	195,056	91	466	–	12	–	213,236
Clonfert	4,761	4	119,082	96	2	–	3	–	123,848
Kilmacduagh	656	1	45,476	99	–	–	–	–	46,132

Diocese	Anglican	%	Roman Catholic	%	Presbyterian	%	Other Protestant Dissenters	%	Total
Elphin	16,417	5	310,822	95	250	–	135	–	327,624
Killala	7,729	5	136,383	95	38	–	139	–	144,289
Achonry	5,417	5	108,835	95	143	–	27	–	114,422
Total	62,301	4	1,383,624	96	1,266	–	381	–	1,437,572
National Total	852,064	11	6,427,712	81	642,356	8	21,808	–	7,943,940

Source: *First Report of the Commissioners of Public Instruction, Ireland*, pp. 9–45 [45], H.C. 1835, xxxiii. The commissioners were unable to determine the religion of 18,951 persons included in the 1831 census. No indication is given of how Jews and nonreligious persons were tallied, if at all. Percentages are rounded to the nearest percentum. "Church Methodists" were tallied as Anglican.

Irish Census of Religion, 1861

County, city or major town	Total no. of inhabitants	Anglican	% of total	R.C.	% of total	Presby.	% of total	Other	% of total
LEINSTER									
C. Carlow	57,137	6,229	10.9	50,539	88.4	106	.2	263	.5
T. Drogheda	14,740	1,031	7.0	13,342	90.5	207	1.4	160	1.1
Dublin City	254,808	49,251	19.4	196,549	77.2	4,875	1.9	4,133	1.5
Dublin Suburbs	50,485	17,668	35.0	29.639	58.7	1,724	3.4	1,454	2.9
C. Dublin	104,959	18,914	18.0	83,556	79.6	936	.9	1,453	1.5
C. Kildare	90,946	10,439	11.5	79,121	87.0	876	1.0	510	.5
Kilkenny City	14,174	1,242	8.8	12,769	90.1	97	.7	66	.4
C. Kilkenny	110,341	4,750	4.3	105,356	95.5	127	.1	108	.1
C. Kings	90,043	9,109	10.1	79,955	88.8	327	.4	652	.7
C. Longford	71,694	6,196	8.6	64,081	90.4	560	.8	137	.2
C. Louth	75,973	5,203	6.8	69,678	91.7	937	1.2	157	.3
C. Meath	110,373	6,492	5.9	103,327	93.6	428	.4	126	.1
C. Queen's	90,650	9,683	10.7	80,025	88.3	240	.3	702	.7
C. Westmeath	90,979	6,336	7.0	83,749	92.1	343	.4	551	.5
C. Wexford	143,954	12,759	8.9	130,103	90.4	287	.2	805	.7
C. Wicklow	86,479	15,285	17.7	70,044	81.0	285	.3	865	1.0
Leinster total	1,457,635	180,587	12.4	1,252,553	85.9	12,355	.9	12,140	.8
MUNSTER									
C. Clare	166,305	3,323	2.0	162,612	97.8	228	.1	142	.1
Cork City	80,121	10,632	13.3	67,148	83.8	881	1.1	1,460	1.8
C. Cork East	286,396	18,279	6.4	264,754	92.4	899	.3	2,464	.9
C. Cork West	178,301	14,543	8.2	162,140	90.9	219	.1	1,399	.8
C. Kerry	201,800	6,200	3.1	195,159	96.7	243	.1	198	.1
Limerick City	44,476	4,238	9.5	39,124	88.0	418	.9	696	.6
C. Limerick	172,801	5,648	3.3	166,604	96.4	148	.1	399	.2
C. Tipp. North	109,220	7,359	6.7	101,171	92.6	194	.2	496	.5
C. Tipp. South	139,886	5,441	3.9	133,710	95.6	304	.2	431	.3
Waterford City	23,293	1,989	8.5	20,429	87.7	234	1.0	639	2.8
C. Waterford	110,959	3,208	2.9	107,225	96.6	245	.2	281	.3
Munster total	1,513,558	80,860	5.3	1,420,076	93.8	4,013	.3	8,609	.6
ULSTER									
C. Antrim	247,564	45,275	18.3	61,369	24.8	131,687	53.2	9,233	3.7
C. Armagh	190,086	58,735	30.9	92,760	48.8	30,746	16.2	7,845	4.1
T. Belfast	120,777	29,832	24.7	41,327	31.4	42,229	35.0	7,482	6.2
Carrickfergus, C. of Town	9,422	1,821	19.3	1,046	11.1	5,582	59.2	973	10.4
C. Cavan	153,906	23,017	14.9	123,942	80.5	5,352	3.5	1,595	1.1
C. Donegal	237,395	29,943	12.6	178,182	75.1	26,215	11.0	3,055	1.3
C. Down	300,127	60,905	20.3	97,409	32.5	133,796	44.6	8,017	2.6
C. Fermanagh	105,763	40,608	38.4	59,751	56.5	1,909	1.8	3,500	3.3
C. Londonderry	184,209	31,218	16.9	83,402	45.3	64,602	35.1	4,987	2.7
C. Monaghan	126,482	17,721	14.0	92,799	73.4	15,149	12.0	813	.6

County, city or major town	Total no. of inhabitants	Anglican	% of total	R.C.	% of total	Presby.	% of total	Other	% of total
C. Tyrone	238,500	52,240	21.9	134,716	56.5	46,568	19.5	4,976	2.1
Ulster total	1,914,236	391,315	20.4	966,613	50.5	503,835	26.3	52,473	2.8
CONNAUGHT									
T. Galway	16,967	837	4.9	15,621	92.1	189	1.1	320	1.9
C. Galway	254,511	7,365	2.9	246,330	96.8	392	.2	424	.1
C. Leitrim	104,744	9,488	9.1	94,006	89.7	338	.3	912	.9
C. Mayo	254,796	6,739	2.6	246,583	96.8	961	.4	513	.2
C. Roscommon	157,272	5,728	3.6	151,047	96.1	277	.2	220	.1
C. Sligo	124,845	10,438	8.4	112,436	90.1	931	.7	1,040	.8
Connaught total	913,135	40,595	4.5	866,023	94.8	3,088	.3	3,429	.4
Ireland total	5,798,564	693,357	11.9	4,505,265	77.7	523,291	9.0	77,054	1.4

Source: derived from *Census of Ireland for the year 1861, report on religion and education*, 10–12, [3204–III], H.C. 1863, lix.

Irish Religious Denominations, 1861–1911

Census Periods	R.C.s No.	% of pop.	Anglicans No.	% of pop.	Presbyterians No.	% of pop.	Others No.	% of pop.	Total population
1861	4,505,265	77.69	693,357	11.96	523,291	9.02	77,054	1.33	5,798,564
1871	4,150,867	76.69	667,998	12.34	497,648	9.20	95,868	1.77	5,412,377
1881	3,960,891	76.54	639,574	12.36	470,734	9.10	103,637	2.00	5,174,836
1891	3,547,307	75.40	600,103	12.75	444,974	9.46	114,366	3.09	4,704,750
1901	3,308,661	74.21	581,089	13.03	443,276	9.94	125,749	2.82	4,458,775
1911	3,242,670	73.86	576,611	13.13	440,525	10.04	130,413	2.97	4,390,219

Source: Census of Ireland for the year 1911, General report, with tables and appendices, 41 [Cd. 6663], H.C. 1912–13, cxviii

Irish Illiteracy Rates, 1861–1911

Proportion able neither to read nor write:

Denominations	1861	1871	1881	1891	1901	1911
		5 years and above				*9 years and above*
Roman Catholic	45.8%	39.9%	31.0%	22.0%	16.4%	11.3%
Anglican	16.0	14.2	10.9	8.6	7.3	4.2
Presbyterian	11.1	9.6	7.1	5.6	4.9	2.7
Methodist	9.0	6.7	5.5	4.4	4.1	1.6
All others	9.6	8.1	5.3	5.0	4.7	2.3

Sources: Census of Ireland, 1901, pt. II: General report with illustrative maps, diagrams, tables and appendix, p. 59 [Cd. 1190], H.C. 1902, cxxix; *Census of Ireland for the year 1911, General report, with tables and appendices*, 44–5 [Cd. 6663], H.C. 1912–13, cxviii

Religion and Occupation of Adult Irish Males, 1861

Occupation	Catholic		Anglican		Presbyterian		Other Protestant		Total	
	No.	%	No.	%	No.	%	No.	%	No.	%
Landed proprietors	2,365	0.1	2,931	0.9	357	0.1	136	0.4	5,789	0.2
Farmers and agriculturalists	728,330	33.0	72,968	21.5	78,592	30.9	7,333	19.5	887,223	31.2
Commerce, manufacturing & mechanical trades	307,615	13.9	68,547	20.2	55,602	21.8	12,675	33.6	444,439	15.7
Law, medicine, clergy	4,875	0.2	5,231	1.5	1,124	0.4	465	1.2	11,695	0.4
Other "liberal professions"	358	0.1	568	0.2	76	0.1	63	0.1	1,065	0.1
Teachers	6,509	0.3	2,496	0.7	976	0.4	246	0.7	10,227	0.4
Civil servants	12,787	0.6	6,006	1.8	1,034	0.4	252	0.7	20,079	0.7
Army and Navy	10,959	0.5	16,110	4.7	2,084	0.8	1,175	3.1	30,328	1.0
Miscellaneous	369,887	16.8	39,415	11.6	22,434	8.8	2,113	5.6	433,849	15.3
No occupation	761,368	34.5	125,042	36.9	92,455	36.3	13,218	35.1	992,083	35.0
Grand total	2,205,053	100.0	339,314	100.0	254,734	100.0	37,676	100.0	2,836,777	100.0

Source: Derived with arithmetical correlations from Census of Ireland for the year 1861. Religion and Occupations, 62 H.C. 1863 [3204-III] lxi.

APPENDIX F

The 1861 Irish Census of Occupations

The hardest thing to do when analyzing Victorian demographic data is to relax and, instead of forcing the data into modern categories, to pay attention to the material on its own terms. The material which follows is derived from the 1861 census of Ireland.* If read with an eye for contemporary ways of thinking about economy and about occupation, it provides a tour through the economy of Victorian Ireland. I am well aware that there are several standard ways of categorizing occupational and social class levels, but most of these have been evolved for describing twentieth-century societies (and thus their use here would be anachronistic) and all of them are used to depict developing societies, not overwhelmingly agricultural ones such as Ireland. I have experimented with the readily available standardized programs of occupational categories developed by historians of nineteenth-century America, but when applied to Ireland these do not work very well. In the heel of the hunt, one discovers that it is better to pay attention to the way people of the last century described themselves and their world rather than to force them into categories derived from present-day social theory.

One of the advantages of using nineteenth-century categories, without any aggregate procedures, is that one gains a feeling for the complex way in which nineteenth-century tradesmen, proprietors, and operatives distinguished themselves one from the other. More important, one gains a feeling for the vertical patterns of the economy, for the way that industries and clusters of industries were distinguished from each other and were arranged in their own hierarchy. This is particularly important because even in the latter half of the nineteenth century, the Irish economy had yet to develop clear social class demarcations that transcended individual boundaries.

These figures deal only with employed males. The 1861 census collected information upon female employment, but most women were lumped together as "wives" so that tallying their occupational profile would be unprofitable.

The religious cross-tabulations are done by Catholic/non-Catholic categories. This is the standard procedure in demographic work adopted in the Republic of Ireland and reflects social reality: the key question in Ireland is whether or not one is Catholic. The 1861 enumeration collected material on each Protestant denomination and much of it is fascinating. For the present discussion, however, it is more revealing to put all the Protestants together.

---

*Census of Ireland. Religion and Occupations, 715–24, H.C. 1863 [3204–III], lx.

Undoubtedly, later historians will find intriguing subpatterns within the Protestant community. For the moment, however, small, simple steps forward are all that can be completed successfully; the complex ones will come later.

In relation to religion, the occupational data are interesting in that they do not show patterns of industrial segregation, but rather of clustering and concentration. (The reference figure for determining whether any occupation was relatively Protestant or relatively Catholic is 78/22 which is the ratio of employed Catholic males to employed Protestant males.) With that in mind, one finds that certain industrial categories tended to be loaded towards one religious group or the other. For example, the clothing industry, finance, and government were relatively weighted with Protestants.

Such relative concentration being noted, it is crucial to realize that at virtually all levels of status there were both Protestants and Catholics. This point is most important in regard to the Protestants, for phrases such as the "Protestant ascendancy" obscure the fact that there was a very large Protestant working class, people doing dirty, unhealthy jobs and just getting by on the margin of society. Most Protestants were not well off. What privilege they had was relative to the even poorer Catholics. Granted, the Protestants were overrepresented in many trades, but merely because Protestants were relatively numerous in certain activities does not mean that these trades were high status – that manure gathering was an activity wherein Protestants were overrepresented does not remove the miasma clinging to that activity.

The limits to the data presented here are obvious. The most important of these is that within cells there is no differentiation of economic level. For farmers and for agricultural labourers and servants this is especially unfortunate. Also, as presented here, the tabulations do not permit one to discern geographic patterns of specialization that intersected with occupational and religious categories. Still, if one scans the occupational profiles with a bit of imagination and with a respect for contemporary ways of thinking about occupation, the lineaments of a complex and fascinating society emerge.

Summary of Occupations, Ireland, 1861

Occupations	Total No.	Catholic No.	Catholic %	Non-Catholic No.	Non-Catholic %
Pertaining to Food					
Vegetable					
Landed proprietors	5,789	2,365	41	3,424	59
Land agents	550	108	20	442	80
Farmers	413,309	315,881	76	97,428	24
Land surveyors	731	540	74	191	26
Land stewards	2,314	1,323	57	991	43
Drainage overseers	8	4	50	4	50
Agricultural teachers	22	8	36	14	64
Nursery and seedsmen	319	187	59	132	41
Manure gatherers and dealers	21	15	71	6	29
Agricultural implement makers	250	181	72	69	28
Ploughmen	52,791	43,544	83	9,247	17
Gardeners	8,273	5,997	72	2,276	28
Farm labourers and servants	374,425	329,614	88	44,811	12
Millstone makers	40	32	80	8	20
Millwrights	808	438	54	370	46
Sieve makers	76	75	99	54	1
Mill owners	105	48	46	57	54
Millers	4,385	3,226	74	1,159	26
Mill stewards and labourers	1,044	863	83	181	17
Sack makers	6	6	100	0	0
Sugar boilers and refiners	17	12	71	5	29
Mustard manufacturers	6	3	50	3	50
Corn and flour dealers	1,130	813	72	317	28
Oven builders	2	1	50	1	50
Bakers	8,996	7,451	83	1,545	17
Confectioners and pastry cooks	540	334	62	206	38
Victuallers	2,415	2,356	98	49	2
Grocers and apprentices	6,623	3,979	60	2,644	40
Tea merchants and dealers	118	33	28	85	72
Fruiterers	351	323	92	28	8
Green grocers	185	169	91	16	9
Huxters and provision dealers	1,555	1,323	85	232	15
Tobacconists and tobacco twisters	994	901	91	93	9
Cigar makers	6	3	50	3	50
Tobacco pipe makers	184	180	98	4	2
Snuff makers	22	21	95	1	5
Animal					
Graziers	182	113	62	69	38
Herds and drovers	26,607	24,753	93	1,854	7
Salemasters	89	69	78	20	22
Cattle dealers	2,957	2,731	92	226	8

Occupations	Total No.	Catholic		Non-Catholic	
		No.	%	No.	%
Dairy keepers and milk dealers	794	743	94	51	8
Cattle doctors	90	82	91	8	9
Pig jobbers	562	551	98	11	2
Fowl and egg dealers	656	568	87	88	13
Rabbit catchers	13	12	92	1	8
Gamekeepers	648	359	55	289	45
Conservators, inspectors and water bailiffs	94	68	72	26	28
Net makers	35	32	91	3	9
Fishing tackle makers	51	39	76	12	24
Fishermen	7,900	7,045	89	855	11
Shellfish collectors	10	10	100	0	0
Butchers	5,671	4,913	87	758	13
Salt manufacturers	80	70	88	10	12
Bacon and provision curers and factors	576	425	74	151	26
Poulterers	250	227	91	23	9
Butter inspectors	11	9	82	2	18
Bee-hive makers	9	8	89	1	11
Fishmongers	626	590	94	36	6
Shellfish dealers	85	82	96	3	4
Fish curers	11	6	55	5	45
Herring packer	1	1	100	0	0
Purveyors	30	27	90	3	10
Cheesemongers	8	4	50	4	50
Churn makers	1	1	100	0	0
Butter dealers and factors	297	230	77	67	23
Forced meat and sausage makers	1	1	100	0	0
Fowl skewer makers	1	1	100	0	0
Drinks and Condiments					
Maltsters	387	360	93	27	7
Malt-house labourers	92	92	100	0	0
Brewers	242	122	50	120	50
Distillers	83	38	46	45	54
Rectifying distillers and cordial makers	14	9	64	5	36
Aerated and mineral water makers	94	71	76	23	24
Cider makers	8	6	75	2	25
Vinegar makers	1	0	0	1	100
Bottle makers	108	86	80	22	20
Bottle dealers	9	8	89	1	11
Cork cutters	488	381	78	107	22
Wine coopers	193	177	92	16	8
Wine and spirit merchants	313	143	46	170	54
Vintners and publicans	4,457	3,688	83	769	17

Occupations	Total No.	Catholic		Non-Catholic	
		No.	%	No.	%
Canteen keepers	25	22	88	3	12
Miscellaneous Foods					
Hotel, tavern and inn keepers	942	499	53	443	47
Messmen and caterers	23	9	39	14	61
Board & lodging-house keepers	368	307	83	61	17
Cooks	173	98	57	75	43
Waiters and potmen	617	541	88	76	12
Dealers in food, miscellaneous	192	165	86	27	14
Total	945,615	772,949	82	172,666	18
Pertaining to clothing					
Wool and woolen stuffs					
Wool merchants	122	85	70	37	30
Woolen manufacturers	103	61	59	42	41
Wool card makers	37	32	86	5	14
Wool carders	136	93	72	38	28
Wool dressers	34	25	74	9	26
Wool staplers	26	19	73	7	27
Wool slubbers	19	18	95	1	5
Wool spinners	135	121	90	14	10
Worsted and yarn manufacturers	11	8	73	3	27
Wool weavers	1,772	1,600	90	172	10
Stuff weavers	7	4	57	3	43
Cloth manufacturers	9	6	67	3	33
Cloth finishers and dressers	68	43	63	25	37
Cloth shearers	2	2	100	0	0
Cloth lappers	22	6	27	16	73
Fringe manufacturers	1	1	100	0	0
Felt manufacturers	15	2	13	13	87
Woolen drapers	854	356	42	498	58
Tailors and clothiers	22,523	19,405	86	3,118	14
Vest makers	17	8	47	9	53
Robe makers	5	1	20	4	80
Clothes renovators	7	3	43	4	57
Dealers in old clothes	91	82	90	9	10
Dealers in miscellaneous clothing	197	181	92	16	8
Cotton					
Cotton merchants	7	5	71	2	29
Cotton manufacturers	11	4	36	7	64
Sewed muslin manufacturers	82	3	4	79	96
Stocking weavers	46	28	61	18	39
Cotton spinners	223	175	78	48	22
Cotton and muslin weavers	4,957	575	12	4,382	88

Occupations	Total No.	Catholic		Non-Catholic	
		No.	%	No.	%
Gingham weaver	1	0	0	1	100
Corduroy weavers	3	3	100	0	0
Corduroy cutters	2	0	0	2	100
Muslin lappers	5	2	40	3	60
Muslin and calico printers	216	44	20	172	80
Embroiderers	11	5	45	6	55
Sewed muslin and tambour workers	133	70	53	63	47
Flax and Linen					
Flax merchants and dealers	291	205	70	86	30
Flax yarn manufacturers	11	2	18	9	72
Linen thread manufacturers	1	0	0	1	100
Linen manufacturers	372	66	18	306	82
Hackle makers	112	58	52	54	48
Flax dressers	3,289	1,834	56	1,455	44
Flax spinners	279	125	45	154	55
Flax twisters and hacklers	731	469	64	262	36
Thread makers	182	54	30	128	70
Damask designers	53	4	8	49	92
Linen and damask weavers	33,074	10,970	33	22,104	67
Canvas weavers	104	95	92	9	8
Tape weavers	2	1	50	1	50
Bleachers	2,026	548	27	1,478	73
Linen lappers	618	126	20	492	80
Lace manufacturers, weavers and workers	61	43	70	18	30
Linen merchants	281	25	9	256	91
Linen drapers	221	57	26	164	74
Drapers (unspecified)	4,879	2,721	56	2,158	44
Skin, Fur, and Leather					
Skinners	164	148	90	16	10
Dealers in hides and skins	109	109	100	0	0
Leather manufacturers	26	15	58	11	42
Tanners and curriers	1,074	366	81	208	19
Leather dressers	60	48	80	12	20
Spanish leather dressers	8	8	100	0	0
Furriers and fur cutters	36	26	72	10	28
Blacking makers	17	16	94	1	6
Leather dealers	219	141	64	78	36
Leather cutters	125	88	70	37	30
Leather breeches makers	4	4	100	0	0
Boot tree, and last makers	67	55	82	12	18
Boot and shoe makers	39,717	30,256	76	9,461	24
Boot and shoe binders and closers	416	271	65	145	35
Brogue makers	970	968	100	2	0
Slipper makers	11	6	55	5	45

Occupations	Total No.	Catholic		Non-Catholic	
		No.	%	No.	%
Clog makers	93	34	37	59	63
Accoutrement makers	18	15	83	3	17
Silk and Silken Stuff					
Silk manufacturers	4	1	25	3	75
Silk pickers	8	4	50	4	50
Tabinet and poplin manufacturers	10	2	20	8	80
Silk weavers	253	176	70	77	30
Velvet weavers	1	1	100	0	0
Tabinet and poplin weavers	20	9	45	11	55
Ribbon weavers	7	5	71	2	29
Silk cord makers	2	1	50	1	50
Silk mercers	49	17	35	32	65
Straw					
Straw platters and workers	6	4	67	2	33
Straw hat and bonnet makers	15	9	60	6	40
Miscellaneous					
Factory overseers	226	62	28	158	72
Factory workers (unspecified)	3,172	1,728	54	1,444	46
Spindle makers	3	1	3	2	67
Reed makers	239	59	25	180	75
Shuttle makers	31	3	10	28	90
Card makers	6	6	100	0	0
Reel makers	5	2	40	3	60
Winders and warpers	1,889	608	32	1,281	60
Lappers (unspecified)	19	3	16	16	84
Spinners (unspecified)	519	295	57	224	43
Girth web makers	5	2	40	3	60
Weavers (unspecified)	16,767	7,843	47	8,924	53
Knitters	16	13	81	3	19
Print cutters	15	3	20	12	80
Chandlers	7	7	100	0	0
Mangle keepers	3	3	100	0	0
Line peg maker	1	1	100	0	0
Chandlers and soap boilers	1,002	752	75	250	25
Starch and blue manufacturers	121	54	45	67	55
Soap sawyers and stampers	2	1	50	1	50
Needle manufacturers	4	0	0	4	100
Thimble makers	2	0	0	2	100
Pin makers	24	20	83	4	17
Lyers	509	354	70	155	30
Hosiers	195	94	48	101	52
Haberdashers	111	33	30	78	70
Vendors of soft goods	147	131	89	16	11
Peddlers	1,418	1,252	88	166	12
Shirt cutters and makers	29	15	52	14	48
Sewing machine stichers	3	2	67	1	33

Occupations	Total No.	Catholic No.	Catholic %	Non-Catholic No.	Non-Catholic %
Hatters	834	544	65	290	35
Hat trimmers	10	4	40	6	60
Cockade and cere cloth makers	2	0	0	2	100
Brace makers	10	9	90	1	10
Button makers	24	16	67	8	33
Hairdressers and barbers	605	472	78	133	22
Wig makers	14	5	36	9	64
Trotter oil makers	1	1	100	0	0
Fancy workers (unspecified)	9	5	56	4	44
Horn presser	1	1	100	0	0
Comb makers	102	90	88	12	12
Smoothing iron maker	1	1	100	0	0
Artificial flower makers	2	4	0	2	100
Glove makers	56	49	88	7	12
Pumassiers	2	2	100	0	0
Whalebone dressers'	5	5	100	0	0
Umbrella makers	88	65	74	23	26
Perfumers	14	10	71	4	29
Artists in pearl and mother-of-pearl	1	0	0	1	100
Gold and silver lace weavers and workers	3	2	67	1	33
Artist in gold, silver, and jewels	1	0	100	0	0
Jewellers	284	104	37	180	63
Bog oak carvers	27	22	81	5	19
Cloth cap makers	52	32	62	20	38
Sewed muslin agents	211	44	21	167	79
Total	150,856	88,624	59	62,232	41
Pertaining to lodging, furniture, and machinery					
Architects	241	76	32	165	68
Builders and contractors	919	566	62	353	38
Clerks of works	78	54	69	24	31
Quarrymen and labourers	1,600	1,316	82	284	18
Miners	2,799	2,535	91	264	9
Lime burners	377	325	86	52	14
Tile and brick makers	514	413	80	101	20
Timber merchants	227	131	58	96	42
Flag and slate merchants	8	5	63	3	37
Marble merchants	8	5	63	3	37
Plaster of paris manufacturers	2	0	0	2	100
Asphalt manufacturers	2	1	50	1	50
Iron merchants	37	17	46	20	54
Stone-cutters	3,156	2,655	84	501	16
Masons	12,300	10,155	83	2,145	17

Occupations	Total No.	Catholic No.	%	Non-Catholic No.	%
Masons' labourers	940	836	89	104	11
Bricklayers	1,571	1,213	77	358	23
Wiggers	2	2	100	0	0
Marble workers	156	137	88	19	12
Marble masons	90	67	74	23	26
Sawyers (hand)	2,715	2,260	83	455	17
Sawyers (machine)	38	17	45	21	55
Carpenters	30,499	23,148	76	7,351	24
Nailers	4,193	3,295	79	898	21
Lead manufacturers	26	20	70	6	30
Plumbers	671	315	47	356	53
Slaters	2,319	2,059	89	260	11
Thatchers	1,212	1,056	87	156	13
Lath makers	82	67	82	15	18
Plasters and stucco workers	1,418	1,138	80	280	20
Riddle makers	43	23	53	20	47
Whitewashers	65	60	92	5	8
Pump sinkers	76	74	97	2	3
Pump makers	165	138	84	27	16
Sash makers	12	12	100	0	0
Window blind makers	18	12	67	6	33
Stained glass makers	17	11	65	6	35
Whitesmiths and locksmiths	1,063	728	68	335	32
Oil and color makers	57	29	51	28	49
Paper stainers	96	63	66	33	34
Glass painters and gilders	8	2	25	6	75
Painters, decorators, paper hangers and glaziers	5,424	3,669	68	1,755	32
Bell hangers	71	53	75	18	25
Gas makers	206	108	52	98	48
Gas meter makers	11	4	36	7	64
Gas fitters	343	239	70	104	30
Pavers	166	152	92	14	8
Measurers	4	3	75	1	25
Furniture					
Size and glue makers	18	11	61	7	39
Cabinet makers	2,236	1,271	57	965	43
French polishers	190	137	72	53	28
Curled hair manufacturers	18	17	94	1	6
Hair cloth weavers	11	10	91	1	9
Bed joiners	5	3	60	2	40
Iron bedstead makers	3	1	33	2	67
Mattress makers	11	9	72	2	18
Feather dealers	185	181	98	4	2
Feather pickers and dressers	17	17	100	0	0
Cushion makers	1	0	0	1	100
Upholsterers	358	166	46	192	54
Patent spring makers	3	3	100	0	0

Occupations	Total No.	Catholic No.	Catholic %	Non-Catholic No.	Non-Catholic %
Chair makers	144	112	78	32	22
Turners of Wood	323	166	51	137	49
Turners of Ivory	8	6	75	2	25
Turners (unspecified)	340	224	66	116	34
Fringe and tassle makers	8	3	37	5	63
Furniture trimming makers	2	2	100	0	0
Furniture brokers	81	74	91	7	9
Bellows makers	49	46	94	3	6
Gold beaters	22	3	14	19	86
Carvers and gilders	368	215	58	153	42
Mat and rug makers	105	90	86	15	14
Carpet weavers	20	15	75	5	25
Carpet cutters and sewers	13	10	77	3	23
Oil cloth makers and dealers	3	2	67	1	33
Coopers	7,218	6,456	89	762	11
Looking-glass makers	7	7	100	0	0
Looking-glass frame makers	2	1	50	1	50
Picture frame makers	73	55	75	18	25
Clock case makers	2	2	100	0	0
Watch case makers	10	2	20	8	80
Watch glass makers	15	3	20	12	80
Watch and clock makers	951	389	41	562	59
Coopersmiths and braziers	281	103	65	98	35
Japanners	29	10	34	19	66
Ironmongers	857	454	53	403	47
Clay makers and cutters	108	62	57	46	43
Earthenware manufacturers	101	54	53	47	47
Delft china and glass dealers	239	169	71	70	29
Pewter workers	2,032	1,620	80	412	20
Pewter and zinc manufacturers	4	2	50	2	50
Gold and silver smiths	123	55	45	68	55
Gold and silver polishers and glasers	25	20	80	5	20
Electro-platers	57	23	40	34	60
Cutlerers	282	178	63	104	37
Lamp makers	15	7	47	8	53
Lusterers and mounters	5	4	80	1	20
Glass muffers	2	2	100	0	0
Crate and basket makers	894	772	86	122	14
Trunk and carpet bag makers	120	94	78	26	22
Dressing case and pocket book makers	19	12	63	7	37
Band box & fancy box makers	51	26	51	24	49
Safe manufacturers	2	1	50	1	50
Scale and weight makers	6	5	83	1	17
Bird cage makers	11	7	64	4	36
Broom makers	368	308	84	60	16
Coal dealers	480	351	73	129	27

Occupations	Total No.	Catholic No.	%	Non-Catholic No.	%
Coal porters and pickers	798	744	93	54	7
Firelight makers	3	1	33	2	67
Match makers and dealers	20	15	75	5	25
Carbonizers	6	5	83	1	17
Turf and bogwood dealers	137	128	93	9	7
Water carriers	110	100	91	10	9
Brush makers	368	271	74	97	26
Domestic servants	39,211	31,581	81	7,630	19
Chimney sweeps	760	717	94	43	6
Dustpit cleaners	2	2	100	0	0
Turncocks (water)	8	4	50	4	50
Gate-keepers	382	249	65	133	35
China and glass menders	3	2	67	1	33
Colliery overseers	6	2	33	4	67
Colliery contractors	11	7	64	4	36
Coal miners	960	926	96	34	4
Mine overseers	2	0	0	2	100
Mine watchmen	14	11	79	3	21
Machinery					
Civil engineers	603	173	29	430	71
Pattern designers	33	17	52	16	48
Sand core maker	1	1	100	0	0
Iron founders and moulders	987	558	57	529	43
Iron rollers	2	1	50	1	50
Iron dressers	16	7	44	9	56
Roller makers	478	265	55	213	45
Iron rollers	169	71	42	98	58
Smiths and fitters	744	515	69	229	31
Metal polishers	2	2	100	0	0
Screw and bolt makers	25	9	36	16	64
Drill makers	3	2	67	1	33
Blacksmiths	18,679	15,413	83	3,266	17
Wheelwrights	591	494	84	97	16
Machine makers	503	160	32	343	68
Lathe makers	2	0	0	2	100
Gun makers and gun smiths	256	109	43	147	57
Medal and die sinkers	6	2	33	4	67
Wire drawers	4	1	25	3	75
Wire workers	130	89	68	41	32
Tool makers (unspecified)	7	3	43	4	57
File makers	31	21	68	10	32
Saw makers and sharpeners	25	12	48	13	52
Heddle makers	23	2	9	21	91
Mangle makers	1	1	100	0	0
Brass founders	527	237	45	290	55
Opticians and mathematical instrument makers	54	22	41	32	59
Total	161,679	126,344	78	35,335	22

Occupations	Total No.	Catholic		Non-Catholic	
		No.	%	No.	%
Pertaining to conveyance and travelling					
Guides	64	58	91	86	9
Sedan chairman	1	1	100	0	0
Road contractors and makers	1,404	1,167	83	237	17
Toll gate keepers	6	6	100	0	0
Toll collectors	39	37	95	2	5
Horse dealers	285	207	73	78	27
Veterinary surgeons	96	42	44	54	56
Riding masters	5	2	40	3	60
Horse trainers and jockeys	638	580	91	58	9
Livery stable keepers	37	27	73	10	27
Hustlers	397	352	89	45	11
Grooms and coachmen	747	578	77	169	23
Grooms and stableboys	4,673	3,932	84	741	16
Horse clippers	41	37	90	4	10
Ferriers and horse-shoers	425	345	81	80	19
Hay and straw dealers	56	47	84	9	16
Ass jobbers	8	8	100	0	0
Saddle tree makers & coverers	14	9	64	1	36
Saddlers' smiths	2	1	50	1	50
Saddle and Harness makers	2,955	2,049	69	906	31
Spur and bit makers	14	6	43	8	57
Whip makers	192	167	87	25	13
Crest makers	2	0	0	2	100
Harness platers	7	3	43	4	57
Collar makers	30	25	83	5	17
Coach and car makers and smiths	1,596	1,183	74	413	26
Box and wheel smiths	41	35	85	6	15
Box fitter	1	1	100	0	0
Carriage spring makers	14	10	71	4	29
Coach painters	566	446	79	120	21
Coach trimmers	178	118	66	60	34
Coach platers	5	3	60	2	40
Coach fitters	12	12	100	0	0
Heraldry painters	6	2	33	4	67
Carriage brokers	2	2	100	0	0
Cart and waggon makers	557	470	84	87	16
Postilions	221	171	77	50	23
Coach and car owners	1,253	1,135	91	118	9
Coach and car men	11,583	9,912	86	1,671	14
Carriers and carters	3,618	2,808	78	810	22
Cab stand runners	10	10	100	0	0
Omnibus conductors	10	6	60	4	40
Secretaries to railway companies	10	5	50	5	50

Occupations	Total No.	Catholic No.	%	Non-Catholic No.	%
Engine drivers	517	329	64	188	36
Engineers, stokers, and firemen	2,161	1,151	53	1,010	47
Coke burners	11	7	64	4	36
Railway officers, police, and labourers	9,018	7,585	84	1,433	16
Tarpaulin maker	1	1	100	0	0
Ship merchants and owners	113	60	53	53	47
Ship agents	158	60	38	98	62
Pursers in merchant service	3	2	67	1	33
Shipwrights	1,398	922	66	476	34
Ship smiths	105	40	38	65	62
Boat and ship builders	374	222	59	152	41
Sail makers	286	198	69	88	31
Block makers	30	20	67	10	33
Rope and twine makers	1,132	872	77	260	23
Ship riggers	13	7	54	6	46
Anchor and chain makers	63	34	54	29	46
Sailors	14,649	7,058	48	7,591	52
Stevedores	35	25	71	10	29
Boat and ferry men	2,869	2,676	93	193	7
Pilots	462	397	86	65	14
Ship stewards	159	58	36	101	64
Ship chandlers	14	3	21	11	79
Lighthouse keepers	119	71	60	48	40
Harbour and dock masters	49	23	47	26	53
Harbour police	18	4	22	14	78
Canal managers	25	17	68	8	32
Lighter men	109	84	77	25	23
Lock-gate keepers	148	108	73	40	37
Telegraph inspectors and clerks	90	52	58	38	42
Telegraph mechanics	9	6	67	3	33
Forage storekeepers	9	8	89	1	11
Walking-stick makers	7	6	86	1	14
Grease manufacturers	3	3	100	0	0
Post masters and mistresses	348	184	53	164	47
Letter sorters and stampers	41	21	51	20	49
Letter carriers	956	676	71	280	29
Post-office officials	141	76	54	65	46
Boat owners	30	30	100	0	0
Canal boatmen	634	611	96	23	4
Total	68,128	49,722	73	18,406	27

Pertaining to Banking and Agency

Bankers and managers	239	52	22	187	78
Bank agents	37	5	14	32	86
Bank clerks	471	77	16	394	84

Occupations	Total No.	Catholic		Non-Catholic	
		No.	%	No.	%
Bank porters	17	11	65	6	35
Stockbrokers	33	6	18	27	82
Public notaries	21	1	5	20	95
Accountants	761	247	32	514	68
Agents (unspecified) and commercial travellers	1,531	556	36	975	64
Pawnbrokers and assistants	719	485	67	234	33
Brokers (unspecified)	112	86	77	26	23
House agents	83	27	33	56	67
Agents for governesses and servants	2	1	50	1	50
Collectors of rents	44	22	50	22	50
Loan fund officers	23	10	43	13	57
Auctioneers and valuators	255	131	51	124	49
Insurance agents	36	8	22	28	78
Total	4,384	1,725	39	2,659	61

Pertaining to Literature and Education

The provost of Trinity College	1	0	0	1	100
Presidents of colleges	17	14	82	3	18
Fellows of Trinity College, Dublin	17	0	0	17	100
Professors of universities and colleges	98	65	66	33	34
Tutors, &c.,	169	76	45	93	55
Astronomers	5	0	0	5	100
Authors	17	4	24	13	176
Education commissioners	1	0	0	1	100
Inspectors of schools	78	35	45	43	55
Superintendent of Irish school books	1	0	0	1	100
Librarians	62	31	50	31	50
Govn't. stationery officer	1	0	0	1	100
School masters and mistresses	3,609	2,190	61	1,419	39
Teachers of Irish	9	2	22	7	78
Teachers of elocution	3	1	33	2	67
Teachers of writing	10	9	9	1	91
Teachers of drawing	16	6	37	10	63
Teachers of music	339	149	44	190	56
Teachers of dancing	88	74	84	14	16
Teacher of fencing	1	0	0	1	100
Teacher of drilling	1	1	100	0	0
Teachers (unspecified)	5,668	3,844	68	1,824	32
Students in training schools	53	34	64	19	36
Students (unspecified)	2,561	1,536	60	1,025	40
Paper manufacturers	289	210	73	79	27

Occupations	Total No.	Catholic No.	%	Non-Catholic No.	%
Envelope manufacturers	6	4	67	2	33
Paper merchants	26	17	65	9	35
Quill pen workers	22	19	86	3	14
Ink dealers	4	2	50	2	50
Sealing wax manufacturers	4	3	75	1	25
Type founders	37	17	46	20	54
Letterpress printers	2,845	1,460	51	1,385	49
Newspaper proprietors, editors and reporters	236	107	45	129	55
News agents	13	10	77	3	23
Newsvendors	200	176	88	24	12
Stationers	275	130	47	145	53
Booksellers	464	200	43	264	54
Bookbinders	448	215	48	233	52
Copperplate printers	15	7	47	8	53
Lithographic printers	202	93	46	109	54
Print-sellers	8	2	25	6	75
Writing clerks	12,365	6,863	56	5,502	44
Steel pen makers	2	1	50	1	50
Total	30,286	17,607	58	12,679	42
Pertaining to religion					
Clergy, Established Church	2,265	0	0	2,265	100
Clergy, Roman Catholic	3,014	3,014	100	0	0
Clergy, Presbyterians	677	0	0	677	100
Clergy, Methodist	227	0	0	227	100
Clergy, Independent	35	0	0	35	100
Clergy, Baptist	21	0	0	21	100
Clergy, Moravians	7	0	0	7	100
Clergy, Unitarians	7	0	0	7	100
Clergy, Jewish	1	0	0	1	100
Clergy, (unspecified)	25	0	0	25	100
Monks	70	70	100	0	0
Vicars choral (lay)	2	0	0	2	100
Choristers	9	3	33	6	67
Reader/Jewish Synagogue	1	0	0	1	100
Missionaries (unspecified)	45	2	4	43	96
Scripture readers	307	0	0	307	100
Parish clerks & sacristans	362	212	59	150	41
Sextons and pew openers	270	26	10	244	90
Bible Society officers	11	1	9	10	91
Agents to missionary societies	28	0	0	28	100
Church warden	1	0	0	1	100
Diocesan registrars	4	0	0	4	100
Divinity students	330	269	82	61	18
Total	7,719	3,597	47	4,122	53

Occupations	Total No.	Catholic		Non-Catholic	
		No.	%	No.	%
Pertaining to Charity and benevolence					
Poor Law commissioners	2	0	0	2	100
Poor Law inspectors	9	2	22	7	78
Poor Law clerks	99	46	46	53	54
Poor Law relieving officers	149	94	63	55	37
Officers of charitable institutions	268	150	56	118	44
Collectors for charitable institutions	6	5	83	1	17
Society collectors	2	2	100	0	0
Fire escape conductors, and fire engine keepers	15	12	80	3	20
Total	550	311	57	239	43
Pertaining to health					
Physicians	1,604	539	34	1,065	66
Surgeons	753	222	28	531	72
Medical teachers	5	2	40	3	60
Inspectors of military hospitals	7	1	14	6	86
Apothecaries and their assistants	419	210	50	209	50
Chemists and chemical students	105	33	31	72	69
Medical students	954	329	34	625	66
Dentists	76	21	28	55	72
Cuppers	4	1	25	3	75
Vaccinators	2	2	100	0	0
Druggists	369	94	25	275	75
Medical electricians	2	1	50	1	50
Chiropodists	5	3	60	2	40
Keepers in lunatic asylums	188	137	73	51	27
Leech dealers	1	1	100	0	0
Surgical instrument makers	10	4	40	6	60
Truss makers and surgeons' artists	5	3	60	2	40
Lint makers	11	8	73	3	27
Herbalists	6	4	67	2	23
Bath keepers and attendants	45	34	76	11	24
Medical storekeepers	2	0	0	2	100
Botanists	3	1	33	2	67
Total	4,576	1,650	36	2,926	64
Pertaining to justice and government					
The Lord Lieutenant of Ireland	1	0	0	1	100

Occupations	Total No.	Catholic		Non-Catholic	
		No.	%	No.	%
Undersecretary for Ireland	1	0	0	1	100
Officers of Lord Lieutenant's household	6	0	0	6	100
Lord Chancellor	1	0	0	1	100
Master of the Rolls	1	0	0	1	100
Judges	21	7	33	14	67
Attorney General	1	1	100	0	0
Ulster King-at-Arms	1	0	0	1	100
Clerks in office of the chief secretary	2	1	50	1	50
State messenger	1	0	0	1	100
Government officers (unspecified)	1,081	420	39	661	61
Officers in the army	1,197	121	10	1,076	90
Surgeons in the army	67	11	16	56	84
Officers (militia)	326	51	16	275	84
Officers in Royal Navy	212	14	7	198	93
Surgeons in Royal Navy	13	3	23	10	77
Soldiers	26,276	9,991	38	16,285	62
Soldiers (militia)	1,045	583	56	462	44
Soldiers (Royal Navy)	1,121	150	13	971	87
Lieutenant, military store department	1	1	100	0	0
Commissariat office keeper	1	0	0	1	100
Barrack masters and sergeants	57	30	53	27	47
Provost sergeants	11	4	36	7	64
Town sergeants	5	2	40	3	60
Mayor	1	1	100	0	0
Sheriffs	15	2	13	13	87
Magistrates	280	67	24	213	76
Coroners	35	16	46	19	54
Consuls	18	7	39	11	61
Clerks of the Crown	13	3	23	10	77
Clerks of the Peace	34	6	18	28	82
County officers	49	13	27	36	73
Affidavit commissioners	2	1	50	1	50
Officers in courts of Justice	384	127	33	257	67
Equity accountant	1	0	0	1	100
Stamp distributors	14	5	36	9	64
Barristers	734	208	28	526	72
Attorneys and solicitors	1,829	665	36	1,164	64
Proctors	6	0	0	6	100
Registrars of marriages	16	1	6	15	94
Bailiffs	337	250	66	127	34
Process servers	627	431	69	196	31
Law students	83	40	48	43	52
Law clerks	1,406	963	68	443	32

Occupations	Total No.	Catholic No.	%	Non-Catholic No.	%
Scriveners	10	4	40	6	60
Parchment and vellum manufacturers	27	25	93	2	27
Interpreters	15	11	73	4	27
Law messengers	76	53	70	23	30
Comptrollers of customs	3	1	33	2	67
Officers of customs and tidewaiters	303	145	48	158	52
Inland revenue officers	551	188	34	363	66
Excise officers	146	75	51	71	49
Coastguard	1,307	605	46	702	54
Barony constables	7	1	14	6	86
Inspector of factories	1	0	0	1	100
City Marshall	1	1	100	0	0
Borough and civic officers	101	64	63	37	37
Parish constables and cess collectors	37	22	59	15	41
Collectors of rates	202	129	64	73	36
Weighmasters	241	181	75	60	25
Scalesman to corporations	1	0	0	1	100
Directors and inspectors of prisons	5	3	60	2	40
Prison officers	661	320	48	341	52
Pound keepers	24	18	75	6	25
Constabulary and metropolitan police	13,846	9,426	68	4,420	32
Total	54,938	25,468	46	29,470	54
Pertaining to amusement					
Organ builders	31	17	55	14	45
Pianoforte makers and tuners	59	18	31	41	69
Harp maker	1	0	0	1	100
Jews' harp makers	9	6	67	3	33
Musical instrument makers (unspecified)	16	14	18	2	12
Music copyist	1	1	100	0	0
Music-sellers	19	9	47	10	53
Fiddlers	332	320	96	12	4
Pipers	176	175	99	1	1
Organ grinders	10	10	100	0	0
Musicians (unspecified)	1,264	1,061	84	203	16
Vocalists	28	14	50	14	50
Scene painters	6	1	17	5	83
Theatrical costume maker	1	1	100	0	0
Actors and actresses	110	52	56	48	44
Public entertainers	51	26	51	25	49
Play bill seller	1	1	100	0	0
Ballad singers	27	26	96	1	4

Occupations	Total No.	Catholic No.	%	Non-Catholic No.	%
Ventriloquists	3	2	67	1	33
Mesmerists	1	0	0	1	100
Pyrotechnists	8	7	87	1	12
Bird catchers and dealers	7	6	86	1	14
Professional cricketers	2	1	50	1	50
Bat maker	1	1	100	0	0
Ball-Court keepers	5	5	100	0	0
Ball and racket makers	26	20	77	6	23
Professional racket players	3	2	67	1	33
Billiard room keepers	14	9	64	5	36
Billiard markers	62	56	92	5	8
Gymnastic artist	1	0	0	1	100
Toy makers and dealers	19	14	74	5	26
Bow and arrow maker	1	1	100	0	0
Judge of horse races	1	0	0	1	100
Sportsmen	9	7	78	2	22
Huntsmen	109	87	80	22	20
Dog trainers	20	17	85	3	15
Billiard table makers	13	11	85	2	15
Shot makers	2	1	50	1	50
Irish harpers	5	3	60	2	40
Total	2,454	2,013	82	441	18

Pertaining to science and art

Occupations	Total No.	Catholic No.	%	Non-Catholic No.	%
Sculptors	50	33	66	17	34
Statuaries	23	20	87	3	13
Figure makers	44	40	91	4	9
Historical painters	4	3	75	1	25
Landscape painters	23	11	48	12	52
Royal hibernian academician	1	100	0	0	
Portrait and miniature painters	45	20	44	25	56
Picture dealers	7	6	86	1	14
Picture restorers	2	0	0	2	100
Transparency painter	1	0	0	1	100
Engravers of wood	4	2	50	2	50
Engravers of copper	3	0	0	3	100
Engravers (unspecified)	111	80	38	131	62
Artists (unspecified)	136	61	45	75	55
Art students	10	6	60	4	40
Artist and ornamental carver	1	0	0	1	100
Seal cutters	11	1	9	10	91
Lapidary	1	0	0	1	100
Dealer in antiques	1	1	100	0	0
Church decorators	5	5	100	0	0
Curators of museums	2	1	50	1	50
Naturalists	5	4	80	1	20
Bird stuffers	3	0	0	3	100

Occupations	Total No.	Catholic		Non-Catholic	
		No.	%	No.	%
Fossil collectors	9	5	56	4	44
Zoological garden keepers	4	2	50	2	50
Optical glass grinder	1	0	0	1	100
Photographers	94	33	35	61	65
Total	701	335	48	366	52
Unclassified					
Peers	31	3	10	28	90
Barons	6	2	33	4	67
Nobles	16	0	0	16	100
Baronets	27	5	19	22	81
Knights	4	1	25	3	75
Gentlemen	1,802	542	30	1,260	70
Half-pay officers	78	13	17	65	83
Retired officers (unspecified)	540	71	13	469	87
Merchants (unspecified)	2,518	986	39	1,532	61
Russia merchants	2	0	0	2	100
Manufacturers (misc.)	79	17	22	62	78
Dealers (misc.)	6,445	5,674	88	771	12
Stewards (unspecified)	2,890	2,071	72	819	28
Stewards and caretakers	66	57	86	9	14
Caretakers (unspecified)	4,654	4,041	87	613	13
Draughtsmen (unspecified)	68	29	43	39	57
Shopkeepers and assistants (unspecified)	15,121	11,182	74	3,939	26
Apprentices (unspecified)	1,868	1,235	66	633	34
Tradesmen (unspecified)	870	271	31	599	69
Registrars in public institutions (unspecified)	9	5	56	4	44
Registrars of burials	6	3	50	3	50
Secretaries to public boards	44	7	16	37	84
Secretaries to societies	21	4	20	17	80
Stockholders	509	175	34	334	66
Annuitants	1,149	449	39	700	61
Householders	1,798	1,190	66	608	34
Vitriol rectifiers	2	1	50	1	50
Gutta percha manufacturers	12	7	58	5	42
Gut manufacturers	12	11	92	1	8
Vermin killers	8	7	88	1	12
Storekeepers (unspecified)	295	177	60	118	40
Rag and bone dealers	1,455	1,344	92	111	8
Stampers (unspecified)	2	2	100	0	0
Pipe polishers	3	3	100	0	0
Plate maker	1	1	100	0	0
Paper bag stamper	1	1	100	0	0
Pensioners	10,931	7,362	67	3,569	33
Collectors (unspecified)	40	24	60	16	40
Quacks	5	5	100	0	0

Occupations	Total No.	Catholic No.	%	Non-Catholic No.	%
Wood rangers	443	290	65	153	35
Wood cutters	101	89	88	12	12
Lamplighters	190	71	79	19	21
Bellmen	44	35	80	9	20
Messengers (unspecified)	2,366	1,896	80	470	20
Labourers	346,816	307,151	89	39,665	11
Divers	6	6	100	0	0
Mill workers (unspecified)	2,600	1,176	45	1,424	55
Porters (unspecified)	3,521	2,563	73	958	27
Overseers (unspecified)	181	122	67	59	33
Watchmen	595	427	72	168	28
Bill stickers and placard carriers	71	51	72	20	28
Scavengers	54	42	78	12	22
Beggars	2,586	2,405	93	181	7
Brothel keepers	7	7	100	0	0
Coffin makers	12	11	92	1	8
Undertakers	26	20	77	6	23
Total	412,907	353,340	86	59,567	14
General Total of Occupations	1,844,793	1,443,685	78	401,108	22

Excess of Female Life Expectancy at Birth Over Male Life Expectancy (in years)

Period	Twenty-six Counties	Northern Ireland	England and Wales	United States
1870–2	1.3	N/A	3.2	N/A
1880–2	0.5	N/A	3.5	N/A
1890–2	0.1	-0.6	3.7	N/A
1900–02	0.3	-4.0	3.9	2.9
1910-12	0.5	-3.2	3.9	3.4
1925–7	0.5	0.7	4.0	2.8

Source: Compiled from Robert E. Kennedy, Jr, *The Irish: Emigration, Marriage, and Fertility* (Berkeley: University of California Press, 1973), 55 and 57, tables 9 and 10.

Permanent Residence of Irish-Born Persons, 1841–1921 (in thousands)

| Year | Population of Ireland (32 Counties) including non-Irish born | Irish-born living in Ireland | Irish-born living in U.S.A., Canada, Australia, and G.B. | Total Irish-born (with exclusions noted in column 3) | Irish-born persons living outside Ireland | | | Great Britain | | | Persons living outside Ireland as % of total of Irish-born (with exclusions noted in column 3) |
					U.S.A.	Canada	Australia	England and Wales	Scotland	Total Great Britain	
1841	8,175	8,141	537 (excluding U.S.A., Australia)	8,678	N/A	122	N/A	289	126	415	6.2
1851	6,552	6,502	1,916 (excluding Australia)	8,418	962	227	N/A	520	207	727	22.8
1861	5,799	5,721	2,703 (excluding Australia)	8,424	1,611	286	N/A	602	204	806	32.1
1871	5,412	5,307	2,854 (excluding Australia)	8,161	1,856	223	N/A	567	208	775	35.0
1881	5,175	5,062	3,035	8,097	1,855	186	213	562	219	781	37.5
1891	4,705	4,581	2,901	7,482	1,872	149	227	458	195	653	38.8
1901	4,459	4,327	2,533	6,860	1,615	102	184	427	205	632	36.9
1911	4,390	4,233	2,134	6,367	1,352	93	139	375	175	550	27.6
1921	4,354(est.)	N/A	1,759	N/A	1,037	93	105	365	159	524	N/A

Source: Derived from *Commission on Emigration and Other Population Problems, 1948–1954* (Dublin: Stationery Office, 1954), 126, table 95.

Emigration from Ireland, 1815–1920, Overseas Only (i.e. Excluding Emigration to Great Britain)

Period	To U.S.A.	% of total	to Canada	% of total	to Australasia	% of total	Other overseas countries	% of total	Total overseas emigration (note exclusions)
1825-30	50,040	38.7	79,142	61.3	N/A	N/A	N/A	N/A	129,182
1831-40	171,087	39.1	262,004	59.8	4,662	1.1	N/A	N/A	437,753
1841-50	908,292	70.0	362,738	27.9	22,825	1.8	4,539	0.3	1,298,394
1851-60	989,880	81.4	118,118	9.7	101,541	8.3	6,726	0.6	1,216,265
1861-70	690,845	84.4	40,079	4.9	82,917	10.1	4,741	0.6	818,582
1871-80	449,549	82.8	25,783	4.8	61,946	11.4	5,425	1.0	542,703
1881-90	626,604	85.3	44,505	6.1	55,476	7.5	7,890	1.1	734,475
1891-1900	427,301	92.7	10,648	2.3	11,448	2.5	11,520	2.5	460,917
1901-10	418,995	86.3	38,238	7.9	11,885	2.4	16,343	3.4	485,461
1911-20	172,490	75.3	32,857	14.3	15,429	6.7	8,463	3.7	229,239

Source: See note 11 to chapter 3.

Male Adult Occupational Types and Place of Birth, Australia, 1921

Place of Birth	Em- ployers	Self- Employed	Working without wages	Wages or salaried	Un- employed	Total for whom information available
Ireland	8.5%	19.1%	0.3%	59.9%	12.2%	100.00%
Scotland	7.6	13.9	0.5	68.1	9.9	100.00
England (excluding Wales)	7.3	16.9	0.5	65.8	9.5	100.00
All European-born (including British Isles)	7.8	17.7	0.4	64.1	10.0	100.00
Australian-born	7.3	16.6	2.2	66.5	7.4	100.00
Total population	7.4	17.0	1.8	65.9	7.9	100.00

Source: Derived from Census of the Commonwealth of Australia, 1921, Part I, 134–5.

Occupation and Place of Birth, Males, New South Wales, 1901

Occupation	Australia and New Zealand	England and Wales	Scotland	Ireland	Entire population
1. Governmental	8,814	3,661	651	1,397	10,809
2. Religion, charity and education	12,888	4,106	867	1,439	16,046
3. Lodging and domestic service	10,167	4,485	828	1,790	20,128
4. Finance and property	5,328	2,245	460	658	8,985
5. Dealing in quality artifacts	2,566	965	161	128	4,144
6. Textile sales	4,568	1,397	240	353	6,957
7. Food and drink sales	13,131	3,034	527	965	19,522
8. Sale of animal products	4,455	724	167	305	5,984
9. Fuel and light sales	1,577	246	42	153	2,084
10. Dealing in minerals	1,480	397	87	85	2,136
11. General merchants	10,151	2,813	587	795	16,689
12. Gamblers	316	71	4	4	424
13. Storage	126	57	6	16	172
14. Communications and transport	37,223	9,437	2,576	3,905	42,822
15. Manufacture of quality artifacts	18,420	5,367	1,479	863	26,346
16. Textile manufacture	6,312	1,724	407	490	9,451
17. Food and drink manufacture	8,233	1,787	486	544	11,638
18. Manufacture of animal and vegetable products	4,397	636	114	198	5,546
19. Jewelry, glass, metalwork manufacture	11,398	2,570	661	494	15,336
20. Fuel and energy production	1,147	539	133	193	2,012
21. Construction	22,374	8,358	2,013	3,132	36,898
22. Morticians and knackers	775	260	51	192	1,278

Occupation	Australia and New Zealand	England and Wales	Scotland	Ireland	Entire population
23. "Imperfectly defined industrial pursuits"	9,642	2,026	502	1,297	14,187
24. Farming	121,306	20,056	5,425	9,908	168,212
25. Independent means	897	1,419	320	702	3,597
Total economically active	317,691	78,379	18,794	30,016	451,403

Source: Derived from *Results of a Census of New South Wales, 1901*, 770–6.

Occupation and Religion, Males, New South Wales, 1901

Occupation	Catholic	Anglican	Methodist	Presbyterian	Entire population
1. Governmental	3,009	7,389	893	1,655	10,809
2. Religion, charity and education	3,889	9,218	1,971	2,680	16,046
3. Lodging and domestic service	5,840	9,445	923	1,571	20,128
4. Finance and property	1,159	4,878	760	1,134	8,985
5. Dealing in quality artifacts	616	1,875	406	415	4,144
6. Textile sales	1,239	3,001	812	698	6,957
7. Food and drink sales	4,629	8,794	1,943	1,645	19,522
8. Sale of animal products	1,589	2,800	437	586	5,984
9. Fuel and light sales	562	1,054	201	108	2,084
10. Dealing in minerals	363	932	231	276	2,136
11. General merchants	3,320	7,231	1,444	1,546	16,689
12. Gamblers	150	186	11	16	424
13. Storage	40	130	14	15	172
14. Communications and transport	15,562	26,923	4,607	5,599	42,822
15. Manufacture of quality artifacts	5,101	13,010	2,789	3,178	26,346
16. Textile manufacture	2,298	3,930	949	832	9,451
17. Food and drink manufacture	2,702	5,380	1,184	1,243	11,638
18. Manufacture of animal and vegetable products	1,387	2,916	436	42	5,546
19. Jewelry, glass, metalwork manufacture	3,364	7,365	1,805	1,517	15,336
20. Fuel and energy production	423	994	206	215	2,012
21. Construction	9,488	17,238	3,310	3,799	36,898
22. Morticians and knackers	470	522	127	88	1,278

Occupation	Catholic	Anglican	Methodist	Presbyterian	Entire population
23. "Imperfectly defined industrial pursuits"	4,519	6,473	1,046	1,059	14,187
24. Farming	43,847	73,483	17,878	17,859	168,212
25. Independent means	688	1,747	253	419	3,597
Total economically active	116,254	216,914	44,636	48,574	451,403

Source: Derived from Results of a Census of New South Wales, 1901, 786–93.

Religious Persuasion and Average Number of Children, Australia, 1911
(Cross-Tabulated by Age of Wives at Census)

Age of Woman	"Roman Catholic"	"Catholic (undefined)"	Anglican	Presbyterian	Methodist	Entire population
Under 14	–	–	–	–	–	.00
14	.40	–	.17	1.00	–	.28
15	.33	.00	.36	.17	.20	.27
16	.45	.75	.48	.41	.46	.50
17	.54	.61	.62	.52	.61	.58
18	.68	.60	.68	.72	.71	.68
19	.81	.81	.83	.86	.85	.82
20	.96	.99	.97	.95	.87	.95
21–4	1.35	1.43	1.35	1.24	1.23	1.31
25–9	2.03	2.20	2.04	1.85	1.94	1.99
30–4	2.92	3.03	2.87	2.65	2.88	2.85
35–9	3.88	3.87	3.74	3.49	3.86	3.75
40–4	4.84	4.89	4.52	4.26	4.71	4.57
45–9	5.57	5.67	5.15	4.95	5.42	5.25
50–4	6.29	6.30	5.84	5.54	6.17	5.92
55–9	6.76	6.70	6.37	6.17	6.75	6.44
60–4	6.86	6.64	6.72	6.59	7.11	6.75
65–9	6.96	6.56	7.00	7.04	7.38	7.03
70–4	6.76	7.83	7.05	7.12	7.40	7.02
75–9	6.75	5.98	6.92	6.82	7.92	6.98
80–4	5.73	5.80	6.91	7.08	7.16	6.60
85–9	6.30	8.00	6.15	6.19	6.54	6.44
90 and Over	5.86	3.50	5.31	5.00	6.86	5.35

Source: Census of the Commonwealth of Australia, 1911, I: 284.

Place of Birth and Average Number of Children, Australia, 1911
(Cross-Tabulated by Age of Wives at Census)

Age of Wives	Australian-born	United Kingdom-born	Entire Population
Under 14	.00	–	.00
14	.29	.00	.28
15	.27	.00	.27
16	.50	1.00	.50
17	.59	.29	.58
18	.68	.47	.68
19	.83	.50	.82
20	.95	.72	.95
21–24	1.32	.99	1.31
25–29	2.02	1.71	1.99
30–34	2.89	2.56	2.85
35–39	3.80	3.50	3.75
40–44	4.63	4.34	4.57
45–49	5.33	4.97	5.25
50–54	6.10	5.48	5.92
55–59	6.78	6.01	6.44
60–64	7.28	6.40	6.75
65–69	7.75	6.70	7.03
70–74	7.88	6.90	7.02
75–79	7.72	6.96	5.98
80–84	7.55	6.59	6.60
85–89	7.29	6.43	6.44
90 and over	9.00	5.47	5.35

Source: Compiled from Census of the Commonwealth of Australia, 1911, I: 282.

APPENDIX O

Migrants from Irish Ports to British North
America as a Percentage of All United Kingdom
Migrants to British North America
1825–52
(unrevised data)

Year	Percentage
1825	78.3
1826	81.8
1827	72.2
1828	55.4
1829	57.9
1830	63.3
1831	70.6
1832	55.9
1833	60.5
1834	71.4
1835	60.7
1836	56.6
1837	75.2
1838	49.9
1839	71.0
1840	74.1
1841	63.1
1842	61.7
1843	46.3
1844	54.1
1845	62.7
1846	73.1
1847	65.0
1848	67.1
1849	64.2
1850	60.0
1851	56.2
1852	53.8

Source: Derived from N.H. Carrier and J.R. Jeffery, External Migration. A Study of Available Statistics, 1815–1890 (London: HMSO, 1953), 95. These figures actually understate considerably the Irish percentage because many Irish migrants sailed from English and Scottish ports. See Akenson, The Irish in Ontario: A Study in Rural History, 14–15 and 29–30 on necessary upward revisions.

Total Irish Migration from All United Kingdom
Ports to British North America as Percentage of
Total U.K. Migration to British North America,
1853–71

Year	Percentage
1853	70.5
1854	64.2
1855	37.9
1856	38.5
1857	26.5
1858	33.2
1859	44.2
1860	43.9
1861	46.7
1862	37.3
1863	40.8
1864	49.3
1865	49.8
1866	39.3
1867	37.7
1868	29.9
1869	15.8
1870	10.6
1871	12.3

Source: Derived from Carrier and Jeffery, External Migration, 95.

Linguistic Preferences of the Irish Population, 1851-1911

	Leinster	Munster	Ulster	Connaught	Ireland
Year 1851					
Total population	1,672,738	1,857,736	2,011,880	1,010,031	6,552,385
No. who spoke Irish only	200	146,336	35,783	137,283	319,602
% of total pop. who spoke only Irish	.01	7.9	1.8	13.6	4.9
No. who spoke Irish and English	58,976	669,449	100,693	375,566	1,204,684
Total who could speak Irish	59,176	815,785	136,476	512,849	1,524,286
% of pop. who could speak Irish	3.5	43.9	6.8	50.8	23.3
Year 1861					
Total population	1,457,635	1,513,558	1,914,236	913,135	5,798,564
No. who spoke Irish only	238	62,039	23,180	77,818	163,275
% of total pop. who spoke only Irish	.02	4.1	1.2	8.5	2.1
No. who spoke Irish and English	35,466	483,492	91,639	331,664	942,261
Total who could speak Irish	35,704	545,531	114,819	409,482	1,105,536
% of pop. who could speak Irish	2.5	36.3	6.0	44.9	19.1
Year 1871					
Total population	1,339,451	1,393,485	1,833,228	846,213	5,412,377
No. who spoke Irish only	374	33,967	19,067	50,154	103,562
% of total pop. who spoke only Irish	.02	2.4	1.0	5.9	1.9
No. who spoke Irish and English	15,873	352,527	65,856	280,057	714,313
Total who could speak Irish	16,247	386,494	84,923	330,211	817,875
% of pop. who could speak Irish	1.2	27.7	4.6	39.0	15.1
Year 1881					
Total population	1,278,989	1,331,115	1,743,075	821,657	5,174,836
No. who spoke Irish only	50	18,422	12,360	33,335	64,167
% of total pop. who spoke only Irish	.004	1.4	.7	4.1	1.3

	Leinster	Munster	Ulster	Connaught	Ireland
No. who spoke Irish and English	27,402	427,344	98,163	332,856	885,765
Total who could speak Irish	27,452	445,766	110,523	336,191	949,932
% of pop. who could speak Irish	2.1	33.5	6.3	44.6	18.2
Year 1891					
Total population	1,187,760	1,172,402	1,619,814	724,774	4,704,750
No. who spoke Irish only	8	9,060	7,053	22,071	38,192
% of total pop. who spoke only Irish	.0007	.8	.4	3.0	.8
No. who spoke Irish and English	13,669	298,573	77,099	252,712	642,053
Total who could speak Irish	13,677	307,633	84,152	274,783	680,245
% of pop. who could speak Irish	1.2	26.2	5.2	37.8	14.5
Year 1901					
Total population	1,152,829	1,076,188	1,582,826	646,932	4,458,775
No. who spoke Irish only	7	4,387	4,456	12,103	20,953
% of total pop. who spoke only Irish	.0006	.4	.3	1.9	.5
No. who spoke Irish and English	26,429	271,881	88,402	233,477	620,189
Total who could speak Irish	26,436	276,268	92,858	245,580	641,142
% of pop. who could speak Irish	2.3	25.7	5.9	38.0	14.4
Year 1911					
Total population	1,162,044	1,035,495	1,581,696	610,984	4,390,219
No. who spoke Irish only	2	2,766	4,737	9,367	16,872
% of total pop. who spoke only Irish	.0002	.3	.3	1.5	.4
No. who spoke Irish and English	40,223	225,728	91,902	207,720	565,573
Total who could speak Irish	40,225	228,494	96,639	217,087	582,445
% of pop. who could speak Irish	3.5	22.1	6.1	35.5	13.3

Source: Derived from *Census of Ireland for the year 1851*, pt. vi: *General Report, etc.*, xlvii [2134], H.C. 1856, xxxi; *Census of Ireland, 1871* pt. iii: *General Report, etc.*, 189 [C 1377], H.C. 1876, lxxxi; *Census of Ireland, 1901*, pt. ii: *General Report, etc.*, 170, 575; *Census of Ireland for the year 1911, General Report*, 46–7 [CD. 6663], H.C. 1912–13, cxviii.

Notes

1 Jean de la Bruyère, *Caractères* (originally published 1688, new ed., Paris: Nelson [1911]), 417.

2 On the near-identity of Catholic and Protestant emigration rates, see the text, 45, chapter 2, n. 2, and chapter 3, nn. 9, 10.

3 There is no trustworthy modern accounting of the losses in the 1920–2 period in Belfast. A well-informed, but not entirely unbiased work is *Fifty Years of Ulster, 1890–1940* (Belfast: The Irish News, 1941) by T.J. Campbell, sometime editor of the *Irish News*, Belfast's leading Catholic newspaper. See esp. 25–30, 116–17. The estimate of 9,000 Catholics forced from employment was put forward by Michael Collins to the United Kingdom government on 27 March 1922 (Ibid., 117).

4 Patrick J. Buckland, "Southern Unionism, 1885–1922," (Ph.D. thesis, Queen's University of Belfast, 1969), 585, 589. This excellent thesis is in some ways more serviceable than the two-volume published version. For reports of outrages during the period 1920–2, *The Church of Ireland Gazette* is particularly useful. See especially 16 June 1922, 1 December 1922, and 12 January 1923. See also the condemnation by Daniel Cohalan, Roman Catholic bishop of Cork, on the murder of Protestants in his diocese (*Irish Catholic Directory*, 1923, entry for 30 April 1922), 566.

On Protestant insecurities, see Patrick J. Buckland, *Irish Unionism, 1885–1923. A documentary history* (Belfast: Her Majesty's Stationery Office, 1973), 366–7, 378, 383.

5 This decline of about 32.5 percent of the Protestant population occurred at a time when the Catholic population of the twenty-six counties was declining by only 2.2 percent (Patrick J. Buckland, *The Anglo-Irish and the New Ireland* (Dublin: Gill and MacMillan, 1972), 285.

Free State politicians and their historians have tried to argue that this sharp decline in the Protestant population was almost entirely ascribable to persons who had "garrison" positions leaving Ireland. However, research has clearly established that, at most, the withdrawal of the British garrisons and its dependents accounted for only one-quarter of the Protestant decline. See Kurt Bowen, *Ireland's Privileged Minority* (Kingston and Montreal: McGill-Queen's University Press, 1983), 20–5.

6 Malcolm P.A. Macourt, "The religious inquiry in the Irish Census of 1861," *Irish Historical Studies* 21 (Sept. 1978): 168–71.

7 Ibid., 171.

8 See the succinct, and erudite, *Anglo-Saxons and Celts: A Study of Anti-Irish Prejudice in Victorian England* by L.P. Curtis, Jr (Bridgeport, Conn.: Conference on British Studies, 1968).

9 Collier Books Edition (New York, 1961), trans. by Joseph W. Swain, 24.

10 R. Kenneth Carty, *Party and Parish Pump: Electoral Politics in Ireland* (Waterloo: Wilfrid Laurier University Press, 1981), xiii.

11 Patrick J. O'Farrell, *Ireland's English Question: Anglo-Irish Relations, 1534–1970* (London: Batsford, 1971), quotation, 303.

12 See also Samuel Clark's "The importance of agrarian classes: agrarian class structure and collective action in nineteenth-century Ireland," *British Journal of Sociology* 29 (March 1978): 22–40; and "The political mobilization of Irish farmers," *Canadian Review of Sociology and Anthropology* 12 (November 1975): 483–99.

13 Kevin O'Neill, *Family and Farm in Pre-Famine Ireland: The Parish of Killashandra* (Madison: University of Wisconsin Press, 1984).

14 See especially A.C. Hepburn's "Work, Class, and Religion in Belfast, 1871–1911," *Irish Economic and Social History* 10 (1983): 33–50; see also, "Catholics in Northern Ireland, 1850–1921: The Urbanization of A Minority," in A.C. Hepburn ed., *Minorities in History* (London: 1978), 84–101.

15 Of the spate of Marxist and neo-Marxist books of the era, to my mind the most successful (if not entirely convincing) was Liam de Paor's *Divided Ulster* (Middlesex: Penguin Books, 1970). Its stance is clearly signposted in its opening two paragraphs (13): "In Northern Ireland Catholics are Blacks who happen to have white skins. This is not a truth. It is an oversimplification and too facile an analogy. But it is a better oversimplification than that which sees the struggle and conflict in Northern Ireland in terms of religion. The Northern Ireland problem is a colonial problem, and the 'racial' distinction (and it is actually imagined as racial) between the colonists and the natives is expressed in terms of religion."

16 The extracts and documents found in the Soviet publication, *Karl Marx and Friedrich Engels: Ireland and the Irish Question* (Moscow: Progress Publishers, 1971) show that both men had read very widely, if selectively, in the contemporary literature on Ireland. Their motives in doing so are impercipient: Marx read everything in any case. I do not take seriously

Owen Dudley Edwards' suggestion that Engels' attachment to his various Irish mistresses gave him an interest in Ireland that was lacking in his English contemporaries who did not experience similar solace. (Owen Dudley Edwards, *The Sins of Our Fathers: Roots of Conflict in Northern Ireland* (Dublin: Gill and Macmillan, 1970), 139.

17 Engels in *Der Schweizerische Republikaner* no. 39 (27 June 1843), translated in *Karl Marx and Friedrich Engels*, 33–4.

18 Engels to Marx, 1 November 1869, ibid., 274. In what one assumes was an intentional music-hall nonsequiter, Engels concluded, "in Ireland it is particularly bad. That is also why the press is so terribly lousy."

19 Sidney and Beatrice Webb to Graham Wallas, 29 July 1892, quoted in Curtis, *Anglo-Saxons and Celts*, 63. Curtis notes (134n47) that Sidney wrote the bulk of the letter but that the last ten "lethal words" were added by Beatrice.

20 One of the most notable, and disappointing, continuations of the tradition is found in E.P. Thompson, *The Making of the English Working Class* (first edition, London: Victor Gollancz, 1963; revised edition, Harmondsworth: Penguin Books, 1968). See, for example, 469–85 for an unpleasant mixture of stereotyping and smarmy "understanding," and certainly no adornment to an otherwise admirable pioneering study.

In Canada, the work of H. Clare Pentland exhibited the same interplay of dialectic and racial-cultural stereotyping, but at a much less sophisticated literary level. On this, see my essay, "H. Clare Pentland, The Irish, and the New Canadian Social History," in D.H. Akenson, *Being Had: Historians, Evidence and the Irish in North America* (Toronto: P.D. Meany, 1985), 109–42.

21 Williams Forbes Adams, *Ireland and the Irish Emigration to the New World from 1815 to the Famine* (New Haven: Yale University Press, 1932). Quotation, 64–5.

22 A particularly unfortunate example is *The Irish Mind: Exploring Intellectual Traditions*, edited by Richard Kearney (Dublin: Wolfhound Press, 1985). In this case the stereotyping and latent prejudice are anti-Protestant. For a devastating (but, nevertheless, excessively kind) comment see the review by Conor Cruise O'Brien in the *Times Literary Supplement*, 1 November 1985.

NOTES TO CHAPTER TWO

1 Kingsley Amis, *One Fat Englishman* (Harmondsworth: Penguin Books edition, 1966), 120.

2 These three measures are the ones which are most promising. There are actually many more potential tests of significant Protestant-Catholic differences, but one has to live within the limits of Irish demographic data.

Three possible measures of religious differences that are not discussed in the text of chapter 2 deserve mention: comparative crime rates, comparative propensity to emigrate, and comparative literacy data.

The Irish authorities did not collect criminal data by religious affiliation. The linkages necessary in the tens of thousands of individual cases would be impossible to make. That throws one back on various indirect measures of criminality and religion (and other factors), and I am skeptical about the value of the various available proxies. In any case, the most sophisticated study yet done along these lines has shown that religious differences in crime rates were not significant. This is David Miller's "The Geography of Discontent in Pre-Famine Ireland," which was delivered as a paper at the American Committee for Irish Studies annual conference, 25 April 1985. (It is at present being revised for publication.) This study shows that although on the surface there was an apparent propensity for Catholics to engage in criminal behaviour relatively more frequently than did Protestants, when regression analysis of several variables is conducted, religion is shown to have no explanatory robustness whatsoever.

The other reason that Irish crime rates are not used is that what crime rates really indicate when they are analyzed, either by religion or by ethnicity, is simple: who was in charge, and that is something we already know. In one of the few historical studies of crime that attempts to control for the hegemony factor, John Weaver has used court records to show that the Upper-Canadian judicial system was biased in the nineteenth century against certain groups. Specifically, the Irish Catholics more frequently were convicted and more severely sentenced for the same behaviour than were members of other groups. It seems likely that the same thing held for nineteenth- and early twentieth-century Ireland where the justice system strongly overrepresented Protestant interests. (See John Weaver, "Moral Order and Repression in Upper Canada: The Case of the Criminal Justice System in the Gore District and Hamilton, 1831–1851," *Ontario History* 87 (Sept. 1986): 176–207.

Concerning comparative calculations of the propensity to emigrate (a) there can be no direct breakdowns by religious groups and (b) what can be inferred does not show a significant difference. The information given in Appendixes A, B and C implies that all religious groups experienced a population decline and this indicates that, in common, they had a rate of emigration that exceeded the rate of increase within their respective groups.

One suspects (but, again, cannot prove directly), that Catholics had a somewhat higher mortality rate than did Protestants (Catholics being relatively overrepresented in the lower occupational groups) and that, therefore, the actual emigration rates of Protestants and Catholics were even closer than might at first appear from examining the data on population decline within each group. (For a useful calculation of intercensal percentage change of each denomination, from 1865 onwards, see Robert E. Kennedy Jr, *The Irish: Emigration, Marriage and Fertility* (Berkeley: University of California Press, 1973), 112, table 36.

As for comparative material on literacy rates, these are not pursued because (a) in my experience literacy data are among the least reliable material collected by the governmental officials and (b) in any case, I once wrote a long book, one of the major themes of which is that the Irish Catholics showed an avidity for learning that was remarkable and in no way less salient than that of the Protestant Irish, even the Ulster Presbyterians, who, in popular mythology, are believed to be particularly keen on education. See D.H. Akenson, *The Irish Education Experiment. The National System of Education in the Nineteenth Century* (London: Routledge and Kegan Paul, and Toronto: University of Toronto Press, 1970).

3 Whether Irish Catholic and Irish Protestant farmers actually farmed differently in the nineteenth century is a tantalizing, albeit unanswerable, question at present. (The digging-with-the-other-foot conceit of Irish folklore may, indeed, point to an important historical reality.) Almost certainly, Catholic farms were smaller and the land generally poorer (a legacy of the eighteenth-century penal laws), so inevitably there were differences associated with these factors. But, for the cultural historian who is interested in causal factors, the question is: on farms of equal size and of equal soil quality, did the two groups act differently? The best hope for answering this question would be to conduct a series of parish-by-parish microstudies.

4 An especially useful edition was published in 1930 (London: Unwin), translated by Talcott Parsons and with a foreword by R.H. Tawney; it included an Introduction written by Weber.

5 The 1938 Penguin Books edition has a valuable reflective new preface by Tawney. It contains a strong defence of Weber against the charge that he ignored the "economic" factor and that he had substituted a simplistic cultural determinism for the equally misleading materialistic determinism. In fact, Weber, like Tawney, argued for the complex interplay of both culture and economic structure.

6 David McClelland, *The Achieving Society* (Princeton: D. Van Nostrand, 1961). Quotation, 8.

7 Ibid., 19. The italics are mine.

8 David S. Landes, *The Unbound Prometheus: Technological Change and Industrial Development in Western Europe from 1750 to the Present* (Cambridge: Cambridge University Press, 1969), 21. For a succinct summary of the Weberian tradition of emphasis upon rationality and the "Protestant ethic," see 22–4.

9 The central tenets of Irish-American literature (of which I am very skepti-

cal) are discussed in D.H. Akenson, "An Agnostic View of the Histori-
ography of the Irish-Americans," in *Labour/Le Travail* 14 (Fall 1984): 123–59.
It is reprinted in Akenson, *Being Had: Historians, Evidence, and the Irish in
North America* (Toronto: P.D. Meany Co., Inc., 1985), 37–76.

10 J.J. Lee, *The Modernisation of Irish Society, 1848–1918* (Dublin: Gill and Mac-
Millan, 1973). Quotation, 16.

11 Ibid.

12 I am assuming that the reader is familiar with the general outlines of the
penal code. The classic description is W.E.H. Lecky's *A History of Ireland in
the Eighteenth Century* 2 vols. (London: Green and Co., new impression,
1913), 1: 136–70. At present, the standard authority is Maureen Wall's *The
Penal Laws 1691–1760: Church and State from the Treaty of Limerick to the Acces-
sion of George III* (Dundalk: Wm Tempest, 1961). This work recently has
been called into question by Sean Connolly who questions Wall's view
that the penal code was not aimed at converting Catholics to Protestantism, but instead at maintaining an economical ascendancy. (See S.J. Connolly, "Religion and History," *Irish Economic and Social History* 10 (1983):
esp. 73–9. Connolly points to the important, but ignored, work of R.E.
Burns, "The Irish Popery Laws: A Study of Eighteenth-Century Legislation and Behaviour," *Review of Politics* 24 (October 1962): 485–508. See also
Burns's "The Irish Penal Code and Some of its Historians," *Review of Politics* 21 (January 1959): 276–99.

13 W. Arthur Lewis, *Racial Conflict and Economic Development* (Cambridge:
Harvard University Press, 1985), 74.

14 As for censuses that might reflect pre-Famine patterns, the manuscript
returns for only one parish exist for 1841. See Kevin O'Neill, *Family and
Farm in Pre-Famine Ireland. The Parish of Killashandra* (Madison: University
of Wisconsin Press, 1984), for their character; for 1851, there are enumerators' books for four County Antrim parishes. See V. Morgan and W.
Macafee, "Irish Population in the Pre-Famine Period: Evidence from
County Antrim," *Economic History Review*, 2 ser. 37 (May 1984): 182–96.

15 A.C. Hepburn, "Work, Class and Religion in Belfast, 1871–1911," *Irish Economic and Social History* 10 (1983): 33–50.

16 A melancholy coda to Hepburn's early twentieth-century work is found
in his article "Employment and Religion in Belfast, 1901–1951," in R.J.
Cormack and R.D. Osborne, eds., *Religion, Education and Employment:
Aspects of Equal Opportunity in Northern Ireland* (Belfast: Appletree Press,
1983), wherein he shows that, if anything, the Catholic position declined
in the first half of the twentieth century (see especially 48, table 3:4).

17 R.L. Miller in "Religion and Occupational Mobility," studied post-World
War II patterns of occupational mobility in Northern Ireland, using
screening data from 2,416 cases, and concluded that "looking at religion,
the net mobility patterns of Protestants and Roman Catholics are not sig-

nificantly different. So, given similar origins and equivalent occupation distributions at present, the mobility experiences of the grouping would be the same. *That is, there is nothing inherent about being either Protestant or Roman Catholic that in itself predisposes one towards better or worse chances of mobility"* (italics mine). (Miller, in Cormack and Osborne, eds., *Religion, Education and Employment,* 75.) As Miller correctly adds, although "net mobility" of the two groups was the same, they did not start off at the same point.

One cannot project this study of the recent past back into the nineteenth century, but Miller's results would form the basis of what seems to me the most reasonable set of hypotheses to test concerning nineteenth-century Ireland (if one had the data!): that the Catholics, because of structural discrimination started lower on the ladder, but that there was nothing in Catholicism that inhibited their rising as rapidly, relative to their starting position, as did Protestants.

18 Cormac O'Grada, "Did Ulster Catholics always have Larger Families?" *Irish Economic and Social History* 12 (1985): 79-80.

19 Brendan M. Walsh, *Some Irish Population Problems Reconsidered* (Dublin: The Economic and Social Research Institute, 1968), 11, tables 9a and 9b.

20 O'Grada, "Ulster Catholics," 80.

21 Particularly tantalizing, in the period 1926-36, are the facts that the Anglicans in the twenty-six counties were shown to have markedly lower birth rates and markedly higher death rates than the Catholics. These differences, though, probably had nothing to do with cultural factors and a great deal to do with the heavy emigration of Protestants from the Free State after independence (see chapter 1 on this phenomenon). In all probability, this emigration left the Church of Ireland population with a relatively large number of older people, thus explaining both the lower birth rate and the higher death rate. For the figures, see Kurt Bowen, *Protestants in a Catholic State: Ireland's Privileged Minority* (Kingston and Montreal: McGill-Queens University Press, 1983), 29, table 4.

22 O'Grada, "Ulster Catholics," 86.

23 Ibid.

24 Hepburn, "Work, Class and Religion," 52. He is referring to the study entitled "Industrial Society: the Structure of Belfast 1901," by A.C. Hepburn and Brenda Collins, in Peter Roebuck, ed., *Plantation to Partition* (Belfast: Blackstaff Press, 1981).

25 O'Grada, "Ulster Catholics," 86.

26 A close study of the one parish for which there is full pre-Famine census data, Killashandra, County Cavan, showed a striking difference between farm labourers and farm operators in family size, as did O'Grada's study. But this was in the opposite direction: farm labourers had smaller families than did their social superiors. See O'Neill, *Family and Farm in Pre-*

Famine Ireland, 167–77, esp. table 5:1. If this has any significance as far as Protestant-Catholic differentials are concerned, it would tend to mean that Protestants, being generally better off, would have been influenced in the direction of having larger families. This would press them *away* from the mid-twentieth century phenomenon of Protestant families being smaller. Unhappily, O'Neill, in his otherwise excellent study, does not deal with religion as one of his categories for analysis.

27 The terms of reference for the debate on pre-Famine Irish family structure were determined by the pioneering work of Kenneth Connell, and anyone reading his work can only be impressed with the skill and verve with which he navigated through an area that was, before his explorations, terra incognita. See especially his: *Irish Peasant Society* (Oxford: Clarendon Press, 1968), 113–63; "The Colonisation of Waste Land in Ireland, 1780–1845," in *Economic History Review*, rev., 2nd ser. 3 (1950): 44–71; "Some Unsettled Problems in English and Irish Population History, 1750–1845," *Irish Historical Studies* 7 (Sept. 1951): 225–34; "The History of the Potato," *Economic History Review*, 2nd ser. 3 (1951): 388–95; "The Land Legislation and Irish Social Life," *Economic History Review*, 2nd ser. 11 (1958): 1–7; "Peasant Marriage in Ireland: Its Structure and Development Since the Famine," *Economic History Review*, 2nd ser. 14 (1962): 502–23; *The Population of Ireland, 1750–1845* (Oxford: Clarendon Press, 1950); "The Population of Ireland in the Eighteenth Century," *Economic History Review*, 1st ser. 16 (1946): 111–24.

28 For a succinct summation of these historiographical trends, see J.M. Goldstrom, "Irish Agriculture and the Great Famine," in J.M. Goldstrom and L.A. Clarkson, eds., *Irish Population, Economy and Society* (Oxford: Clarendon Press, 1981), 155–8, 171.

29 The classic studies on the manner in which the Irish stem family system operated are: Conrad M. Arensberg and Solon T. Kimball, *Family and Community in Ireland* (Cambridge: Harvard University Press, 1940), and Conrad M. Arensberg, *The Irish Countryman: An Anthropological Study* (New York: MacMillan, 1937).

30 On the sources of data on age of marriage, see Robert E. Kennedy Jr, *The Irish*, 139*n*–140*n*. Data on the marriage age of women are illuminating. In 1864, 18 percent were under twenty-one when first married; the figure for 1911 was 5 percent. In 1864 71 percent of women were under twenty-five when first married; by 1911 the figure was down to 51 percent. (See Connell, "Catholicism and Marriage in the Century After the Famine," in *Irish Peasant Society*, 113n3).

31 Ibid., 140–5.

32 Ibid., 113–61.

33 The controversial relationship between celibacy and mental illness in modern Ireland is discussed in Nancy Scheper-Hughes, *Saints, Scholars,*

and Schizophrenics: Mental Illness in Rural Ireland (Berkeley: University of California Press, 1979). For comparative diagnostic data, some of them dating back to 1911, see 65–74. Scheper-Hughes' study has not been well-received in Ireland. Nor has the work on sexual repression in certain Irish "museum areas" on the west coast, conducted by John Messenger. See Messenger's comments on both the character of repression and on the resistance of Irish scholars to acknowledge its existence in his "Sex and Repression in Irish Folk Communities," in Donald S. Marshall and Robert C. Suggs, eds., *Human Sexual Behavior: Variations in the Ethnographic Spectrum* (Philadelphia: Basic Books, 1971), 3–37. Findings of scholars such as Scheper-Hughes and Messenger often are mistakenly taken as an attack on the churches. However, as Joseph Lee notes, "it seems probable that only the consolation offered by the Churches to the celibate victims of economic man prevented lunacy rates, which quadrupled between 1850 and 1914, from rising even more rapidly." (Lee, *Modernisation of Irish Society*, 6).

34 Irish marital fertility was at a high of 307 legitimate births per 1,000 married women aged from 15 to 44 years in 1871. Fertility declined thereafter until 1946 (in southern Ireland) when it levelled off. Even so, in 1961 the southern Irish marital fertility rate was as high as that of El Salvador, Panama, and Chile, nations that exhibited at that time some of the highest population growth rates in the world. See Walsh, *Irish Population Problems*, 5–7 and Kennedy, *The irish*, 174–6.

35 This population decline was a matter of grave domestic social concern and of some international embarrassment to the government of the Irish Republic and in the 1940s and '50s a major public study of the problem was conducted: *Commission on Emigration and Other Population Problems, 1948–1954* (Dublin: Stationery Office, 1954). Various influential Irish clergymen, academics, and writers felt the same concern and contributed to the somewhat stunned volume edited by John A. O'Brien, *The Vanishing Irish, The Enigma of the Modern World* (London: W.H. Allen, 1954).

36 Walsh, *Irish Population Problems*, 9.

37 Given that nineteenth-century Ireland was overwhelmingly an agricultural economy, the most important question related to social class is whether families of farm labourers or farm operators had a higher birth rate. O'Neill's work, on pre-Famine Killashandra, showed a significantly large family size among farmers (168, table 5:1); O'Grada, with a larger sample in Ulster for 1911 found the opposite ("Ulster Catholics," 83). And, census data for the Irish Republic in 1961 showed a virtual identity in marriage and family patterns as between farmers and "other agriculture" (meaning labourers). See Walsh, *Irish Population Problems*, 4, table 3, and 13, table 11. The case, then, is very much an open one.

38 S.J. Connolly, "Illegitimacy and Pre-Nuptial Pregnancy in Ireland before

1864: The Evidence of Some Catholic Parish Registers," *Irish Economic and Social History* 6 (1979): 5–23.

39 Walter McDonald, *Reminiscences of a Maynooth Professor*, edited by Dennis Gwynn (London: Jonathan Cape, 1925), 19.

40 S.J. Connolly, *Priests and People* in *Pre-Famine Ireland, 1780–1845* (Dublin: Gill and MacMillan, 1982), 188. For example, Connolly quotes the ordnance survey concerning Islandmagee, Co. Antrim, in the 1830s, that "conjugal fidelity is among any class a virtue but little practiced on the part of either husband or wife," and most girls, the survey said, either were pregnant or mothers of illegitimate children when they came to the altar. Yet, a study of the records of the Presbyterian churches of Island-magee in the second half of the nineteenth century shows an illegitimacy rate of only 1.6 percent which is *lower* than the all-Ireland rate. It also shows that 13.5 percent of the girls were pregnant at the altar. There was no radical social change in Islandmagee that would permit one to argue that a new stricter morality came after the Famine. See D.H. Akenson, *Between Two Revolutions: Islandmagee, County Antrim, 1798–1920* (Toronto: P.D. Meany, 1979), esp. 122–3. Also, see below, note 63.

This is not to argue that the ordnance survey was wrong in pointing out the Antrim Presbyterians' vices, but that the exact degree of this behaviour should not be credulously accepted, unless corroborated by other evidence.

This is especially true when such statements correspond to modern day stereotypes. Connolly, in *Priests and People* (188) states that the laxity of these attitudes is "fully borne out by the regional pattern revealed when official statistics on the incidence of illegitimacy became available for the first time in 1864." Actually, the regional variation is accounted for by higher levels of urbanization and by economic modernization in Ulster, rather than by any religious factor.

The same tying of Protestantism to illegitimacy is found in Connolly's essay, "Marriage in Pre-Famine Ireland," in Art Cosgrove, ed., *Marriage in Ireland* (Dublin: College Press, 1985), 91.

41 The 1833–6 report of the Commissioners for Inquiring into the Condition of the Poorer Classes in Ireland is one of nineteenth-century Ireland's more impressive parliamentary documents. Unlike most such commissions, its activities were directed along the lines of what today would be called good experimental design. Strenuous efforts were made to avoid evidentiary bias. For instance, assistant commissioners collected evidence in pairs, one person Irish, the other English. In collecting oral testimony "triangulation" was employed. And, fortunately for the historian, the commissioners' evidence, both written and oral, was published in six massive volumes. (The effort was far from perfect, of course, as will be indicated in the text.) In both the experimental design and in its conclu-

sions (especially that the English Poor Law should not be applied to Ireland), the Commission's work was thoroughly Whatelian. On the report's unfortunate fate, see D.H. Akenson, *A Protestant in Purgatory: Richard Whately, Archbishop of Dublin* (Hamden: published for the Conference on British Studies and for Indiana University, by Archon Books, 1981), 128-9.

42 For English figures, see Peter Laslett, *Family Life and Illicit Love in Earlier Generations. Essays in Historical Sociology* (Cambridge: Cambridge University Press, 1977), 140-2.

43 David Miller, review of Connell's *Irish Peasant Society* in *Journal of Modern History* 42 (Sept. 1970): 387-9. Specifically, what Connell did was highlight the figures for 1871-80, the first complete decade of civil registration when the illegitimate births were at an all-time low level of 1.63 percent of total births. Connell then draws a line of continuity between these figures and pre-Famine figures. As Miller points out, he should have emphasized as his sightline the earliest available numbers, namely those of 1864, when illegitimacy was 3.8 percent. On rates, see Connolly, "Illegitimacy and Pre-nuptial Pregnancy," 9.

44 Less debilitating, but unfortunate nonetheless, was Connell's comparing the number of illegitimate births in the Catholic parish with the population of the parish as defined by the Protestant Established Church. The units were far from being identical and multiple errors were introduced into his work. However, these were not necessarily in one direction. Presumably, the laws of chance operated and for every one in which Connell overestimated the illegitimate rate through his methods, he underestimated it in another. The only problem is that he did not have a large enough number of cases to make this self-cancelling occurrence an overwhelming probability.

45 Connell's data are found in "Illegitimacy Before the Famine," in *Irish Peasant Society*: 80-1. If one wishes to use Connell's calculation of illegitimate children as a percent of total baptisms one should realize that his number would translate into a somewhat higher level of illegitimacy, because not all illegitimate children were baptized.

46 See Laslett, *Family Life*, 125, table 3:2.

47 See, for example, *The Poor Law Inquiry (Ireland). First Report, Appendix A*, H.C. 1835 (369), xxxii, pp. 52, 53, 59, 60; and Connell, "Illegitimacy Before the Famine," 55.

48 The County Roscommon priest who told the Poor Law Commissioner that he several times had refused to celebrate "subsequent marriages" was a rarity. (*The Poor Law Inquiry (Ireland). First Report, Appendix A*, 54, 70.) Virtually every other priest who gave information on the matter indicated that "subsequent marriages" were performed and several of them stated that they themselves helped bring pressure on the young man to produce this desirable result.

49 John Revans, *Evils of the State of Ireland; their Cause and their Remedy: A Poor Law* (London: John Hatchard, 1835), 56.

50 Ibid.

51 Ibid.

52 Connell, "Illegitimacy Before the Famine," 54.

53 David Miller, "Irish Catholicism and the Great Famine," *Journal of Social History* 9 (Fall 1975): 94n8.

54 The result of the 1942 study of a parish in County Limerick, conducted by C. Lee and D. MacCarthaigh, is conveniently incorporated by Connolly along with his own data, and published in "Illegitimacy and Pre-Nuptial Pregnancy," 5–23.

55 Connell, "Illegitimacy Before the Famine," 82–3.

56 Allan Greer, *Peasant, Lord and Merchant: Rural Society in Three Quebec Parishes 1740–1840* (Toronto: University of Toronto Press, 1985), 59. There is a problem of comparability here. Greer counted as premarital conception all *births* recorded within eight months of marriage. Connolly recorded as premarital conception all *baptisms* within nine and a half months of marriage.

    Professor Peter Ward's study of St. Raphael's Roman Catholic parish, Charlottenburg (in the mostly highland Scots' area of Upper Canada), 1815–53, showed an illegitimacy rate of 2.2 percent and a premarital conception rate of 7.1 percent to 9.6 percent, figures closely in line with the Irish experience. See Peter Ward, "Unwed Motherhood in Nineteenth-Century English Canada," Canadian Historical Association, *Historical Papers* (1981): 36, 39.

57 Angus McLaren, *Reproductive Rituals: The Perception of Fertility in England from the Sixteenth Century to the Nineteenth Century* (London: Methuen, 1984), 46–7.

58 Ibid., 65–6.

59 M. O'Riordan, *Catholicism and Progress in Ireland* (1905), 272n, quoted in Connell, "Illegitimacy Before the Famine," 86. The italics are mine.

60 Connolly, *Priests and People*, 188.

61 Akenson, *Between Two Revolutions*, 123.

62 Ibid., 206n16. This procedure was to allow for the incidence of possible prematurity of birth.

63 I do not have Islandmagee illegitimacy rates for 1845–67. Between 1854 and 1920, however, of the 1,338 baptisms on the register of the Second Islandmagee Presbyterian Church, only 1.6 percent were illegitimate, a figure considerably below the national average (Ibid., 122). Projecting these figures back into the first half of the nineteenth century is problematical, but less so than for most parts of Ireland, because Islandmagee had very little in the way of an economic or social revolution in the nineteenth century.

64 I am grateful that the late Dr. Hugh Calwell of Whitehead, County Antrim, shared with me his unrivaled knowledge and his material on eighteenth- and nineteenth-century Presbyterianism in the area.

65 Lee, *Modernisation of Irish Society*, 6. One is not precluding the possibility that there were interesting marginal differences among the various Protestant denominations.

66 The reader is aware that ever since the beginning of civil registration in 1864, Ulster had a higher illegitimacy rate than did the rest of the country. This, I would suggest, had nothing to do with the higher proportion of Protestants in that province than elsewhere, but was instead a function of Ulster being the only part of Ireland in which modernization was well in train. The affects of the industrial revolution in the north included a reduction in the parental control over children and a parallel reduction of sanctions against illicit love. This was a general, not a denominationally specific phenomenon.

That said, although I am arguing that in the nineteenth- and early twentieth-centuries there was no significant difference between Protestant and Catholic families that had its basis in religion, I do *not* think that such culturally determined differences are implausible at other moments in Irish history. Indeed, it seems that in the present day such differences exist and these stem from an adoption of a different ideology of the family by the two groups – that is, the Protestants' acceptance of scientific methods of family limitation and the Catholics rejection of them. But it is easy to forget what a recent phenomenon this is. Theological roadblocks to scientific birth control were not removed in the Anglican community until the decision of the 1930 Lambeth Conference.

67 Kennedy, *The Irish*, 51–65.

68 David Fitzpatrick, *Irish Emigration, 1801–1921* (Dundalk: Dundalgan Press, published for the Economic and Social History Society of Ireland, 1984), 7. See also, Pauline Jackson, "Women in 19th Century Irish Emigration," *International Migration Review* 18 (Winter 1984): 1007, table 1.

69 Lest my saying that the indicator does not work be found too direct for methodophiles, I shall translate: as a proxy for relative levels of female abuse, either between nations or within any given nation, the excess of female over male life expectation as between two or more populations, considered comparatively, is open to grave objections, because the comparative differences are not necessarily reflective of differences in levels of female abuse, but are often reflective of other, more directly and demonstrably causal factors, such as age and sex, specific emigration differentials, regional and national variations in urbanization, and to regional and national variations in social stratification at the lower, more economically vulnerable end of the socioeconomic spectrum.

70 See, for example, Hasia R. Diner, *Erin's Daughters in America: Irish Immi-*

grant Women in the Nineteenth Century (Baltimore: Johns Hopkins University Press, 1983), esp. 1-29; and Margaret MacCurtain and Donncha O'Corrain, eds., *Women in Irish Society: The Historical Dimension* (Westport: Greenwood Press, 1979), esp. J.J. Lee's, "Women and the Church Since the Famine," 27-45.

NOTES TO CHAPTER THREE

1 To extend the point: There are, of course, many cultural patterns that run for several generations. But, for the purposes of supposition, assume that one were interested only in two generations born abroad, and, assume also that Irish emigration had a ridiculously low birth rate (say only two children for each emigrant). Even so, in the late decade of the nineteenth century, well over half of the people in the world who had parents born in Ireland were living outside of Ireland.

2 David Fitzpatrick, *Irish Emigration, 1801-1921* (Dundalk: Dundalgan Press Ltd, 1984, published for the Economic and Social History Society of Ireland), 30.

3 J.J. Lee, in *Emigration: The Irish Experience* no page given, quoted in P.J. O'Farrell "Emigrant Attitudes and Behaviour as a Source for Irish History," in G.A. Hayes-McCoy, ed., *Historical Studies* (Galway: published for the Irish Committee of Historical Science, 1976), 10: 120.

   In much the same vein, M.A.G. O'Tuathaigh has argued: "Emigrant behaviour, in addition to its intrinsic interest, can tell us much about the society from which the emigrants have emigrated." O'Tuathaigh, "Ireland, 1800-1921," in *Irish Historiography, 1970-80*, edited by J.J. Lee (Cork: University Press, 1981), 106.

4 D.H. Akenson, *The Irish in Ontario: A Study in Rural History* (Kingston and Montreal: McGill-Queen's University Press, 1984), 335-7.

5 O'Farrell, "Emigrant Attitudes and Behaviour," 120.

6 I am fully aware that there is a rich and diverse theoretical literature on the nature of migration as a worldwide phenomenon. However, the present discussion is better served by a concrete vocabulary focused on the Irish historical experience than by theoretical constructs derived from international literature.

7 This point was most forcefully established by S.H. Cousens, "The Regional Pattern of Emigration during the Great Irish Famine, 1846-51," *Institute of British Geographers. Transactions*, 28 (1960), 119-34. See also, Cousens: "The Regional Variation in Emigration from Ireland between 1821 and 1841," *Institute of British Geographers. Transactions*, 37 (1965), 15-30. Corrections to Cousens' procedures, which change his county-by-county figures, but not his overall conclusions, are found in Joel Mokyr, *Why Ireland Starved: A Quantitative and Analytical History of the Irish Economy,*

1800-1850 (London: George Allen and Unwin, 1983), 68ff.

8 This point is worth underscoring because there has arisen a small scholarly industry in Ireland bent on establishing, contrary to the available demographic evidence, that the Irish language held a strong position well into the middle and late nineteenth century. It is not entirely coincidental that most of the scholars engaged in this Lazarus-like effort are also the financial beneficiaries of the programs of the Irish Republic government that are aimed at reviving the Irish language, or that many of their publications are subsidized. This would be no great harm in the present instance, except that this industry has had its influence on emigration historians, some of whom have greatly overstated the influence of the Irish language upon the behaviour of emigrants. What frequently (and misleadingly) is done is to lump together two census categories – the small minority who spoke only Irish and the larger group who spoke both Irish and English – to call them "Irish-speakers" and to imply that their being Irish speakers somehow impaired their functioning in the New World*

People who knew both Irish and English did not go to Melbourne or Toronto, or Dunedin, or Chicago to spend their time trying to communicate with the natives in Irish.

For a summary of the demographic data on Irish language usage, see Appendix Q. The fact is that by 1851 less than 5 percent of the population could not speak English and among the emigrants the percentage was inevitably much less than that, in part because the emigrant stream was heavily weighted towards young persons who had experienced the goverment's English-language educational system, set up in 1831.

9 Robert E. Kennedy, Jr points out that in the census years relevant for this study, 1861–1921, the differences in the dicennial rate of decline as between any two successive census periods never was more than 4 percent. (As noted in chapter 1, there was a major Protestant out-migration following the creation of the Irish Free State, but that is beyond the time line of this study.) See Kennedy, *The Irish: Emigration, Marriage, and Fertility* (Berkeley: University of California Press, 1973), 119.

10 That this reminder of the importance of Protestant emigration in the Irish diaspora is necessary is puzzling, for nineteenth-century Irishmen were well aware of it and, among Protestants, there was a literature of alarm concerning the large number of "the lower orders" of Protestants leaving – that is, the small farmers and minor capitalists. See for example, "Emigration of the Protestants of Ireland," *Dublin University Magazine* 4 (July 1834): 1–12. A recent observer, writing about twentieth-century Protestant emigration, has noted that "one of the most interesting and frequently overlooked aspects of Irish emigration in the present century is the very substantial Protestant component." Sean Glynn, "Irish Immigra-

tion to Britain, 1911-1951: Patterns and Policy," *Irish Economic and Social History* 8 (1981): 52.

11 The basic form for Appendix I, upon which figure 6 is based, is taken from *Commission on Emigration and other Population Problems, 1948-1954* (Dublin: Stationery Office, 1954), 125, as is the data for 1851-1920. However, for the years before 1851, this commission's report left several holes which are filled in by N.H. Carrier and J.R. Jeffrey, *External Migration: A Study of the Available Statistics, 1815-1950, being No. 6 In the General Register Office's "Studies on Medical and Population Subjects"* (London: HMSO, 1953), 95. In turn, the Carrier and Jeffrey material has been corrected for undercounting for sailings to the U.S.A. and to British North America according to the work of William Forbes Adams, *Ireland and Irish Emigration to the New World from 1815 to the Famine* (New Haven: Yale University Press, 1932), 413-14. For 1836, for which Adams made no estimate, I have interpolated the data myself. For the years 1846-50 (for which Adams made no correction for undercounting) I have used his formula. See Akenson, *The Irish in Ontario*, 14-15, 29-30.

One suspects that the Australian figures for 1831-40 are an underestimate.

12 Deirdre M. Mageean, "Nineteenth-Century Irish Emigration: A Case Study Using Passenger Lists," in P.J. Drudy, ed., *The Irish in America: Emigration, Assimilation, and Impact* (Cambridge: Cambridge University Press, 1985), 40.

13 The observation is Cormac O'Grada's, "A Note on Nineteenth Century Irish Emigration Statistics," *Population Studies* 29 (1975): 143-9, cited by Mageean, "Irish Emigration," 60*n*1. For an early example of such discrepancies between numbers collected in countries of arrival and origin, compare the corrected estimates for Irish migration to the U.S.A. in the period 1831-40, given in Appendix I (171,087) with the numbers given by the U.S. immigration service (207,381). These are cited in D.H. Akenson, *Being Had: Historians, Evidence, and the Irish in North America* (Toronto: P.D. Meany, 1985), 47.

14 David Fitzpatrick, "Irish Emigration in the Later Nineteenth Century," *Irish Historical Studies* 22 (Sept. 1980): 127.

15 See particularly, David Fitzpatrick, "The Disappearance of the Irish Agricultural Labourer, 1841-1912," *Irish Economic and Social History* 7 (1980): 66-92.

16 For bibliographies of the literature see: R.A. Burchell, "The Historiography of the American Irish," *Immigrants and Minorities* 1 (Nov. 1982): 281-305; David Noel Doyle, "The Regional Bibliography of Irish America, 1800-1930: A Review and Addendum," *Irish Historical Studies* 23 (May 1983): 254-83; Seamus Metress, *The Irish American Experience: A Guide to the Literature* (Washington, D.C.: University Press of America Inc., 1981);

Michael F. Funchion, "Irish-America: An Essay on the Literature Since 1978," *The Immigration History Newsletter* 17 (Nov. 1985): 1–8.

17 The literature on the Irish in America is discussed in D.H. Akenson, "An Agnostic View of the Historiography of the Irish-American," *Labour/Le Travail* 14 (Fall 1984): 123–59; reprinted in Akenson, *Being Had*, 37–75 and 205–16. The quotations which follow in the text are from the most widely read of the synthesizers of Irish-American history, and, of course, individual specialists' studies will vary on specific points of emphasis. The noteworthy point, however, is that almost all of the specialized studies take some version of this general consensus as their framework.

See also, D.H. Akenson, "Data: What is known about the Irish in North America?" in Oliver MacDonagh and W.F. Mandle, eds., *Ireland and Irish-Australia: Studies in Cultural and Political History* (London and Sydney: Croom Helm, 1986), 1–17.

18 Carl Wittke, *The Irish in America* (New York: Russell and Russell, 1956), 26–7.

19 Lawrence J. McCaffrey, *The Irish Diaspora in America* (Bloomington: Indiana University Press, 1976), 63.

20 William V. Shannon, *The American Irish* (New York: MacMillan, 1963), 27.

21 George Potter, *To The Golden Door. The Story of the Irish in Ireland and America* (Boston: Little Brown, 1960), 171.

22 Kerby A. Miller, *Emigrants and Exiles: Ireland and the Irish Exodus to North America* (London and New York: Oxford University Press, 1985), quotation, 238.

23 Ibid., 240.

24 Ibid., 259.

25 Ibid., 277.

26 Ibid., 119.

27 Ibid., 7–8.

28 One has to say "highly probable" because it is conceivable that the hypotheses might be confirmed, but eventually shown to have been a function of some as yet unspecified exogenous variable or set of variables.

29 See, for example, the suggestion in Fitzpatrick's "Irish Emigration," 130–3.

30 Fitzpatrick, *Irish Emigration*, 5.

31 As is the case with virtually all Irish emigration data for the nineteenth and early twentieth centuries, the figures in table 2 should be taken as only roughly indicative of the dimension of the outflow. The material is derived from the emigration information collected by the United Kingdom registrar general and it clashes on virtually every category with that collected from other sources and presented in the Irish Republic's *Report on Population*, 125. I know of no way to resolve the difficulty. (In fact, the data in the *Report on Population* clashes with itself: compare tables 93 and 94, at 124–5.)

32 Glynn, "Irish Immigration," 56–7.

33 Ibid., 51.

34 Fitzpatrick, "Irish Emigration," 137.

35 Ibid., 138.

36 Lynn Hollen Lees, *Exiles of Erin. Irish Immigrants in Victorian London* (Ithaca: Cornell University Press, 1979).

37 A useful, if frequently inaccurate, bibliography is *The History of the Irish in Britain. A Bibliography* (London: The Irish in Britain History Centre, 1986). For a discussion of demographic data – lacking, however, any significant religious analysis – see John Archer Jackson, *The Irish in Britain* (London: Routledge and Kegan Paul, 1963). For a collection of studies of the Irish as urban Catholics, see Roger Swift and Sheridan Gilley, eds., *The Irish in the Victorian City* (London: Croom Helm, 1985).

38 C.J. Houston and W.J. Smyth, "The Irish Abroad: Better Questions Through a Better Source, the Canadian Census," *Irish Geography* 13 (1980): 3.

39 Malcolm P.A. Macourt, "The Religious Inquiry in the Irish Census of 1861," *Irish Historical Studies* 21 (Sept. 1978): 172.

40 It is diagnostic of the problem that even Lees's excellent book contains fifty pages on the Irish-Catholic culture of her London parishes, without any direct data on the religious affiliation of the Irish-born.

41 The only study I have encountered that analyzes the impact of Irish cultural patterns on immigrant behavior in Great Britain at the necessary level of sophistication, is "Household Structure and Overcrowding Among the Lancashire Irish, 1851–1871," by John Haslett and W.J. Lowe, *Histoire sociale/Social History* 10 (May 1977): 45–58.

42 The historical material on the Irish in New Zealand is largely anecdotal. Richard P. Davis kindly provided me with bibliographic advice. His *Irish Issues in New Zealand Politics* (Dunedin: University of Otago Press, 1974) is required reading. See also, John Morris, "The Assisted Immigrants to New Zealand, 1871–79" (M.A. thesis, University of Auckland, 1973); and Arthur J. Gray, *An Ulster Plantation. The Story of the Katikati Settlement* (Wellington: A.H. and A.W. Reed, first ed. 1938; second ed., 1950).

43 For a useful introduction to the New Zealand data, see E.P. Neale, *Guide to New Zealand Official Statistics* (Christchurch: Whitcome and Tombs Ltd., third ed., 1955).

44 Compiled from *Results of a Census of the Dominion of New Zealand, 1878,* 10; *1886,* 14; *1921, General Report,* 101.

45 Fitzpatrick, "Irish Emigration," 133, 138, 139.

46 *Results of a Census of the Dominion of New Zealand . . . 1921. General Report,* 101.

47 *Results of a Census of the Dominion of New Zealand . . . 1916,* 58.

48 *Results of a Census of the Dominion of New Zealand . . . 1921. General Report,* 128.

49 *Results of a Census of the Dominion of New Zealand . . . 1921. Birthplaces,* 9.

50 One obstacle that might present itself in taking up the New Zealand data

is that those on the settlement pattern of the foreign-born lump together everyone, no matter how long the immigrant had been in New Zealand. That opens the possibility that the Irish arrived earlier and therefore their rural orientation as compared to other groups reflects their having arrived while land was easier to obtain. However, such length of residence in no way changes the fact that in absolute numbers a near-moiety of the Irish immigrants settled in rural areas.

51 New Zealand Census, 1921. *General Report*, 130. For more detailed breakdown of occupational categories and religious affiliations, see New Zealand Census, 1921, *Religions*, 36–42. This 1921 census was the first for which cross-tabulations of religion and occupation were done.

52 New Zealand Census, 1921. *General Report*, 130.

53 For a relevant methodological discussion, see Robert W. Fogel, "Circumstantial Evidence in 'Scientific' and Traditional History," in David Carr, ed., *Philosophy of History and Contemporary Historiography* (Ottawa: University of Ottawa Press, 1982), 61–112.

One should note that the circumstantial evidence of Irish Protestants and Irish Catholics being neither occupationally disadvantaged nor excessively urban is very slightly loaded towards making that case because the Irish profile group generally (and presumably the Irish Catholics within that group) had been in New Zealand a bit longer than had the general population.

One can infer this fact if one reworks the (quite incomplete) data found in the 1921 census (*General Report*, 99, 106):

Entire Population		*Irish (Catholic and Protestant)*
First generation	312,630	34,419
Second generation	509,221	76,080
Third and fourth generations	397,062	N/A

If one can take the first and second generations as a guide, then the Irish ethnic cohort had a somewhat smaller proportion of immigrants in it and a larger proportion of second, third, and fourth. This would mean that if one could control for recency of arrival, the Irish profile would have been slightly lower.

54 Professor Patrick O'Farrell of the University of New South Wales has recently published a monumental pioneering work, *The Irish in Australia* (Kensington, NSW: New South Wales University Press, 1987). It supplements, but does not significantly duplicate the material in his *The Catholic Church and Community: An Australian History* (Kensington, NSW: New South Wales University Press, new ed., 1985). Other material by O'Farrell that is of value includes: "Irish-Australia at an End," *Papers and Proceedings*,

Tasmanian Historical Research Association 21 (Dec. 1974): 142–60; "Irish-Australian Diplomatic Relations," *Quadrant* (March 1980): 11–20; "The Irish and Australian History," *Quadrant* (Dec. 1978): 17–21; "The Irish in Australia: Some Aspects of the Period 1791–1850," *Descent* 7 (March 1975): 43–56.

The first census of the Commonwealth of Australia, 1911, contained a useful historical survey of all the earlier censuses of the Australian states, including a tally of the questions on which information was collected. See *Census for the Commonwealth of Australia . . . 1911*, 1: 36–40.

55 O'Farrell, "The Irish in Australia," 43. For related analysis, see Manning Clark, "The Origins of the Convicts Transported to Eastern Australia, 1787–1852, Part I," *Historical Studies* 7 (Melbourne, May 1956): 121–35; and Part II, Ibid. 7 (Nov. 1956): 314–27.

56 *General Report on the Eleventh Census of New South Wales* (Sydney: 1894), 90.

57 Oliver MacDonagh, "The Irish in Victoria, 1851–91: A Demographic Essay," in T.D. Williams, ed., *Historical Studies* (Dublin: Gill and MacMillan, 1971) 8: 82.

58 O'Farrell, "The Irish in Australia," 43–5. For a valuable discussion both of the shortcomings of many previous estimates of the character of the convict force, see James Waldersee, *Catholic Society in New South Wales, 1788–1860* (Sydney: Sydney University Press, 1974). See also, George Rudé, "Early Irish Rebels in Australia," *Historical Studies* 16 (Melbourne, April 1974): 17–35.

59 R.J. Shultz, "Immigration into Eastern Australia, 1788–1851," *Historical Studies* 14 (Melbourne, April 1970): 228 and 281, tables IV and V.

60 See Neil Coghlan, "The Coming of the Irish to Victoria," *Historical Studies* 12 (Melbourne, Oct. 1965): 68–86, and esp. 73.

61 Computed from Eleventh Census of New South Wales, *General Report*, 87.

62 Fitzpatrick, "Irish Emigration," 32.

63 Derived from Australia Census, 1911, 2: 128–9.

64 Charles Price, "Ethnic Composition and Origins," *Australian Immigration. A Bibliography and Digest Number 4, Supplement* (Canberra: Australian National University, 1981), 46, table 5:1.

65 Ibid.

66 If one uses Price's data and embraces the useful fiction that virtually all the south Europeans were Catholics, that half the eastern Europeans were, and that one half of the Germans and Austrians were, and that the French and Belgians were virtually all Catholic, then one infers that 3.94 percent of the population was European Catholic in background. Of course, in this kind of approximation one is not really assuming, for example, that *all* Frenchmen were Catholics, but that the numbers of Frenchmen who were not Catholics were compensated for by, say, the odd Scandinavian who was not Protestant, but Catholic. Obviously, the

result is an approximation only, but a serviceable one, as long as it is not overread.

67 Oliver MacDonagh, "The Irish in Victoria," 72. The equation of Irish and Catholic is elaborated in MacDonagh, "The Irish in Australia: A General View," in Oliver MacDonagh and W.F. Mandle, eds., *Ireland and Irish Australia: Studies in Cultural and Political History* (London and Sydney: Croom Helm, 1986), 155–74.

68 Nor, indeed, would a strong negative correlation prove that all Irishmen were Protestants and all Protestants Irishmen. The same rules of logic apply to a negative correlation as to a positive one.

69 Australia Census, 1911 II: 254–5.

For reference it is worth noting that the religious percentages of the Irish-born population, not just in Victoria, but throughout the entire Commonwealth of Australia in 1911:

Catholics	71.28%
Church of England	14.09
Presbyterian	8.70
Methodist	2.58
Other Christian	2.84
Non-Christian	0.03
Indefinite and no religion	0.48
Sub-total, Non-Catholic	28.72
Total	100.00

Source: Australia Census, 1911, 1: 152–3.

70 Ibid., 200.

71 Patrick O'Farrell (with Brian Trainor), *Letters from Irish Australia 1825–1929* (Sydney: New South Wales University Press, and Belfast: Ulster Historical Foundation, 1984) marks an important innovation in the history of the Irish in Australia: including the Protestant Irish in that story. O'Farrell portrays the Irish Presbyterians and Anglicans as people with "non-Gaelic names, with non-Catholic cultural roots – all of which, in their different ways, were firmly and intensely Irish and proud of it" (5).

For quantitative data on the Australian religious structure, see the following by Walter Phillips: "Christianity and Its Defence in New South Wales, circa 1880 to 1890" (Ph.D. thesis, Australian National University, 1969); "Religious Professions and Practice in New South Wales, 1850–1901: The Statistical Evidence," *Historical Studies* 15 (Melbourne, Oct. 1972): 378–400; "Statistics on Religious Affiliation in Australia, 1891–1961," *Australian Historical Statistics* 4 (Nov. 1981): 5–15. See also, "Religious

Adherence and Population Mobility in 19th Century New South Wales,"
Australian Geographical Studies 10 (Oct. 1972): 193–202.

72 Fitzpatrick, "Irish Emigration," 136.

73 Chris McConville, "Catholics and Mobility in Melbourne and Sydney, 1861–1891," *Australia 1888* 1 (August 1979): 56.

74 O'Farrell, "Emigrant Attitudes," 126.

75 MacDonagh, "Irish in Victoria," 75.

76 See Australia Census, 1911, 2: 188–9. If anything, the nearly 80 percent figure understates the length of residence of these people, for there were 9,119 persons whose length of residence was unspecified and some, probably most of these, would have been in the twenty-plus years residence group.

77 Derived from ibid., 128–9, 296–7.

78 David Fitzpatrick, "The Settlers: Immigration from Ireland in the Nineteenth Century," in Colm Kiernan, ed., *Ireland and Australia* (Cork: Mercier Press, 1984), 28.

79 Derived from data in Australia Census, 1911, 2: 128–9, 296–7.

80 David Fitzpatrick, "Irish Immigrants in Australia: Patterns of Settlement and Paths of Mobility," *Australia 1888* 1 (Feb. 1979): 52.

81 If one wishes to engage in the exercises indicated in the text, the raw data are found in Australia Census, 1911, 2: 128–9, 242–3, 296–7.

82 Derived from ibid., 200, 212. One must add together "Roman Catholics," and "Catholics (undefined)" as the census takers allowed these as separate categories. The census reports make clear, however, that these were really a single denomination.

83 Derived from ibid., 128–9, 296. European is defined so as to exclude the British Isles and British possessions.

84 Is there any chance at all that some fragment of hypothesis no. 1 – that the Irish were a city people – can be rescued? Yes, although the odds for its occurring are almost as great as the chances of catching a piece of a descending meteor in a baseball glove.

There is one problem that keeps the chain of logic specified in the text from being completely, 100 percent, certain: the census gives us data on settlement patterns of (a) the European-born and (b) on Catholics as a group, but (c) not specifically on the settlement pattern of European-born Catholics.

So, under very special circumstances, it is theoretically possible that (a) the Irish-born in 1911 were huddled together in cities, and (b) that the European Catholics were completely dispersed in rural areas, and (c) that the second and third generation of Irish Catholics, as contrasted to the first generation, were settled almost entirely in the countryside, and (d) that the second and third generation of European-heritage Catholics were settled overwhelmingly in the cities. Only if *each* of these conditions pertained would it be possible to accept the government statistics and still argue that a significant subset of the Irish Catholics were city people. Obviously, this requires special pleading on an heroic scale. Better, instead, to accept that in all generations the Irish Catholics were mostly people of the countryside and rural hamlets.

85 Source: Australia Census, 1911, 2: 212, 215.

86 Fitzpatrick, "Irish Immigrants in Australia," 52.

87 O'Farrell, "Emigrant Attitudes," 122–3.

88 O'Farrell, "The Irish in Australia," 47.

89 Derived from *General Report on the Census for New South Wales ... 1901*, 211.

90 The full funding of private schools in Australia did not become law until 1964.

On the history of education in Australia in the nineteenth century see: Rupert Goodman, *Secondary Education in Queensland, 1860–1960* (Canberra: Australian National University Press, 1968); D.C. Griffiths, *Documents on the Establishment of Education in New South Wales, 1789–1880* (Melbourne: Australian Council for Educational Research, 1957); Denis Grundy, *'Secular, Compulsory, and Free.' The Educational Act of 1872* (Melbourne: Melbourne University Press, 1972); Patrick O'Farrell, *The Catholic Church and Community*, esp. chapter 3, "The Education Question, 1865–84;" W.W. Phillips, 'Christianity and its Defence in New South Wales."

91 Derived from Australia Census, 1911, 1: 134–5. The literacy rate of non-European immigrants was considerably lower than for the groups cited in the text.

92 Compiled from Australia Census, 1911, 1: 283.

93 Compiled from ibid., 281.

94 Computed from ibid., 149.

95 The following were the average number of children classified according to the occupation of the male head of household in 1911:

Class I Professionals	3.37
II Domestic	3.24
III Commercial	3.39
IV Transport & Communication	3.61
V Industrial	3.81
VI Farming, Mining, Forestry and Fishing	4.37
VII Independent Means	6.27
Total: All Breadwinners	3.89

Source: Australia Census, 1911, 1: 286

96 Computed from ibid., 208–9. The "Roman Catholic" and "Catholic (undefined)" categories have been aggregated and the percentage recalculated.

97 Ibid., 151. Because of the vastly divergent age structure between the

foreign-born and the native-born, there is no profit in comparing the celibacy rate of the Irish-born to that of any native-born group.

98 Derived from ibid., 208.

99 Derived from ibid., 272.

100 Compiled from ibid., 270.

101 Pastoral quoted in Patrick O'Farrell and Deirdre O'Farrell, eds., *Documents in Australian Catholic History, 1788-1884*, 2 vols. (London: Geoffrey Chapman, 1969), 1: 350-1.

102 Chris McConville, "The Victorian Irish: Emigrants and Families, 1851-1891," *Australia 1888* (Sept. 1982): 71. See also, P.F. McDonald, *Marriage in Australia: Age at First Marriage and Proportions Marrying, 1860-1971* (Canberra: n.p., 1975), 52-53, cited in McConville, "Catholics and Mobility in Melbourne and Sydney, 1861-1891," *Australia 1888* 1 (August 1979): 59.

103 McConville, "The Victorian Irish," 71.

104 Derived from Australia Census, 1911, 1: 269.

105 Fitzpatrick, "Irish Immigrants," 52.

106 Derived from Australia Census, 1911, 1: 106, 271, 272. The calculation of percentages is done upon a base of the total number of marriages for which the religion both of the husband and the wife is known and only for instances where both husband and wife were residing together at the time of the census.

107 Derived from ibid., 271. "Roman Catholic" and "Catholic (undefined)" are combined. The combination reduces somewhat the number of marriages tallied as mixed and that explains why the combined percentage of mixed marriages of the "Roman Catholic" and "Catholic (undefined)" group is lower than the mixed marriage rate for both "Roman Catholic" men and women.

108 For an analysis of the bounty system in the first half of the nineteenth century, see Robert J. Shultz, "The Assisted Immigrants, 1837-1850," (Ph.D. thesis, Australian National University, 1971).

109 Fitzpatrick, "Irish Immigration," 131-4.

110 Ibid., 132n12.

NOTES TO CHAPTER FOUR

1 E.P. Hutchinson, "Notes on Immigration Statistics of the United States," *American Statistical Association Journal* 53 (Dec. 1958): 974-5, 980-1. Fitful attempts at recording land crossing had begun in 1853 and been abandoned during the Civil War; they were reintroduced in 1865 and then again abandoned, as being illegal, in 1885. Accurate counts only began in 1908.

2 Edward Jarvis, "Immigration," *Atlantic Monthly* 29 (April 1872), quoted in Hutchinson, "Immigration Statistics," 976.

3 For a more detailed discussion of the problems with the U.S. data, see D.H. Akenson, *Being Had: Historians, Evidence, and the Irish in North America* (Toronto: P.D. Meany, 1985), pp. 37–76. For a comparative discussion of U.S. and Canadian sources of data see D.H. Akenson, "Data: What is Known about the Irish in North America?" in Oliver MacDonagh and W.F. Mandle, eds., *Ireland and Irish-Australia: Studies in Cultural and Political History* (London and Sydney: Croom Helm, 1986): 1–17.

4 Kerby A. Miller, *Emigrants and Exiles. Ireland and the Irish Exodus to North America* (New York: Oxford, 1985), 323.

5 Even in Hamilton, Ontario, one of the places where the Irish Catholics were most disadvantaged, "there was little of the virulent Know-Nothingism that disfigured American urban politics in the same period." Michael B. Katz, *The People of Hamilton, Canada West. Family and Class in A Mid-Nineteenth Century City* (Cambridge: Harvard University Press, 1975), 3.

6 The Canadian laboratory is not perfectly clean, only much moreso than the American. On one form of prejudice, see J.R. Miller, "Anti-Catholic Thought in Victorian Canada," *Canadian Historical Review* 66 (Dec. 1985): 474–94.

7 See 1870–71 Dominion of Canada Census, reproduced in *Census of Canada, 1931, Summary*, 1: 710.

8 A. Gordon Darroch and Michael D. Ornstein, "Ethnicity and Occupational Structure in Canada in 1871: The Vertical Mosaic in Historical Perspective," *Canadian Historical Review* 61 (Sept. 1980): 312, table 1. The large Irish adhesion to Anglicanism is noteworthy on two grounds. First, it pre-empts the tendency to label the Protestant-Irish immigrants to North America as chiefly of Ulster Presbyterian origin (called "Scotch-Irish" in the American historical literature). Second, it reminds one that what was called "the Church of England" in Canada would more accurately have been termed "the Church of England and Ireland" (in the homeland, indeed, the episcopal churches of England and Ireland were united from 1801 until 1871, under the terms of the Act of Union of Great Britain and Ireland of 1800). Gordon Darroch kindly retabulated for me his data on religion and ethnicity and found that in Ontario, a large sample cross-tabulation revealed that the Anglican church's membership was 47.3 percent of English origin and 42.2 percent of Irish origin. To this demographic data, one should add that Irish-trained clergy, particularly from Trinity College, Dublin, were a large and influential group.

9 Akenson, *Being Had*, 87.

10 Ibid., 88.

11 D.H. Akenson, *The Irish in Ontario: A Study in Rural History* (Kingston and Montreal: McGill-Queen's University Press, 1984), 35–7.

12 For sources and methods of this calculation, see ibid., 38.

13 Ibid., 39.

14 Darroch and Ornstein, "Ethnicity and Occupational Structure in Canada," 305-33.
15 Ibid., 314.
16 Ibid. In a footnote, the authors note that if one excluded the farm category from their tables, one would be struck by "how similar the proportional distribution of the remaining population would be to that found in the nineteenth century urban studies." (314n18). This is an extremely delicate way of saying that the interpretation of the Irish Catholics as a nineteenth-century urban group can come about only if one ignores all non-urban data.
17 Ibid., 314.
18 Ibid.
19 A. Gordon Darroch and Michael D. Ornstein, "Ethnicity and Class, Transitions Over A Decade: Ontario, 1861-1871," Canadian Historical Association, Historical Papers, 1984, 111-37.
20 Ibid., 111.
21 Compare tables 1a and 1b (Ibid., 121, 122) with table 6 (135). What I think these tables point to is a situation in which (a) for the most part Irish-Catholic immigrants had as rapid economic mobility as did the general population, including Irish Protestants, but (b) within this larger whole there was a small subgroup of genuinely disadvantaged Irish Catholic individuals.
22 Ibid., 127.
23 D.H. Akenson, "Ontario: Whatever Happened to the Irish?" in Canadian Papers in Rural History 3 (1982): 238. Computed from Census of Canada, 1880-81, 1: 58-93, 262-95, 360-94.
24 On the Orange Order, see Cecil J. Houston and William J. Smyth, The Sash Canada Wore. A Historical Geography of the Orange Order in Canada (Toronto: University of Toronto Press, 1980); Hereward Senior, Orangeism: The Canadian Phase (Toronto: McGraw-Hill Ryerson, 1972); and Gregory Kealey, Toronto Workers Respond to Capitalism, 1867-1892 (Toronto: University of Toronto Press, 1980), chapter 7.
25 The most solidly documented study involving ghettoized Irish is found in Katz, The People of Hamilton, Canada West.
26 See, for example, John Clarke and Karl Skof, "Social Dimensions of an Ontario County, 1851-52," in D.B. Knight, ed., Our Geographic Mosaic: Research Essays in Honor of G.C. Merrill (Ottawa: Carleton University Press, 1985), 107-36. In this area, "in contradistinction to stereotypes of the Irish as a whole, the poor Irish were Irish Anglicans." (135) See also the study of the Irish in Leeds and Landsdowne township in Akenson, The Irish in Ontario, 139-331.
27 On the agenda for Darroch and Ornstein's future work is an analysis of the "farmer" category, according to the various sizes and levels of suc-

cess of the farm occupation. Pioneering work on the analysis of farm enterprise has been conducted by R. Marvin McInnis of the economics department of Queen's University, Ontario. In a "two-stage random sample" he found that Irish-Catholic immigrant farmers were not as successful as Irish-Protestant immigrant farmers although the differences were not black-and-white, but ones of close degree. Because of the limited sample (1,200 farm enterprises) and the absence of information on length of time in the New World, this study should not be taken as definitive. (I am grateful to Professor McGinnis for communicating to me the unpublished results of his Canada West farm survey. These data are discussed in Akenson, *The Irish in Ontario*, 339–44.)

28 David Fitzpatrick, *Irish Emigration, 1801–1921* (Dundalk: Dundalgan Press Ltd, 1984, published for the Economic and Social History Society of Ireland) 13.

29 Ibid.

30 Oliver MacDonagh, "The Irish Famine Emigration to the United States," in Donald Fleming and Bernard Bailyn, eds., *Perspectives in American History* 10 (1976): 410.

31 David Fitzpatrick, "Irish Emigration in the Later Nineteenth Century," *Irish Historical Studies* 22 (Sept. 1980): 131n9.

32 Ibid.

33 Fitzpatrick, *Irish Emigration*, 32.

34 For bibliographies of the work on the Irish in the United States, see chapter 3, note 16.

35 William V. Shannon, *The American Irish* (New York: MacMillan, 1963), 27.

36 For a discussion of the Irish-American literature in detail, see Akenson, *Being Had*, 37–75.

37 Derived from U.S. Immigration and Naturalization Service, *Annual Report, 1975* (Washington: D.C., 1976), 62–4, quoted in Stephan Thernstorm, ed., *Harvard Encyclopedia of American Ethnic Groups* (Cambridge: Harvard University Press, 1980), 528.

38 The standard definition of "city" used by historical demographers of this period in the United States is 25,000 and above. The proportion is computed from data found in *The Population of the United States . . . 1870*, 1: 388–9. In arguing that the Irish were not a city people, I am being true both to the spirit and the letter of the Irish-American literature. I am not, at this point, suggesting that the Irish immigrants were a rural people (there is a wide band of human experience between the boundaries of ruralness – under 2,500 population – and the lower boundary of cities – 25,000). The Irish-American literature has suggested that in the nineteenth century the Irish settled in cities and the data here presented are enough to disprove that.

39 U.S. Bureau of the Census, *Historical Statistics of the United States, Colonial*

Times to 1970 (Washington, D.C., 1975), vol. 1, cited in Thernstorm, ed., *Harvard Encyclopedia*, 528.

40 Using the standard line of 2,500 to denominate an urban area, the following were the levels of urbanization in the United States: 1830: 8.8 percent; 1840, 10.8 percent; 1850, 15.3 percent; 1860, 19.8 percent; 1870, 25.7 percent. See David Ward, *Cities and Immigrants* (London: Oxford University Press, 1971), 6, and Robert E. Kennedy, Jr, *The Irish. Emigration, Marriage, and Fertility* (Berkeley: University of California Press, 1973), 82.

41 There are notable exceptions to the usual belief that the Irish-Americans were overwhelmingly a product of the post-Famine migration, and that they were a city people, characteristically locked into urban environments. For example, David Noel Doyle's *Ireland. Irishmen and Revolutionary America, 1760–1820* (Cork: Mercier Press, 1981), argues for a strong Catholic presence long before the Famine era. Jay P. Dolan, in *The Immigrant Church. New York's Irish and German Catholics, 1815–1865* (Baltimore: Johns Hopkins University Press, 1975) has presented a microstudy of parts of New York City and shown that "the tendency to remain in the city was greater among Germans than among Irish." (41) In a sophisticated quantitative study entitled "Patterns of Childbearing in Late Nineteenth-Century America: Determinants of Marital Fertility in Five Massachusetts Towns in 1880," Tamara K. Hareven and Maris A. Vinovskis have argued against the belief in strong ethnic social differences. Their work suggests that "there may be considerable flexibility in social behaviour of the various ethnic groups, so that generalizations about 'the Irish' or other immigrant groups in the United States, without adequate reference to their specific location and condition, can be misleading." See *Family and Population in Nineteenth-Century America*, edited by Tamara K. Harevan and Maris A. Vivovskis (Princeton: Princeton University Press, 1978), 123. One of the few studies of rural Irish people is by Kiernan D. Flanagan, "Emigration, Assimilation, and Occupational Categories of the Irish Americans in Minnesota, 1870–1900," (M.A. thesis, University of Minnesota, 1969), which deals with an era and a jurisdiction in which the Irish immigrants were overrepresented (as compared to Scandinavians) in agricultural occupations. This overrepresentation preceded the Catholic colonization movement in the state. As Cormac O'Grada has pointed out, the work of Lowell Gallaway and Richard Veder has established through quantitative studies that the Irish migrants to nineteenth-century America were not locked into the eastern cities, but first took jobs on the seaboard and then, having gained skills and money, moved on both geographically and economically. See Cormac O'Grada, "Irish Emigration to the United States in the Nineteenth Century," in David Noel Doyle and Owen Dudley Edwards, eds., *America and Ireland, 1776–1976. The American Identity and the Irish Connection* (Westport, Conn.: Greenwood Press, 1982), 93–103, and

Richard K. Vedder and Lowell E. Gallway, "The Geographic Distribution of British and Irish Emigrants to the U.S. after 1800," *Scottish Journal of Political Economy* 19 (1972): 19-35.

42 "Statistics showing the native counties of emigrants were first compiled in May 1851, but for another quarter-century they were to remain highly misleading." Fitzpatrick, "Irish Emigration," 127.

43 The Irish-born were 42.8 percent of the foreign-born in the United States in 1850, 33.3 percent in 1870, 15.6 percent in 1900, and 7.54 percent in 1920. Niles Carpenter, *Immigrants and Their Children. A Study Based on Census Statistics Relative to the Foreign born and the Native Whites of Foreign or Mixed Parentage* (Washington, D.C.: U.S. Government Printing Office, 1927), 79.

44 David Noel Doyle, "Unestablished Irishmen: Immigrants and Industrial America, 1870-1910," in Dirk Hoerder, ed., *American Labor and Immigration History, 1877-1920s: Recent European Research* (Urbana: University of Illinois Press, 1983), 207.

45 Ibid., 199.

46 Fitzpatrick, "Irish Emigration," 129.

47 Ibid., 131.

48 The reader will notice that I have not mentioned speciation by religion in the migration pattern. This is because the U.S. data preclude such a discussion. I do not accept the assumption that is virtually universal in Irish-American studies that Protestants migrated to the United States in only negligible numbers. Certainly this was not the case in the era of greatest immigration into the U.S., 1846-70.

49 Doyle, "Unestablished Irishmen," 201.

50 See David Fitzpatrick, "The Disappearance of the Irish Agricultural Labourer, 1841-1912," *Irish Economic and Social History* 8 (1980): 66-92. Although the methods employed by Fitzpatrick and the historical geographer S.H. Cousens are not entirely compatible, the latter's contention that the dissolution of the link between the poorest Catholic peasants of the south and west of Ireland and the land occurred quite late, roughly in the last quarter of the nineteenth century, fits quite well with Doyle's point about the "new" Irish immigration of the 1870s and thereafter, and with Fitzpatrick's description of the final stages of the class collapse of the Irish countryside. See S.H. Cousens, "Emigration and Demographic Change in Ireland, 1851-1861," *Economic History Review*, 2 ser., 14 (1962): 278-88; and "The Regional Variations in Population Changes in Ireland, 1861-1881," *Economic History Review*, 2 ser., 17 (1964): 301-21; "Population Trends in Ireland at the Beginning of the Twentieth Century," *Irish Geography* 5 (1968): 387-401.

51 Ward, *Cities and Immigrants*, 58.

52 Ibid.

53 *Abstracts of Reports of the Immigration Commission* (Washington, D.C.: Government Printing Office, 1911), 1: 145.

54 U.S. Immigration and Naturalization Service, *Annual Report, 1975*, quoted in Thernstorm, ed., *Harvard Encyclopedia*, 528.

55 The data available in American sources stem largely from the concern with the perceived threat of immigrants and their descendants to native American culture. The classic use of two-generation data is found in the massive Dillingham Commission Report of 1911.

56 In using the concept of ethnicity to refer to persons of the third and fourth generation in America, I realize that I am in danger of becoming involved in the almost-theological *methodonenstreit* which swirls around such concepts. Instead of becoming involved in that controversy, let us keep in mind that in this book persons "of Irish ethnicity" has been used consistently to refer to the people who migrated from Ireland and their descendants. That many of these individuals lost all visible marks of Irish descent is just as important and makes them no less historically significant (and their actions no less indicative of the holding-power of the Irish culture) than individuals whose families lived within a stone's throw of the same Catholic church for three generations.

The Dillingham Commission made an interesting observation about farmers and farm workers: "Of the 2,105,766 males of foreign origin [that is, immigrants] in agriculture, about thirty percent belonged to the English-speaking races – Canadian, Irish, English, Scotch and Welsh – nearly all of them comparatively early immigrants who are scattered the country over, and are so thoroughly Americanized, on the whole, that they have lost their racial characteristics." (Report of the Immigration Commission, *Immigrants in Industries*. Part 24. *Recent Immigrants in Agriculture*, 3). If one excises the word "race" and inserts "cultural" or "ethnic," the report has relevance and is thought provoking: is an Irish-born farmer who migrated to the United States in, say, 1860, any less significant as a datum point than one of the city-bound Irish-born industrial labourers who migrated, say, in 1900, and found his way into the Dillingham Report of 1911? If one says "yes" then all one is doing is deciding on grounds external to the evidence, what the "correct" profile of the Irish-American immigrant was and then excluding data that do not conform to that preconception.

57 See D.H. Akenson, "Data," 15–17.

58 Thomas Kuhn, *The Structure of Scientific Revolution* (Chicago: University of Chicago Press, 1962).

NOTES TO CHAPTER FIVE

1 James Joyce, *Ulysses* (New York: Vintage Books Edition, 1966), 331.

2 The four original volumes and the coda were published by MacMillan of London. The supplement was republished in 1968 by Dawsons of Pall Mall.

3 For an excellent study of this matter see Kurt Bowen, *Protestants in a Catholic State. Ireland's Privileged Minority* (Kingston and Montreal: McGill-Queen's University Press, 1983), esp. 40ff.

4 William E.H. Lecky, *A History of Ireland in the Eighteenth Century* 5 vols. (London: Longmans and Co., New Impression, 1913), 1: 152.

5 S.J. Connolly, *Priests and People in Pre-Famine Ireland, 1780–1845* (Dublin: Gill and MacMillan, 1982), 197; Patrick J. Corish, "Catholic Marriage Under the Penal Code," in Art Cosgrove, ed., *Marriage in Ireland* (Dublin: College Press, 1985), 67–77.

6 Lecky, *History of Ireland*, 1: 152.

7 Ibid.

8 Connolly, *Priests and People*, 197.

9 Ibid.

10 Ibid.

11 Ibid., 201–2; Corish, "Catholic Marriage," 68–70; Patrick J. Corish, *The Irish Catholic Experience. A Historical Survey* (Dublin: Gill and MacMillan, 1985), 107, 124.

12 Corish, "Catholic Marriage," 73–4. See also, Corish, *Irish Catholic Experience*, 219–21.

13 Cullen was concerned that there would be a rash of appeals to Rome against the Thurles decree against interfaith marriages. "It seems to me that it will become necessary to take a firm stand, otherwise the abuse will never be corrected," he wrote to Monsignor Barnabo, secretary of the Sacred Congregation of Propaganda in 16 February 1852. (Reproduced in Peadar MacSuibhne, *Paul Cullen and His Contemporaries with their letters from 1820–1902*, 4 vols. (Naas: Leinster Leader Ltd., 1965), 3: 108.

One should point out that in practice, as distinct from synodical decree, Cullen could be flexible on the intermarriage issue. Desmond Bowen has shown that Cullen was wont to approve mixed marriages when they brought significant financial gain or social status to the Catholic church. See Desmond Bowen, *Paul Cullen and the Shaping of Modern Irish Catholicism* (Dublin: Gill and MacMillan, 1983), 176.

14 See Emmet Larkin, *The Making of the Roman Catholic Church in Ireland, 1850–1860* (Chapel Hill: University of North Carolina Press, 1980), 258.

15 Owen Dudley Edwards, *The Sins of Our Fathers. Roots of Conflict in Northern Ireland* (Dublin: Gill and MacMillan, 1970), 196.

16 Denis P. Barrit and Charles F. Carter, *The Northern Ireland Problem* (London: Oxford University Press, 1962), 26; *Oxford Dictionary of the Christian Church*, 947–8.

17 Corish, "Catholic Marriage," 76; Corish, *Irish Catholic Experience*, 221.

18 Edwards, *Sins of Our Fathers*, 193*n*. Edwards notes that this degrading atmosphere was expunged by the Vatican II decrees that came into force in 1964. At the same time, the clause requiring the Catholic partner to try to convert the non-Catholic was removed from the written contract. Other liberalizations were introduced in the 1970s (see Kurt Bowen, *Protestants*, 43–4).

19 How well these canonical decrees fit the values of Catholic-dominated Ireland as it existed after 1922 is shown by the *ne Temere* contracts being adjudged to be enforceable in civil law. On the Tilson case of 1950, see Kurt Bowen, *Protestants*, 43; and J.H. Whyte, *Church and State in Modern Ireland 1923–1970* (Dublin: Gill and MacMillan, 1971), 169–71.

20 John M. Mogey, *Rural Life in Northern Ireland* (London: Oxford University Press, 1947), 87.

21 Edwards, *Sins of Our Fathers*, 193.

22 On the Protestant education societies, see D.H. Akenson, *The Irish Education Experiment: The National System of Education in the Nineteenth Century* (London: Routledge and Kegan Paul and Toronto: University of Toronto Press, 1970), 72–107.

23 Edward Maginn to Paul Cullen, 16 August 1848, quoted in Desmond Bowen, *Cullen*, 71.

24 Larkin, *Roman Catholic Church*, xx.

25 The standard, and excellent, history of the founding of the colleges is found in T.W. Moody and J.C. Beckett, *Queen's Belfast, 1845–1949: The History of a University*, 2 vols. (London: Faber, 1959), see especially, 1: 1–39.

26 Larkin, *Roman Catholic Church*, 35.

27 Akenson, *Irish Education Experiment*, 197–202, 285–94.

28 The data, available from 1861 onwards, are found in ibid., 377.

29 Ibid., 41–58.

30 *Second Report of Evidence from the Select Commission on the State of the Poor in Ireland*, 426–7, H.C. 1830 (654), vii, quoted in Moody and Beckett, *Queen's Belfast*, 1: lvi.

31 For a more detailed discussion of the evolution of the national system, see the following by D.H. Akenson, *Irish Education Experiment*; "National Education and the Realities of Irish Life, 1831–1900," *Eire-Ireland* (Winter 1969), 4: 42–51; *A Protestant in Purgatory. Richard Whatley, Archbishop of Dublin* (Hamden, Conn.: Archon Books, 1981, published for the Conference on British Studies and for Indiana University), 165–204.

32 For a history of the intermediate schools, see T.J. McElligot, *Secondary Education in Ireland, 1870–1921* (Dublin: Irish Academic Press, 1981).

33 *Freeman's Journal*, 20 August 1851, quoted in Larkin, *Roman Catholic Church*, 101.

34 Larkin, *Roman Catholic Church*, 490.

35 *Acta et Decreta Synodi Plenariae Episcoporum Hiberniae Hibitae apud Mayn-*

niutium, 1875 (Dublin: Brown and Nolan, 1877), 160.

36 Larkin, *Roman Catholic Church*, 34.

37 National Programme Conference (Ireland) *National Programme of Primary Instruction* (Dublin: Educational Company of Ireland Ltd., 1922), 24.

38 On these and related matters see D.H. Akenson, *Education and Enmity. The Control of Schooling in Northern Ireland, 1920–1950* (published for the Institute of Irish Studies, the Queen's University Belfast, Newton Abbot: David and Charles and New York: Barnes and Noble, 1973), 12–18.

39 For a discussion of southern education see: D.H. Akenson, *A Mirror to Kathleen's Face. Education in Independent Ireland, 1922–1960* (Montreal and London: McGill-Queen's University Press, 1975), and E. Brian Titley, *Church, State, and the Control of Schooling in Ireland, 1900–1944* (Kingston and Montreal: McGill-Queen's University Press, 1983).

40 See Akenson, *Education and Enmity*, passim.

41 Kurt Bowen, *Protestants*, 134.

NOTES TO CHAPTER SIX

1 Milton Rokeach, *The Open and Closed Mind. Investigations into the Nature of Belief Systems and Personality Systems* (New York: Basic Books, 1960), 3. Several of Rokeach's other works repay study. See *The Nature of Human Values* (New York: The Free Press, 1973); *Beliefs, Attitudes, and Values. A Theory of Organization and Change* (San Francisco: Jossey-Bass Inc., 1969); (editor) *Understanding Human Values. Individual and Societal* (New York: The Free Press, 1979).

2 S.J. Connolly, *Priests and People in Pre-Famine Ireland, 1780–1845* (Dublin: Gill and MacMillan, 1982), 15.

3 Engels to Borkheim, March 1872; reproduced in *Karl Marx and Frederick Engels. Ireland and the Irish Question* (Moscow: Progress Publishers, 1971), 300.

4 Engels to J. Bloch, 21 March 1890, quoted in Patrick Lynch, "Political Economy, The University and Modern Ireland," *The Crane Bag* 7, no. 2 (1983): 15.

5 F.S.L. Lyons, *Culture and Anarchy in Ireland, 1890–1939* (Oxford: Clarendon Press, 1979), 2.

6 "Emigration of the Protestants of Ireland," *Dublin University Magazine* 4 (July 1834): 9.

7 L. Paul-Dubois, *Contemporary Ireland* (Dublin: Maunsel and Co., 1911), 463.

8 Hewitt's work has stimulated a fine collection of essays. See *Across a Roaring Hill. The Protestant Imagination in Modern Ireland. Essays in Honour of John Hewitt* (Belfast: Blackstaff Press, 1985), edited by Gerald Dawe and Edna Longley. Quotation, i.

9 Sean O'Faolian, *King of the Beggars* (Dublin: Allen Figgis, Ltd., 1970), originally published 1938), 75.

10 I am indebted to W.T. Stace's *Religion and the Modern Mind* (Philadelphia: Lippincott, 1960) for the concepts that are here employed. For a perceptive general discussion, historically oriented, see Hugh McLeod's *Religion and the People of Western Europe 1789–1970* (Oxford: Oxford University Press, 1981).

11 Emile Durkheim, *The Elementary Forms of the Religious Life* (New York: Collier Books ed., 1961), 52.

12 One of the anonymous appraisers of this manuscript shrewdly pointed out that in many ways the situation was similar in nineteenth-century England. There, nonconformity, with its opposition to the Established Church in the early and mid-century, entered into a tacit system with the church: each side needed the other for the positive affirmation of its own character.

13 L.P. Curtis, Jr, *Anglo-Saxons and Celts. A Study of Anti-Irish Prejudice in Victorian England* (Bridgeport, Conn.: Conference on British Studies, 1968), 109. This entire volume, tightly focused and sharply argued, bears careful reading.

14 For Anglo-Saxons in general and for Ireland in particular, the Scots were a problem. The solution was to make the lowland Scots honourary Anglo-Saxons and then cede the highlanders to the Celtic mists.

15 A.T.Q. Stewart, *The Narrow Ground. Aspects of Ulster, 1609–1969* (London: Faber and Faber, 1977), 26.

16 J.C. Beckett, *The Anglo-Irish Tradition* (London: Faber and Faber, 1976), 10. For a very perceptive related study, see the essay by G.C. Bolton, "The Anglo-Irish and the Historians, 1830–1980," in Oliver MacDonagh, William F. Mandle, and Pauric Travers, eds., *Irish Culture and Nationalism, 1750–1950* (Canberra: Humanities Research Centre, 1981), 239–357.

17 Desmond Keenan, *The Catholic Church in Nineteenth Century Ireland. A Sociological Study* (Dublin: Gill and MacMillan, 1983), 29.

18 Quote, ibid.

19 For a particularly graphic example of this phenomenon, see Richard Kearney, ed., *The Irish Mind: Exploring Intellectual Traditions* (Dublin: Wolfhound Press, 1985). This is a large collection of essays by several authors which excludes from the "national mind" all Protestants with the exception of the rare few who took up Irish nationalism and, further, excludes such writers as Sean O'Faolain as being too much tainted by British colonial influence to be truly Irish.

20 Curtis, *Anglo-Saxons and Celts*, 108.

21 Oliver MacDonagh, *States of Mind. A Study of Anglo-Irish Conflict, 1780–1980* (London: George Allen and Unwin, 1983), 104.

22 Maureen Wall, "The Decline of the Irish Language," in Brian O'Cuiv, ed., *A View of the Irish Language* (Dublin: Stationery Office, 1969), 82.

23 MacDonagh, *States of Mind*, 104.

24 Wall, "Irish Language," 83.

25 Lyons, *Culture and Anarchy*, 30–6.

26 MacDonagh, *States of Mind*, 86.

27 Like most things in Ireland, these words cut both ways. They went down well with the more arrogant of the Anglo-Irish, but they spurred Gaelic revivalists to further action. Mahaffy's testimony was reprinted in *Gaelic Language Pamphlets, no 12. The Irish Language and Irish Intermediate Education* (Dublin: Gaelic League, 1901), 1–2.

28 Patrick O'Farrell, *Ireland's English Question. Anglo-Irish Relations 1534–1970* (London: B.T. Batsford, 1971), 11.

29 I should emphasize that I use "Protestant" in the modern sense to include Anglicans, Methodists, Presbyterians, Quakers, and so on. In the first half of the nineteenth century "Protestant" in official documents and, frequently in contemporary usage, referred to the Church of Ireland as the Established Episcopalian Church. Other Protestants were "dissenters" or, less frequently, "non-conformists." This usage gradually died out and from 1870 onwards, when the Church of Ireland was disestablished, "Protestant" was usually taken to mean all non-Roman Catholic Christians. This is not quite the same thing as the category invented by the government of the Irish Free State which usually lumped together everyone who was not Roman Catholic as "non-Catholic." There was some practical advantage in this, but putting Roman Catholics in one category, and atheists, Muslims and Jews in the same category as the various Protestant denominations indicated a certain cultural blindness – precisely the kind of mindset that is discussed in this chapter.,

30 David Miller, *Church, State and Nation in Ireland, 1898–1921* (Pittsburgh: University of Pittsburgh Press, 1973), 1.

31 Paul-Dubois, *Contemporary Ireland*, 491. For international context, see Sheridan Gilley, "The Roman Catholic Church and the Nineteenth Century Irish Diaspora," *Journal of Ecclesiastical History* 35 (April 1984): 188–207.

32 *American Hsitorical Review* 71 (June 1972): 625–52. For Larkin's very interesting reflections on this article and on subsequent scholarship, see his preface to a reprinting of his various articles: *The Historical Dimensions of Irish Catholicism* (Washington, D.C.: Catholic University of America Press, new edition, 1984), 1–11.

33 David Miller, "Irish Catholicism and the Great Famine," *Journal of Social History* 9 (Fall 1975): 81–98.

34 Larkin and Sean Connolly, (*Priests and People*) are at odds on this. Connolly holds that not much in the way of preparations for the devotional revolution occurred before the Great Famine. Larkin looks further back. For Larkin's comments, see *Irish Catholicism*, 7–8.

35 See ibid., 6–11.

36 The chief dissentient from this point of view is the historical sociologist

Desmond J. Keenan. See his *The Catholic Church in Nineteenth-Century Ireland. A Sociological Study*. For a useful critique of Keenan's work see S.J. Connolly, *Religion and Society in Nineteenth Century Ireland* (Dundalk: Dundalgan Press Ltd, 1985, published for the Economic and Social History Society of Ireland), 55–8.

37 S.J. Connolly, "Catholicism in Ulster, 1800–50," in Peter Roebuck, ed., *Plantation to Partition* (Belfast: Blackstaff Press, 1981), 159.

38 Patrick J. Corish, *The Irish Catholic Experience. A Historical Survey* (Dublin: Gill and MacMillan, 1985), 199; Larkin, "The Devotional Revolution," 644.

39 D.H. Akenson, *The United States and Ireland* (Cambridge: Harvard University Press, 1973), 132.

40 With both the Protestant and the Catholic religious revivals in the nineteenth century, it is well to remember the international context. Revivals were widespread throughout the Christian world. Timothy Smith has identified nineteenth-century revivals in a wide range of European faiths, Lutheran, Orthodox, Catholic, and evangelical Protestant. See Timothy L. Smith, "Religion and Ethnicity in America," *American Historical Review* 83 (December 1978): esp. 1161–8.

41 The schisms and rejoinings in Irish Presbyterianism are well laid out in John M. Barkley, *A Short History of the Presbyterian Church in Ireland* (Belfast: Publications Board, Presbyterian Church in Ireland, 1959). For useful background, see J.C. Beckett, *Protestant Dissent in Ireland 1678–1780* (London: Faber and Faber, 1948).

42 David W. Miller, "Presbyterians and 'Modernisation' in Ulster," *Past and Present* 80 (August 1978): 66–90.

43 For a case study in changing social mores in a Presbyterian community, see D.H. Akenson, *Between Two Revolutions. Islandmagee, County Antrim, 1798–1920* (Toronto: P.D. Meany; Dublin: Academic Press; Hamden, Conn.: Archon Books, 1979).

44 See D.H. Akenson, *The Church of Ireland. Ecclesiastical Reform and Revolution, 1800–1885* (New Haven: Yale University Press, 1971).

45 Jay P. Dolan, *Catholic Revivalism. The American Experience, 1830–1900* (Notre Dame: University of Notre Dame Press, 1978).

46 The way that various magical and other religious nonofficial beliefs about the invisible world coexisted with formal religion is well depicted in Connolly's *Priests and People*. On similar beliefs in a Protestant community, see Akenson, *Between Two Revolutions*, 119–69; and Akenson and W.H. Crawford, *Local Poets and Social History: James Orr, Bard of Ballycarry* (Belfast: Public Record Office of Northern Ireland, 1977), 110–11.

47 Quoted in Keenan, *Catholic Church*, 191.

48 On the union as a "problem" and various answers to it, see Akenson, *The United States and Ireland*, 18–33.

49 A perceptive observer of present-day Northern Ireland has written the following:

The contemporary northern Protestant's sense of history is, I would argue, markedly similar to that of the Catholic nationalist. That his history seems impoverished by comparison with nationalist historical awarenesss is because that history has had to perform fewer functions and is necessarily simpler ... Northern Protestants, as inheritors of those who have prosecuted the political cause of the Protestants of Ireland, have in the last analysis only the one historical requirement – to uphold the settlement of 1689 and to try to ensure that the principle of Protestant hegemony is recognised and supported.

(Terence Brown, *The Whole Protestant Community: the Making of a Historical Myth* [Derry: Field Day Pamphlets, 1985], 8)

50 Dr Marianne Elliott has percipiently noted: "The highly stylised vocabulary of Irish Presbyterianism creates an illusion of continuity between the seventeenth century – a period when the battle for Protestant survival was fought and won – and the present. Above all it is a language of crusade in which Popery is still seen as the enemy and the sense of insecurity which surrounded the earlier struggle persists." Marianne Elliott, *Watchmen in Sion: the Protestant Idea of Liberty* (Derry: Field Day Pamphlets, 1985), 14-15.

51 Patrick O'Farrell, "Whose Reality? The Irish Famine in History and Literature," *Historical Studies* (Melbourne) 20 (April 1982): 1-13; O'Farrell, *Ireland's English Question*, 112-13.

For an especially atrabilious study indicating the durability of the Mitchell tradition, written by an Irish-American, see Thomas Gallagher, *Paddy's Lament, Ireland 1846-1847: Prelude to Hatred* (New York: Harcourt Brace Jovanovich, 1982).

The difficult matter of proselytizing is dealt with in Desmond Bowen, *Souperism: Myth or Reality?* (Cork: Mercier Press, 1970). Bowen's study indicates that there were some instances of proselytizing but that these were quite rare and that actual cases of souperism can be dismissed as "not proved" in the areas which he intensively studied. He explains, however, how the actions of a few Protestant fanatics, when combined with the deep division between the two major faiths, could easily lead to the myth of endemic souperism.

52 It will not have escaped the notice of anyone who has read much recent Irish historical writing that there is a present-day counterpart to this kind of thinking. It comes from those politically engaged who claim that the Northern Ireland problem has nothing fundamentally to do with reli-

gion and instead is the product of the illegitimate hegemony of the ruling class (unspoken word: Protestant) that for its own purposes divides from each other the Protestant and the Catholic working class, or is an artifact of British imperialism. Or both. And that without the actions of the ruling class and of the British, the good Protestant people of Northern Ireland could get along in peace with the good Catholic people. Would that it were so!

In logical terms, this school of thought is best described as suffering from the nominalist fallacy, under which renaming things is thought to make them go away. They do not. The religious gulf is deep, indigenous, and real.

53 For a pioneering attempt to understand religious tensions at a local level, see Thomas G. McGrath, "Interdenominational Relations in Pre-Famine Tipperary," in William Nolan and Thomas G. McGrath, eds., *Tipperary: History and Society. Interdisciplinary Essays on the History of the Irish County* (Dublin: Geography Publications, 1985), 256–87. There are several other very strong essays in this collection, including Kevin Whelan's revealing, "The Catholic Church in County Tipperary, 1700–1900," 215–55. Another study of local relations, somewhat less discerning but useful nonetheless, is Ian d'Alton's, *Protestant Society and Politics in Cork, 1812–1844* (Cork: Cork University Press, 1980).

54 Sigmund Freud, *Group Psychology and the Analysis of the Ego*. Translated by James Strachey (London and Vienna: International Psycho-Analytic Press, 1922), 52–9. *Civilization and Its Discontents* (London: English edition, Hogarth Press, 1963), 51–2.

Index

Adams, William Forbes, 13-14
Adelaide, 66
American-Irish. *See* Irish-Americans
Amis, Kingsley, 15
Anglican, definition of, 219n8, 229n29
Anglo-Irish, emigration studies, 100
Anglo-Irish Tradition. See Beckett, J.C.
"Anglo-Saxonism," 133-4
apartheid, 115
association. *See* correlation
Aughrim, 143-4
Australia: early settlement, 59-60; Irish-born, 60-2, 66-7; ethnic structure, 61-2; religious composition, 62-6; Oliver MacDonagh's views, 62-6; urban/rural 67-9; occupational structure, 70-3; literacy, 73-4, 84; family structure, 74-81; mixed marriages, 81-4

Ballycarry, 37
bastardy. *See* illegitimacy
Beckett, J.C., 5, 134
Belfast, 126; pogroms, 3-4, 131; occupational structure, 24
belief systems, 127-49
Beresford family, 134
Bible in schools, 121-5 passim
"Black Protestants," 143
Bloom, Leopold, 108
Blythe, Ernest, 137
Borkheim, Sigismund, 128
Boyne, 144
Brisbane, 66
British North America. *See* Canada
Broadisland. *See* Ballycarry
brothel keepers, 22
Bruyère, Jean de la, 3
Buffalo, 86

Calwell, Hugh, 207n64
Canada: sources of data, 87-8; Irish immigration, 88-91; urban/rural, 91-4; occupational structure, 93-7; Orange Order, 97-8; summary, 98-9
Canadian-Irish. *See* Canada
Cashel, province of, 112
Catholic Defence Association, 121-2
causality, 8-9
celibacy, 27-38 passim, 79

"Celticism," 133-9
censuses (esp. of religion): Irish, 5-6, 7, 19-21, 24, 153-6, 157, 200n14; English, 53; US, 87-8, 101; Canadian, 87-101 passim. *See also* Australia; New Zealand
Chinese, 17
Church Education Society, 117
Church of Ireland, definition of, 219n8, 229n29
"city people." *See* urban/rural
Clark, Samuel Jr., 12
class. *See* social class
class collapse, 105, 223n50
classical economists, 129
coeducation of the sexes, 122-3
Cohalan, Daniel, 195n4
Collins, Michael, 4, 195n3
community studies, 53-4, 88, 98, 101-2
Congregationalists, 22
Connell, Kenneth, 29-38, 205nn43, 44, 45
Connolly, Sean, 28, 29-30, 34-6, 200n12, 204n40, 206n56, 229n34, 230n46
correlation, 8
Council of Trent, 112, 113
Cousens, S.H., 26-7

Craig, James, 146
crime data, 198n2
Crotty, R.D., 26-7
Cullen, Paul, 113, 116, 121-2, 128, 140, 143, 225n13
cultural determinism, 11
Culture and Anarchy in Ireland. See Lyons, F.S.L.
Curtis, L.P., Jr, 133-4, 135

Darling Downs, 66
Darroch, A. Gordon, 94-9
Davis, Richard P., 212n42
"demographic transition," 28
denominational schooling. *See* education
Derry, 126, 143
"devotional revolution," 139-40
Dillingham Commission, 105, 224n56
discrimination, 22-4, 101, 130
Dolan, Jay P., 142-3, 222n41
Doyle, David N., 103-5
Doyle, James, 119-20
Durkheim, Emile, 10, 111, 132-3
"Dutch precedent," 113, 114

Edinburgh University, 116
education, 115-26
Edwards, Owen Dudley, 113, 115, 197n16
emigration: as standardizer, 43-5; propensity of Irish religious groups toward, 45, 153-7, 198-9n2. *See also* Australia; Canada; Great Britain; New Zealand; United States
endogamy. *See* intermarriage. *See also* family structure
Endowed Schools Commission, 138
Engels, Friedrich, 12-13,

128, 129, 131, 197n16, 197n18
English language. *See* linguistic preferences
English migrants: to New Zealand, 56; to Australia, 61, 62; to Canada, 89, 90, 97
Enniskillen, 144
Episcopalian. *See* Anglican ethnicity: Charles Price on Australian, 61-2; lack of US data on, 87-8, 101; Canadian data, 90-9
Evangelicalism, 140-3, 230n40

fallacies, 9-10, 53-4, 231-2n52. *See also* community studies
family structure: Ireland, 15, 24-38, 201nn21, 26, 203nn34, 37; Australia, 74-81
family size. *See* family structure. *See also* marital fertility
famine, of 1846-9, 26-7, 51, 60, 87, 100, 102, 136, 139, 140, 144-5, 147, 231n51
farming. *See* occupational structure
Ferguson, Samuel, 137
Fisher, R.A., 17
Fitzpatrick, David, 43, 51-2, 66, 69, 99, 104, 223n50
Flanagan, Kiernan, 222n41
Frazer, Sir James, 109-10
Freud, Sigmund, 149

Gaelic. *See* linguistic preferences
Germans, 17-18
"Godless colleges," 116
Grattan, Henry, 134
Great Britain, 50-4
Great Famine. *See* famine
Greer, Allan, 206n56

hedge schools, 118-19

Hepburn, A.C., 12, 24, 26
Heslinga, M.W., 11
Hewitt, John, 131, 132
historical sense of Irish, 144-5
Hobart, 66, 67
Houston, C.J., 53
Hyde, Douglas, 137
hypotheses *re* Protestant-Catholic differences, 47-50

illegitimacy, 26-8, 204n40, 206n43, 207n77. *See also* Connell, Kenneth
illiteracy rates. *See* literacy
illicit love. *See* celibacy; illegitimacy; premarital pregnancy
integration. *See* education
intermarriage, 81-4, 109-15, 126, 218n107, 225n13, 226n18
intermediate schools, 121
Ireland's English Question. See O'Farrell, P.
Irish-Americans: historiography of, 19, 47-50, 86-8, 99-107, 211n17; urban/rural, 102-6; shifts in origin, 103-5
Irish-Canadians. *See* Canada
Irish language. *See* linguistic preferences
Irish national school system, 119-26
Islandmagee, 36-7, 204n40, 206n63
Israel, 16
Italians, 105

Jews, 17

Kennedy, Robert E., Jr, 38-41
Kuhn, Thomas, 107

"laboratories," 54, 84-5, 108, 208n3
Landes, David, 18

Larkin, Emmet, 116–17, 122, 139–40, 229n34
lay involvement in education, 123–5
Lebanon, 16
Lecky, W.E.H., 111–12
Lee, Joseph J., 19, 37–8, 43
Lees, Lynn, 52, 212n40
"liberal virus," 122, 123–4
life expectancy of women, 38–41, 181
linguistic preferences, 49, 135–9, 193–4, 209n8
literacy, 7, 9–10, 73–4, 85, 117–18, 158, 199n2
"Liverpool divorce," 80–1
Londonderry Act, 125
Londonderry, Charles Stewart, seventh marquis of, 124, 125
Londonderry, city of. See Derry
Lower Canada. See Quebec; Canada
Lyons, F.S.L., 5, 129–30

McCaffrey, Lawrence, 48
McClelland, David, 16–17
McDonagh, Oliver, 62–6, 100, 135, 136, 215n69
McDonald, Walter, 29
McInnis, R. Marvin, 221n28
McLaren, Angus, 35
Mageean, Deirdre, 45
Maginn, Edward, 116
Mahaffy, John Pentland, 128, 138, 229n27
marital fertility, 25–8 passim, 189, 190, 203nn34, 37
marriage age, 26, 27
marriage breakdown, 79–80
Marx, Karl, 12, 13, 129
Marxist historiography, 12–13, 129, 196n15
Melbourne, 66
mental illness, 27, 202–3n33
Miller, David, 30, 33, 139,

140–1, 205n43
Miller, Kerby A., 48–50, 70
Mitchell, John, 145, 231n51
"mixed education." See education
"mixed marriages." See intermarriage
Montreal, 86
multicollinearity, 9
Murray, Daniel, 112

"n Achievement," 17–18
national identity, 145–7, 231nn49, 59
Ne Temere, 113–14, 226nn18, 19
New Brunswick, 86–90 passim
Newfoundland, 90
New France. See Quebec; Canada
New South Wales. See Australia
New York City, 86
New Zealand: Irish-born in, 54; religious composition, 54–5; urban/rural, 55–7; occupational structure, 58–9
Ninety-eight rising, 131
Nova Scotia, 86–90 passim

occupational structure: in Ireland, 15–24, 159–80, 199n3, 201n17; hypotheses concerning, 49–50; in New Zealand, 58–9, 84; in Australia, 69–73, 184–8, 217n95; in Canada, 93–9, 100, 220n21; in US, 101, 104
O'Connell, Daniel, 132, 134, 135, 146
O'Farrell, Patrick J., 11, 43–4, 66, 70, 139, 145, 213–14n54, 215n71
O'Grada, Standish, 137
O'Neill, Kevin, 12
Ontario, 90–9
Orange Order, 99, 125, 143–4

ordnance survey, 30
O'Riordan, M., 18
Orkney Islands, 123
Ornstein, Michael D., 94–9
Oxford University, 116

Paor, Liam de, 196n15
Paul-Dubois, L., 130, 139
pauper emigrants, 44
pay schools, 118–19
Pearse, Patrick, 137
penal code, 22–3; on intermarriage, 111–13; on education, 118–19
Pentland, H. Clare, 96, 197n20
Perth, 66
Petrie, George, 137
Pius IX, 116
Plunkett, Sir Horace, 18
Polish migrants, 105
political prisoners, 60
Poor Law Commission, 1833–6, 30–6 passim, 204–5n41
Port Phillip, 60
Portugal, illegitimacy in, 34
premarital pregnancy, 26–38, 204n40, 205n48, 206n63
"Presbyterian," usage of, 229n29
Price, Charles, 61–2, 214–15n66
prohibited degrees, 110
propensity to emigrate, of religious groups, 104, 209n10, 223n48
"Protestant," usage of, 229n29
The Protestant Ethic. See Weber, Max

Quakers, 22, 229n29
Quebec City, 86, 100
Quebec, province of, 34–5, 86–90 passim, 100

racial thinking, 133–5

rape, 32, 33
religion. *See* belief systems
residential segregation.
   See urban/rural
Revans, John, 32-3
Revival of 1859, 141
Rokeach, Milton, 127, 146
Russian emigrants, 105

St John, 86, 100
Sarsfield, Patrick, 144
"Sassenach," 135
schizophrenia. *See* mental
   illness
school attendance, 122-3
Scotch-Irish. *See* Ulster-
   Scots
Scottish migration: to
   New Zealand, 56; to
   Australia, 61, 62; to
   Canada, 89-90
segregation. *See* education
sexual repression, 27. *See
   also* celibacy; illegitimacy; illicit love
Shannon, William, 102
Shepparton, 66
"significance," 8
Smyth, W.J., 53
social class, 12, 85, 140. *See
   also* occupational structure

split labour market, 96
Stanley, Edward, 119-25
   passim
stem family, 27, 28
stereotyping, 9-14 pas-
   sim, 28-38 passim,
   204n40, 228n19
subsets, 9. *See also* community studies
Sydney, 66

Tawney, R.H., 16, 18,
   199n5
Thompson, E.O., 197n20
Thurles, synod of, 113,
   116-17, 225n13
Toronto, 86
Totemism and Exogamy. See
   Frazer, Sir James
Transportation of con-
   victs, 60
Treaty of Limerick, 136,
   144
Trinity College, Dublin,
   116, 117
Troy, John T., 111
Tuam, province of, 112

Ulster-Scots, 100, 219n9
unionism. *See* national
   identity
Ulster-Scots, 100, 219n9

United States. *See* Irish-
   Americans
urban/rural patterns of
   Protestants and Catho-
   lics: hypotheses, 49-50;
   in Great Britain, 52-4; in
   New Zealand, 56-8,
   212-13n50; in Australia,
   66-9, 84; in Canada,
   91-3, 98-9, 220n16; in
   US, 102-6, 221n38,
   222n40, 222-3n41

Victoria. *See* Australia
violence, 3-5

Wall, Maureen, 135, 136,
   200n12
Wallas, Graham, 13
Ward, David, 105
Ward, Peter, 206n56
Weaver, John, 198n2
Webb, Sidney, and Bea-
   trice, 13, 197n19
Weber, Max, 16, 18, 199n5
Whately, Richard, 30,
   205n41
Wilde, Oscar, 128
William III of Orange, 128,
   144
women, Irish treatment
   of, 15, 38-41

Also by D.H. Akenson

SOCIAL AND RELIGIOUS HISTORY
Between Two Revolutions: Islandmagee, Co.
  Antrim, 1798–1920
The United States and Ireland
The Church of Ireland: Ecclesiastical Reform and
  Revolution

BIOGRAPHY
A Protestant in Purgatory; Richard Whately:
  Archbishop of Dublin
Local Poets and Social History: James Orr, Bard
  of Ballycarry.
  With W.H. Crawford

EDUCATIONAL HISTORY
A Mirror to Kathleen's Face: Education in
  Independent Ireland, 1922–60
Education and Enmity: The Control of Schooling
  in Northern Ireland, 1920–50
The Irish Education Experiment: The National
  System of Education in the Nineteenth
  Century
The Changing Uses of the Liberal Arts College:
  An Essay in Recent Educational History.
  With L.F. Stevens

NORTH AMERICAN STUDIES
Being Had: Historians, Evidence and the Irish in
  North America
The Irish in Ontario: A Study in Rural History
(Editor) Canadian Papers in Rural History, 6 vols.

FICTION
The Edgerston Audit
The Orangeman. The Life and Times of Ogle R.
  Gowan
Brotherhood Week in Belfast
The Lazar House Notebooks